Riding the Whirlwind

Riding the Whirlwind

Connecting people and organisations
in a culture of innovation

Fons Trompenaars

Copyright © The Infinite Ideas Company Limited, 2007

The right of Fons Trompenaars to be identified as the author of this book has been asserted in accordance with the Copyright, Designs and Patents Act 1988.

First published in 2007 by

The Infinite Ideas Company Limited

36 St Giles

Oxford, OX1 3LD

United Kingdom

www.infideas.com

A CIP catalogue record for this book is available from the British Library

ISBN   978–1–905940–36–3

Brand and product names are trademarks or registered trademarks of their respective owners.

Cover designed by Cylinder

Typeset by Sparks, Oxford

Printed and bound by TJ International, Padstow, Cornwall

This book is printed on 100% recycled paper. The board used for the cover is from sustainable forests and PEFC certified (www.pefc.org).

For Cens

CONTENTS

PREFACE

This book is intended to fill a gap in the market between books that show how to develop more creative people and those that show how organisations can create a culture of innovation that can harness this creativity. In the increasingly oligopolistic world of business, in which old ideas can be copied and replicated at lower and lower costs, it is the constant renewal of creative solutions that is the ultimate differentiator of survivors.

Much has been written (separately) about creativity and innovation. Much has also been written about corporate culture and mechanistic and structural approaches to innovation in organisations. What is severely lacking is a single body of knowledge in the form of an easily digestible book that integrates these subjects.

The core philosophy of this book is thus the connection between the development of people first as individuals, then as teams and then across the organisation (which contributes to the long-term sustainability of the organisation) and the constant renewal of talent and motivation of its workforce.

As you will discover, to apply the concepts presented in this book you will need a change in mindset in the way you approach problems – away from more simplistic linear and bi-modal ideas, characteristic of Western cultures. Weighing the relative merits of 'this *or* that' action along a linear scale where you can only have more of one at the expense of the other, or assuming that action is limited in choosing between 'this *or* that', too often results from the consumer idea of choice and from suffering from (Cartesian-based) Western education. Do you want tea *or* coffee?

To become more creative and to harness the talent of being creative requires us to think in terms of asking 'Can we have our cake *and* eat it?' or, more succinctly, as explained throughout this book, 'How can we combine and not simply choose between options to open up new avenues to deal with today's fast-changing world?' So it is not about choosing a beer *or* a whisky, but asking if we can combine the two (as in a 'chaser') to create something more.

Organisations often focus on systems and process changes. But the key message from this book is the importance of behaviours and actions by leaders and managers that can lead to a supportive climate that respects and reinforces creativity and innovation essential to the longer term sustainability of the organisation. When creativity is put in the context of realising business objectives and solving business issues, its results are greatly enhanced.

The author has an exceptional talent for blending rigorous research with professional practice so that one informs the other within an entertaining and easy-to-read format. This book will therefore be of value to managers to help them understand how their behaviours have consequences for the working context of their employees and thereby how they can synergise the needs of the organisation with the needs of the individual employee and secure the best for all. It will also be of value to individual employees and students of business and management who need to learn and understand the increasing importance of these 'soft issues' of work and organisations, over and above functional disciplines and business economics.

This book includes a comprehensive exploration of creativity and innovation from this new perspective with a business focus. You can test yourself on some of the profiling instruments described in this book and access interactive cases studies and further content at www.ridingthewhirlwind.com.

Professor Peter Woolliams, PhD
Emeritus Professor, Anglia Ruskin University, UK

ACKNOWLEDGEMENT

Fons writes:

It all started on the evening of 13 October 2005 when I was invited to join a Gala dinner of Abbott Diagnostics in Wiesbaden. Because there was no 'Dutch table', I was asked if I would join the Scandinavian table, where Norwegians, Swedes and Danes were hospitable enough to invite both me and the Finns. At the end of the evening, one of the Swedish clients wished me good luck and told me that I would most probably see him next year in Stockholm. Indeed, I had been invited to a bestseller conference, but how did he know this? 'Haven't you seen the programme?' No, I said. 'But you are on stage with John Cleese.' WHAT? With John Cleese? *The* John Cleese ...? YES!

And indeed, on 1 June 2006 I was on stage with John Cleese, who talked about creativity, while I talked about the importance of diversity for innovation. It inspires me, particularly because his presentation complemented (in the broad sense of the word) my own so well. We travelled together on the train to Gothenburg, and the idea was born to do some joint workshops and seminars in the fall of 2007. What better way to prepare than to write a book?

The first part of the book integrates more traditional thoughts on creativity into our culture and dilemma framework. The following chapters draw heavily on the work of Charles Hampden-Turner, whose creative mind continues to be a main source of inspiration. And it was very much inspired by the dialogues I had with Peter Woolliams, who contributed and did the final editing. Here the question becomes 'where does co-authorship start and editing stop?' It's a grey area. Thank you, Peter, for all the support you gave me.

Thank you David Lewis for the great graphic support. Your talents go beyond being a good graphic artist; you have an unusual talent to capture in drawings that which we couldn't say in words.

And last but not least, a big thank you to John Cleese, who keeps on reminding me that the ultimate creative act is to make people laugh – then they realise that humour is the ultimate way to appreciate opposite ends of a spectrum.

As I write this on a terrace looking out over Darling Harbour in Sydney, I realise how important it has been to test my concepts in front of large audiences. Thank you to all the organisations that have allowed me to speak on the creation of a innovative culture – in particular AHRI, the professional organisation of HR managers of Australia, for allowing me to withdraw for a moment and test the latest idea on 1,400 of their members.

June 2007, Sydney
Fons Trompenaars

INTRODUCTION

'Life is a bursting unity of opposition barely held.'
'A nation should be just as full of conflict as it can contain ... but of course, it must contain.'

Robert Frost

In an impressive study of Global CEOs, Expanding the Innovation Horizon (2006)[1], IBM concluded that leaders in every industry and in every part of the world are emerging from a period of retrenchment and cost-cutting and moving toward a vision of sustained growth. The study indicated a growing recognition that new innovation is the preferred path to achieving organic growth and brand value. After interviewing 765 CEOs around the world, IBM asserted that the CEOs' view of innovation is evolving beyond the traditional focus on pure invention and new product or process development, and that they are placing increasing emphasis on differentiation through innovation in the basics of their business models. In short, innovation has regained its central place in corporate life. So it should. However, the innovation of today is of another shape and reveals itself in different types of processes than traditionally conceived.

In this book I seek to describe these new processes and how the leadership of an organisation can guide its staff into a more creative mindset. This is perhaps more essential now than ever because of the increasing speed with which one needs to innovate. In addition, there are many

---

1   *Expanding the Innovation Horizon*, the Global CEO study 2006, IBM Global Services, New York, USA, 2006

counterproductive forces related to the process of innovation. First, we find that the commoditisation of education – a prime killer of creativity – has not helped to make our graduates more innovative. In fact, the contrary is true. Second, organisational conditions, from Sarbanes Oxley to the Hay system of job evaluation, have not been an effective framework for the creative person in enabling breakthrough services. In contrast, there seems to be an increasing drive for us to control our processes as much as we can and avoid mistakes at all costs. But, despite the fact that we seem to have tried to numb our creative processes more and more, the countervailing powers are at least as big. With the globalisation of the world's business, we are increasing the diversity of our business partners. And through mergers and acquisitions, and less formal co-operations like joint ventures (JVs) and partnerships, we have also added diversity to the gene pool.

So we see two trends occurring together: on the one hand, an increasing standardisation of the world; and on the other hand, an ever-growing diversity. And our position is that, when we connect the two, we have the essence of what the new innovation is all about. The joining of things we share, as well as the things that differ, is the essential task of leadership. And it is, perhaps, this mode of leadership that we are currently missing the most.

The crisis of education

One of the key factors that inhibits the development of an innovative culture is embedded in our education system. Russell Ackoff[2] made it clear that what schools want is children who think the way their parents want them to think: conservatively, not creatively. And he demonstrates this eloquently by an extra-credit problem that one of his daughters got to solve in a mathematics class.

Everyone who has studied for an MBA knows this puzzle. Can you connect the following nine dots with four straight lines without lifting the pen from the paper?

---

2   Ackoff, Russell L., *The Art of Problem Solving*, p.5, Wiley Inter-Science, 1978

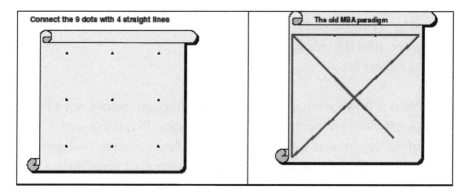

Fig 1.1 Traditional approach to the 'nine dots' problem

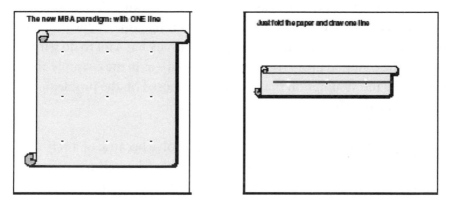

Fig 1.2 New approach to the 'nine dots' problem

And almost every MBA student knows the answer. You have to think out of the box. But look what happened to Ackoff's daughter. She asked her father what to do and he came up with a brilliant solution, since he is known to be fond of going beyond 'known' solutions. He told her that you could fold the paper in such a way that the dots would overlap. In other words, you could do it with *one* line rather than with four. The teacher asked the class who had found the solution (yes, *the* solution). Five people raised their hands. Four of them gave the known and less creative solution. When Ackoff's daughter asked if she could try an alternative solution, the teacher agreed with reservation. She asked for a flip-chart because she needed the paper to fold, rather than the blackboard.

The teacher got angry and told her she couldn't do that: 'She told the teacher that the instructions didn't say she couldn't do it. The teacher replied by saying she didn't care what the instructions said; that was what she meant. And she told her to sit down.'

As Ackoff says:

> 'This is how creativity is suppressed, although usually not so overtly. The teacher made it clear to her class that the objective of the assignment was not to find the solution, but to find *the solution she knew* and could pretend to have discovered on her own. She had no interest in any other solution.'

So creativity can be described as the process of breaking the assumptions one has accumulated quite unconsciously through one's education, upbringing and/or culture. The teaching of creativity has a lot to do with revealing the common property of solutions, and – as in the example above – breaking the assumption that the solver imposed on the problem.

As Ackoff[3] observes:

> 'A puzzle is a problem that one cannot solve because of a *self-imposed constraint*. Creativity is shackled by self-imposed constraints. Therefore the key to freeing it lies in developing an ability to identify such constraints and deliberately removing them.'

Children's education might not help us to remove self-imposed constraints. On the contrary, it might even add some more. And very often, this doesn't stop simply in the academic educational environment: in business too, we have to focus on what MBA education and in-service training has done to our creativity.

There are three 'serial killers' of the creative mind of the MBA student. One is the assumption that there is *one best way* to solve almost any business challenge. The second is the assumption that the best way to model the complex business world is *linear*, where one side excludes the other. Just look at how students are graded. You make a mistake and it is deducted from the total number of points you can get. And what about 'the one-day MBA' that is so popular in many parts of the world?

---

3   ibid, p.9

Finally, education is very often geared towards the *control* of the business environment and the avoidance and elimination of mistakes. As demonstrated in this book, all these components are creativity killers.

New aspirations for increasing creativity

If creativity and innovation are the result of reconciling standardisation and diversity through leadership, then there are hopeful developments. The internationalisation of business and the increased number of inter-organisational activities give an enormous boost to creative energy. Even American culture is becoming increasingly aware that pushing harder to have the world follow one standardised logic (forgetting to add that it happens to be theirs) hasn't worked; not in business, nor in politics. The world might become flat in some ways, as Friedman[4] assumes, but it is quite spiky as well, as Richard Florida[5] shows.

The structure of this book

The aim of this book is to offer a new set of approaches to the leaders to make their organisations more innovative and thereby more sustainable in the increasingly turbulent future.

We will deal with three crucial levels of the innovative culture: the individual, the team and the organisation. An organisation cannot be innovative if there are no creative individuals working to fulfil their personal dreams. Yet you can put creative individuals together and end up with a team that is actually very *un*creative. Creative people need to have people with complementary competences around them to make the team inventive. And haven't we all seen organisations where the Research and Development (R&D) and marketing teams are (separately) excellent, but the organisation is dysfunctional because they can't work together? Indeed, an innovative organisation needs to develop a pattern of interac-

---

4   Friedman, Thomas L., *The World Is Flat: A Brief History of the Twenty-first Century*, Farrar, Straus and Giroux; expanded and updated edition, 18 April 2006

5   Florida, Richard, 'The World is Spiky', *The Atlantic Monthly*, October 2005

tions where individuals and teams work effectively together for the larger objective of the organisation.

The second chapter focuses on individual creativity and how to enhance it, but from a new perspective. It covers the tensions with which the creative person needs to deal, such as the quandary between our rushed 'hare brain' and the more reflective, investigating 'tortoise mind', as originally discussed by Guy Claxton. We revisit the well-established psychological frameworks that are closely linked to creativity, such as the Myers Briggs Type Indicator typology (MBTI), Kolb's Learning Style Inventory and even Kirton's Adaptation-Innovation Inventory (KAI). The concern is to draw attention to the fact that all of these (and other) frameworks are essentially based on linear models that cannot fully capture a person's creativity. We offer both practical and conceptual arguments supporting the premise that the creative individual essentially reconciles all the mutually exclusive poles that underlie these models. Exercises and alternative measurement tools show how effective the concept and practice of 'dilemma reconciliation' can be for your organisation.

The work of comedy writers such as John Cleese (including *Monty Python* and *Fawlty Towers*), John Sullivan (*Only Fools and Horses*) and Matt Groening (*The Simpsons*) and that of myself as an academic and consultant, (consulting daily in the largest and most successful international organisations in the world) are quite different, but complementary. We seem to have one thing in common: the functional use of humour. Like Arthur Koestler, they all believe that humour is very much linked with creativity. Why? Because humour is the process of discovering that two apparently opposite logics turn out both to be logical. That is what makes you laugh. So this book will try to take utmost advantage of this both theoretically and practically.

The third chapter deals primarily with how to encourage and facilitate inventions from teams that consists of individuals with complementary talents. We begin from a description of the eight roles of the innovative team as described by Meredith Belbin, but we will extend the basic model by also describing the reconciliation of the main characteristics across those roles. You might have a team that is not inventive even though all roles are covered. Again, it is important that, for example, roles like the idea-generating Plant are challenged by the role of the Monitor-Evaluator. We focus on how to find the particular roles and facilitate the tensions between the roles. The role of the Chair – as the reconciler in chief – gets particular mention.

The fourth chapter is devoted to the patterns of interactions one needs to create to get the whole organisation innovating. Yes, the creation of an innovative culture assumes creative individuals and inventive teams. But these are just necessary pre-conditions, and are not sufficient alone. The dynamics that exist between teams (as well as between individuals in teams) are crucial. This chapter is underpinned by the research we have undertaken at THT (Trompenaars Hampden-Turner), into several thousand dilemmas of the participants at our workshops over the past ten years. We use this evidence to discuss not only the many dilemmas that need to be reconciled but also how to create what we will define as an integral culture of innovation. This culture consists of a focus on adaptation/flexibility, tasks/goals, structure/reliability *and* loyalty/commitment. We show the results of hundreds of organisations – ones that are innovative compared to those who struggle – and how their respective cultures differ.

The final fifth chapter proposes some ideas and actions for leaders and managers to help their organisations innovate.

I trust you will enjoy the book and have fun reading it.

Fons

INDIVIDUAL CREATIVITY 2

'There is a phrase I learned in college called "Having a healthy disregard for the impossible". That is a really cool phrase. You should try to do things that most people would not'

Larry Page, co-founder of Google Inc.

The creation of a culture of innovation often starts with the individual. There are few innovative organisations that don't have some unusually creative individuals. They are constantly challenging the organisation's routines, irritating their more conservative colleagues and making many mistakes on their way, from which they constantly learn.

People like actors and sculptors sometimes think that they all have creativity. But not everybody who has new ideas is creative. In the past it was a luxury; now, in the global economy, it is a necessity for survival. If you are not creative, you are dead. It is nonsense to say that you are creative or not – anybody can become creative, but this is counter-cultural. Researchers have had to overcome the prevailing wisdom that creativity is possessed by only a gifted few.

What kind of special competence(s) does the creative person possess? And is it innate or can you teach it? A great deal of effort has been made to try and define creativity. Early Greek philosophers thought it was a mystical inspiration from the seven muses and later Freud viewed creativity as resulting from the tension between conscious reality and unconscious.

One of the problems is the enormous range of implicit notions, that is, what people think creativity is implicitly, rather what has been explored systematically and rigorously through scientific research. Many of us have various ideas about creativity often based on 'great man' theories (such as Leonardo da Vinci or Einstein) but cannot explicitly state what this is. Most of the explicit theories generated in the field of creativity have focused on identifying how much creativity a person possesses rather than what it is. This approach is interested in measuring the capacity or ability to create, evaluating the 'correctness' of responses. Ability or level of creativity might be measured by fluency, flexibility, originality and elaboration; it is specific to the situation being examined. This is called the *level approach*. Thus we might contrive an instrument that 'measures' how much creativity a person has based on the following dimensions:[1]

- Connections: the capacity to make connections between things that don't initially appear to have connections
- Perspective: the capacity to shift one's perspective on a situation in terms of space and time and other people
- Curiosity: the desire to change or improve things that everyone else accepts as the norm
- Boldness: the confidence to push boundaries beyond accepted conventions and the ability to eliminate fear of what others think of you
- Complexity: the capacity to carry large quantities of data and to be able to manage and manipulate the relationships between information
- Persistence: the capacity to force oneself to keep trying and derive more and stronger solutions even when good ones have already been generated
- Abstraction: the capacity to abstract concepts from ideas.

Since the 1950s, researchers have focused on understanding how people manifest their creativity. This is called the *style approach*. It recognises that people express their creativity in different ways or cognitive styles. The style approach aims to answer the question 'How are you creative?'

---

1   As used by CREAX NV, Belgium, in their 'Creativity' Profiling tool

The need for identifying highly creative individuals generated an impressive amount of research that focused on the level approach. This situation reinforced a commonly held belief that creativity is limited to a minority capable of generating creative thinking. A corollary of this argument is that geniuses use cognitive processes that are radically different from those employed by most individuals. Most researchers conclude that we are all, or can be, creative to a lesser or greater degree if we are given the opportunity.

In summary, the spectrum of components that various authors come to include when defining creativity comprises four characteristics:

1   They always involve thinking or behaving imaginatively.
2   Overall this imaginative activity is purposeful: that is, it is directed to achieving an objective.
3   These processes must generate something original.
4   The outcome must be of value in relation to the objective.

Imagination is definitely a key part of creativity. But are all imaginative ideas creative? Suppose someone imagined a green and white spotted lion. Would this be creative? It may be that no one has conjured up a lion like this before. But what is the point of the idea? If someone thinks of an imaginative idea like this and then does not take it any further, are they creative? Creative people are purposeful as well as imaginative. Their imaginative activity is directed at achieving an objective (although this objective may change over time). Imaginative activity can only be creative if it is of value in relation to its purpose. This means asking questions such as, 'Does it do the job?', 'Is it aesthetically pleasing?', 'Is it a valid solution?', 'Is it useful?'

Sometimes our views about what is worthwhile and valuable may differ. Sharing judgments together can provide useful insight into what other people value. An act can be highly imaginative and original, but harm someone or destroy something. Are we happy with this kind of creativity?

An additional aspect has to do with dissecting creative thought into a process of dual exchanges through the interaction of two types of thinking – convergence and divergence. Definitions of divergent thinking usually include the ability to elaborate and to think of diverse and original ideas with fluency and speed. Ideating and brainstorming are premiere examples of this type of thinking. Convergent thinking is defined as the ability to use logical and evaluative thinking to critique and narrow ideas to ones best suited for given situations, or set criteria. We use this type of thinking when we make crucial and well-formed decisions after appraising an array of ideas, information, or alternatives. One needs to be able to weave in and out of divergent and convergent thought patterns in arriving at an appropriate conclusion specific for a given situation.

Once the level of creativity could be identified[2], consistently and reliably, the next wave of research examined whether or not those levels of creativity could be enhanced. Torrance[3] and Torrance and Presbury[4] identified a total of 384 studies that examined the effectiveness of creativity training. The majority of these studies concluded that creativity can be enhanced through formal training. Perhaps one of the most extensive studies on the effects of creativity training was conducted by Parnes and Noller[5].

Creative people are more...	Creative people are less...
Intuitive	Sensing
Perceiving	Judging
Thinking	Feeling
Extrovert	Introvert
Tortoise brain	Hare brain
Lateral	Focused
Risk taking	Securing
Hunting	Gathering
Individualistic	Consensus seeking
Right brain	Left brain
Etc.	Etc.

2   Guilford, J.P., *Way beyond the IQ*, Buffalo, NY: Beady Limited, 1977; Torrance, E. P., *Torrance tests of creative thinking: Norms and technical manual*, Bensenville, IL: Scholastic Testing Service, 1974

3   Torrance, E.P., 'Can we teach children to think creatively?', *Journal of Creative Behavior 6*, pp.236–262, 1972

4   Torrance, E.P. and Presbury, J., 'Criteria of success of 242 recent experimental studies of creativity', *Creative Child Quarterly 30*, pp.15–19, 1984

5   Parnes, S. J. and Noller, R.B., 'Applied creativity: The creative studies project Part 11', *Journal of Creative Behavior 6*, pp. 164–186, 1972

Unfortunately, the various measures are most often represented on linear-scale models, where one orientation excludes the other. Let's try it:

We argue that there might indeed be relationships between certain dominant orientations and the creative competence of an individual, but an important point has been missed. 'Stop!' some would say. Many have done solid research that shows a correlation between certain of the above preferences and creativity. Take the work of Kirton, the renowned British psychologist, who developed the well-regarded instrument, the KAI Inventory[6]. This measures individual styles of problem definition and solving. Kirton conducted a study showing the relationship between the KAI and the MBTI. The primary correlations of the KAI were with the MBTI's Sensing-Intuiting (S-N) and Judging-Perceiving (J-P) scales (Thinking-Feeling and Introvert-Extrovert were not highly correlated)[7]. Other studies went further, and one claimed that all four MBTI preferences correlate with creativity. Creative individuals tend to be more intuitive (N) than sensory (S), more perceiving (P) than judging (J), more extroverted (E) than introverted (I) and more thinking (T) than feeling (F)[8].

We don't dispute the relationship (statistical reliability) between these characteristics and preferences. However, we have found that the essence of the creative process is not in one or other position of a continuum, but in how the opposites of the scale interact. How are the faculties of imagination, holism, emotions and connectedness of our right brain interacting through our *corpus callosum* with the preferences of our left brain to be realistic, analytic and rational? Creative people integrate *all* those faculties and, in the process, discover new ideas and solutions.

Let's see what that means for the major models of distinctive orientations in the human brain:

---

6   Kirton, M.J., *Journal of Applied Psychology 61*, pp.622–629, 1980

7   Kirton, M.J., 'Adaptors and innovators: A description of a measure', *Journal of Applied Psychology, 61*, pp.622–629, 1976. Kirton, M.J., *Manual of the Kirton Adaption-Innovation Inventory*, London, England: National Foundation for Educational Research, 1977

8   Thorne, Avril and Gough, Harrison, *Portraits of Type: An MBTI Research Compendium*, Palo Alto, California: Consulting Psychologists Press Inc, 1991

1 Hare brain and tortoise mind (Guy Claxton)
2 MBTI (originally Carl Jung)
3 Adaptors versus Innovators (Michael Kirton)
4 The role of humour (Arthur Koestler)
5 NLP (Neuro linguistic programming)
6 HBDI (Ned Hermann's and cerebral dominance and whole brain concept)

We'll examine how powerful these ways of looking at reality are and, in addition, extend them by going beyond their inherently linear scales.

Hare brain and tortoise mind

Guy Claxton[9] makes a fundamental distinction between 'hare brain' and 'tortoise mind'. Hare brain with its faster thought-processing speed is analytical, calculating, self-conscious, and language-dependent (and given to 'monkey chatter' in its worse moments). As Claxton emphasises, 'hare brain' is the right tool for many situations, but not all.

But when creative solutions are needed, when a problem is fuzzy and imprecise, then the much slower, pondering and meditative strengths of the 'tortoise mind' give answers. Others have named this 'tortoise mind' as intuition, or the unconscious, and the id. Claxton goes on to name it the 'undermind'.

Based on research of electrical activity of the brain, Claxton describes that the brain unconsciously initiates action one-third of a second before conscious intention, which in turn precedes action by one-fifth of a second. The obvious question is, does the 'undermind' will things to happen that the conscious mind can only veto, not initiate? And who instructs the undermind, if it might not be our conscious mind? This would seem to violate the notion of human 'free will'.

Freud suggested the hidden, unconscious mind, the id, was the pressure cooker for much neurotic pain. Claxton wants us to see the under-

---

9 Claxton, Guy, *Hare Brain, Tortoise Mind: How Intelligence Increases When You Think Less,* Harper Perennial, 2000

mind 'tortoise mind' as a wondrous endowment of the brain and ever the equal of the conscious mind, the 'hare brain'.

Beyond the reach of conscious language, the undermind, to do its best, needs time to ponder and meditate. Claxton suggests that among religions, Buddhism best cultivates the undermind.

Confusion has to become our friend

Thus Claxton explores why intelligence increases when you think less. He builds a thesis on the dichotomy between the privileged mode of intelligence-conscious, result-oriented problem solving and the less respectable unconscious intelligence. This unconscious, or 'undermind', approaches problems playfully, examines the questions themselves and keeps us in touch with our poetic nature. His multidisciplinary approach is beautifully executed, with a constant dialogue on the virtues of intuition and a peaceful mind drawing on the works of poets, novelists and Buddhist teachings. In the West, 'intelligence' is measured by how well we can verbalise what we do, and therefore much of human capability suffers when put under the spotlight of conscious attention. He contrasts this Western approach with the actions of the 'unconscious intelligence', claiming that much of our best thinking takes place below consciousness.

That is why in management we go from one fad to another, because in the long term none of them seem to work. Management writers often say there are just five points, or seven habits, written in a very concise, rational way. You get excited, but the next day you have forgotten 50%, and by the next Tuesday 98%. The problem in business is that these commandments leave no room for the tortoise mind – a terribly dangerous development that stifles creativity and innovation and inevitably leads to bad decision making. These commandments are the widely held, but misguided, beliefs that being decisive means making decisions quickly, that fast is always better, and that we should think of our minds as being like computers. Sadly, most of us today believe that a computer is of more use to us than a wise person.

If you want to change your behaviour or incorporate a new habit, you have to continually practise and 'live' it for 30 to 40 days after you first learn it – otherwise it is gone forever. It is in the ongoing practice that you finally understand what was meant on that PowerPoint slide that was flashed up in front of you. And it seems very much like learning to speak a language. You start with some words and some basic grammar, then you get the holistic feel for the structure and flow of the language. And when you go to a shop and speak to the shopkeeper in her local language, do you still calculate the total cost of what you are buying in your mother tongue? It takes time to 'think' and 'calculate' in the new language.

Guy Claxton noted that to clarify by hare brain, you need to refer to the sort of deliberate, conscious thinking that we do when we apply reason and logic to known data. By tortoise mind he refers to a less purposeful, clear-cut, making less assumptions, more playful, more dreamy way of experiencing; we mull things over, we ponder a problem, we bare the problem in mind when we see the world go by. These leisurely ways of knowing are part of our intelligence. Hare brain works best when the problem is known and so is the answer. All the info is there to solve the problem. But real-world problems are not like that. When the problem is complex the tortoise mind works best. You may need measurements but you don't have them. In our Western culture, things that can't be measured are often ignored. Problems which are a bit dubious and loaded with assumptions are often either avoided or disregarded as not serious. In tortoise mind we like 'big buzzing confusions'. Where the measurements and data don't match. Answers are not clear-cut.

However, hare brain can solve small creative problems. The Japanese educational system stops people thinking for themselves. Yet, the Japanese are very good in solving tiny incremental problems. But when you want a new picture, you need tortoise mind. With our nine-dot problem discussed in the intro we see that hare brain tends to look within the imaginary frame. While our tortoise mind invites us to think outside of the box, to leave our self-imposed assumptions. Since creativity is inviting the tortoise mind to overcome your hare brain assumptions. These assumptions are what Scheerer calls 'fixations'. In our normal mode of operation we are so used to thinking mechanistically, linearly, conservatively and with no full inspiration, we take the problem and 'kill it'. And when it doesn't work we attack even more aggressively, with the same approach. Insight is often delayed or thwarted by 'fixation' on an inappropriate solution. Hare brain seems to dominate our automatic pilot. There are more sources of fixation. Here are some exercises that show it.

The match problem
Six matches must be assembled to form four congruent equilateral triangles each side of which is equal to the length of the matches.

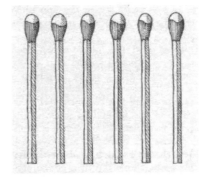

Solution: The match problem is solved by building a three-dimensional pyramid. Most people assume that matches must lie flat.

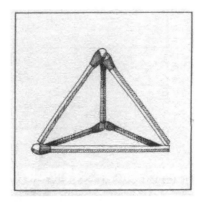

Like the nine dots problem we discussed in Chapter 1 we see that the matches problem cannot be solved, as one assumes that the matches must lie in one plane, and virtually everyone who tries it assumes just that. And the assumption is implicit. And the solution is obvious when one 'reformulates' or 're-centres' one thoughts. This is exactly what happens with the next riddle as well.

Perceptual fixation exercise:
Place element B on element A in such a way that two closed figures are formed.

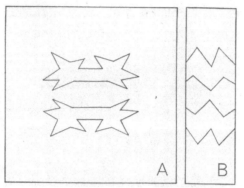

Solution: Recentering also solves this problem. The abstract shapes of A are broken up and rotated 90 degrees, B then fits properly.

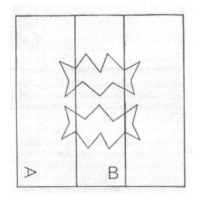

Sheerer quotes some experiments where fixation has been reported to be a function of involvement in a situation. When observers were given a conscious 'psychological distance', while watching 'subjects' running through the motions of solving problems, a significantly higher percentage of observers were able to solve the problem than those involved in the problem. And don't we all find this when watching games on television? Another reason for fixation is goal-directedness. A large majority of people are unwilling to accept a detour that delays the achievement of their goal and can be strengthened by too much motivation. A final quoted factor of fixation is habituation. In all cases fixation is overcome and insight attained by a sudden shift in the way the problem or the objects involved in it our viewed. It is our tortoise mind that can get the habits and goal-orientation of our hare brain broken.

Working together between hare brain and tortoise mind

Your hare brain you might easily conclude that it is in the tortoise mind that creativity is born. Yes, no doubt, using your tortoise mind made the difference. If you overcame your assumption that the matches should be lying flat, then it becomes easy. And if you overcome your assumption that the pictures need to be horizontal, the answer becomes obvious. But let's explore the following exercise. Here's a picture. What do you see?

Fig 2.1 What do you see?

Some people interpret the integrated picture as a skull and some as an older man drinking wine with a younger lady. Even looking at the integrated picture we can see the 'other image'. This might require you to let your mind drift (as in 'tortoise' mode). Both the hare brain of detail and analysis and the tortoise 'undermind' of the larger picture are in and

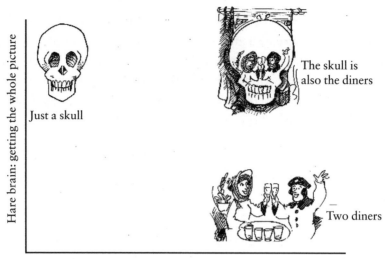

Fig 2.2 The whole picture in detail

of themselves deceptive. It is in the interplay between these orientations that we create our reality. Which you see first may be based on your expectation.

Let's go back to the question we asked at the beginning of this chapter. What were the circumstances in which your best creative idea was born? Where did it happen?

Let us take a guess. You weren't working hard and pushing for the breakthrough. Neither were you just relaxing and meditating waiting for ideas to drop into your mind. You got to some great ideas when you used the tension between hard work and relaxation. It was on vacation, when you suddenly got the new ideas that could make that difficult project so much easier.

In a nutshell, Claxton describes the hare brain as logical, fast, machine-like thinking. The tortoise mind, on the other hand, is slower, less focused, less articulate, much more playful, almost dreamy. In his book, Claxton says that the two sides *need each other* to come up with not just ideas, but good ideas. It is important to note that you need the hare brain. You need to get the information first and work hard on it through the hare brain. Only with that work will you make the tortoise mind effective and creative. You only get the solutions because you work hard. You need to do the hare brain thinking first! Then you must think through the situation and finally, when you have the ideas, you need to evaluate them logically and systematically (hare brain again). It becomes a spiral, reconciling the tension between hare brain and tortoise mind.

You may think that you consciously make moment-to-moment decisions about your life. But Claxton convincingly demonstrates that the mysterious 'undermind' has more to do with who we are and what we do than our conscious, logical, linear mind. The 'd-mode', our *deliberative* thinking style – the one we perfect in our years of schooling – is the most commonly accepted model of how our minds work. However, the experimental evidence suggests that d-mode thinking has relatively little to do with how we make most of the decisions in our lives. The d-mode actually comes up with plausible reasons that justify our actions, but it isn't the *source* of those actions. The conscious mind's job is to focus attention on a particular problem and maintain a coherent sense of ourselves; but these processes all come after the fact of our inner decision making. People often seem happier with their decisions in the long run if they think less about them from the outset. It is in this sense that 'think less' makes one more intelligent.

How to create the conditions for tortoise mind

Often the only difference between creative and uncreative people is self-perception. Creative people see themselves as creative, and give themselves the freedom to create. Uncreative people do not think about creativity, and do not give themselves the opportunity to create anything new. Being creative may just be a matter of setting aside the time needed to take a step back. Ask yourself if there is a better way of doing something. Edward de Bono calls this a 'Creative Pause'. He suggests that this should be a short break of maybe only 30 seconds, but that this should be a habitual part of thinking. This needs self-discipline, as it is easy to forget. On a corporate level 3M and Google have successfully experimented with the notions of '15 or 20 percent time'. It is borrowed from the academic world, where professors are given an average one day a week to pursue private interests. At Google, individual employees are expected to allot 20 percent of their time to whatever ideas interest them most. It is the refocusing between projects that makes tortoise mind and hare brain interact creatively:

'The 20 percent rule was a way of encouraging innovation, and both Brin and Page (the two co-founders of Google FT) saw this as essential to establishing and maintaining the right culture and creating a place where bright technologists would want to work and be motivated to come up with breakthrough ideas ... People talk over lunch about the things they are playing with.'[10]

Much earlier 3M developed a 15 percent rule to spin innovation. The extra time to dream yielded amongst other things, the idea for Post-it notes.

MBTI revisited While few people would argue against the desirability of employing creative people, how to accurately identify creative people is less clear. There are instruments that claim to measure almost anything, so wouldn't it be wonderful if we could simply test a person's creativity? The goal of making personality traits measurable is the fundamental quest of professional tools that seek to offer an objective assessment. Of these, the champion is the MBTI instrument, the most widely used personality inventory in history, which is administered to over three million people a year[11]. Human Resources professionals depend on it when their clients need to make important business, career, or personal decisions.

One of Jung's most important discoveries was the realisation that, by understanding the way we typically process information, we can gain insights into why we act and feel the way we do. In particular, he noted that, in order to understand ourselves better, we need to understand the way we typically perceive, and then act upon, information. Jung identified two core psychological processes: *perceiving*, which involves receiving, or taking in, information; and *judging*, which involves processing

---

10 Vise, David A., *The Google Story*, fully updated edition, Pan Books 2005, p.7

11 Myers, Isabel *Gifts Differing*, Palo Alto, California: CPP Inc, 1995. And look at http://www.winovations.com/NFmbti.htm Myers, Isabel Briggs, and McCaulley, Mary H., *Manual: A Guide to the Development and Use of the Myers-Briggs Type Indicator*, Palo Alto, California: Consulting Psychologists Press Inc, 1992

that information (e.g. organising the information and coming to conclusions from it).

Jung identified two further ways of perceiving information, which he termed *sensing* and *intuiting*, and two alternative ways of judging information, which he termed *thinking* and *feeling*. Moreover, he noted that these four mental process can be directed either at the external world of people and things, or at the internal world of subjective experience. He termed this attitude towards the outer world *extraversion*, and this attitude towards the inner world *introversion*.

MBTI limitations

So, can this widely used instrument also give some clues to the creativity of the individual being evaluated?

One such variation of the basic tool that we have found to be particularly useful is the MBTI Creativity Index, or MBTI-CI. The MBTI-CI is calculated by taking MBTI scores and applying an algorithm, developed out of 30 years of creativity research at the Institute for Personality Assessment and Research (IPAR)[12].

Creative individuals tend to be more intuitive (N) than sensory (S), more perceiving than judging (J), more extroverted (E) than introverted (I) and more thinking (T) than feeling (F)[13]. In another study, the MBTI profiles of innovators varied greatly. The great majority had an ENT combination, while the split between judging and perceiving was approximately 50:50. Other studies have shown that up to 95% of senior corporate managers are STJs[14], with Americans tending to be an E type and British managers a dominant I type.

And the frequently occurring difference between innovators and managers is a source of potential conflict. Intuitives and sensers view the

---

12 Gough, Harrison, 'Studies of the Myers-Briggs Type Indicator in a personality assessment research institute', paper presented at the *Fourth National Conference on the Myers-Briggs Type Indicator*, Stanford University, California, July 1981

13 Thorne, Avril and Gough, Harrison, *Portraits of Type: An MBTI Research Compendium*, Palo Alto, California: Consulting Psychologists Press Inc, 1991

14 Kroeger, O. and Thuessen, J. *Type Talk at Work,* Dell Publishing: New York, pp 394–399, 1992

world very differently. A change will always seem greater to an ST than to an NT, because STs are typically more comfortable with continuous change than with discontinuous change. An NT, however, may actually enjoy discontinuous change.

But what happens when users try to apply methodologies and instruments to measure things that go beyond the environment and delimitations in which they were developed?

Personality and creativity

What we really need to ask is why the underlying models were designed around mutually exclusive values in the first place. It is because our Western, hare brain way of thinking is based on Cartesian logic and forces us to say it is *either/or*, not to say *and ... and*. This contradicts what Jung had in mind when he originally construed the underlying conceptual framework behind MBTI[15].

We want to consider how we can extend MBTI by slightly adjusting the context and thereby make it a more reliable instrument, measuring creativity far beyond any cultural preference.

Although there is some evidence that the typologies are statistically related to creativity, we believe that the assumptions on which the instrument is based prohibit its potential to measure creativity. We need a different approach, and a different context.

First of all, it needs to be redesigned into an Integrated Type Indicator that overcomes the limitation of the linear model; and secondly, we need to adjust the process in which it is embedded.

The big advantage of the MBTI is how readily recognisable it is. We have all encountered extroverts or overwhelming introverts at social gatherings. We have all tried to reason in vain with someone whose feelings are so strong that our efforts were useless, or have witnessed someone calculating while others visibly suffer in the process. The MBTI is a 'ready reckoner' of personality types, but there are serious problems of superficiality and of proper application.

---

15 Jung, Carl G, *Psychological Types*, Routledge & Kegan Paul, 1971

The superficiality problem stems from *either/or* classifications. Is it really the case that we judge *or* perceive, think *or* feel, etc.? Jung himself arranged his 'opposite' archetypes in the shape of Tao and wrote of *effectance through synthesis*. He warned us that ESTJ was the dominant profile of relatively young, brash people in the practical world. He regarded these as the dominant Western industrial values. But is this related to the process of creation? Our research suggests not!

What Jung advocated was that we move *out* of this pattern and mature over time, especially in our later years. He believed that introversion should qualify extraversion, that intuitive faculties should guide sensing, that our feelings could tell us which thoughts were more profound and that good judgment was based on the fullness of perception. In short, Jung sought to *reconcile* his four functions, not polarise them. He regarded the less preferred end of any function as lying beneath the *persona* (the superficial character armour). Where personalities over-emphasised their dominant preferences, they could be haunted by their 'shadow sides' – that is, the values that are repressed and pushed down into unconsciousness. But these values were always there, and all the more pervasive for being denied!

The problem of applicability is even more troublesome (in staff selection, for example). Suppose a company *is* predominantly ESTJ: does that mean that a candidate with this profile should be preferred or *not* preferred? Clearly he or she would 'fit in', but is this necessarily desirable, particularly if we are looking for innovation? Haven't we missed an opportunity to make the company more diverse? After all, customers come in every shape, size and type. Might it not be wise to match the preferences of our customer base with our employee base and listen to someone *different* for a change?

The problem of applicability doesn't end here either. Suppose we decided to achieve a balance. Should this be an aggregate balance (i.e. all employees), a departmental balance or a peer group balance? And where should this balance take place: *within* the personality or *between* personalities? Jung wanted a better balance and a synthesis within the personality, but the MBTI is of little use in this respect, because it fails to register our less preferred types. We are left with the possibility of creating balance within the group, but what do we do when the first INFPs we hire feel rejected by the ESTJs?

And might it be actually harmful to just accept your type as fixed? Might you not, like the tragic heroes of world drama, *overplay your winning combination*, go on doing what you have habitually done and not change? In our experience, those who administer the MBTI work hard to bring to the surface the less preferred type, and so make their subjects more whole – but are these efforts enough to compensate for the selective reinforcement of one's customary façade? Perhaps not.

It's also instructive to consider what the MBTI does *not* measure. It does not measure the capacity to reach out to another person with the opposite profile, and it does not measure how severely the 'shadow sides' are repressed within the candidate. Severe repression would, according to Jung, make it very difficult to communicate with someone with the characteristics you so dislike in yourself.

Can the MBTI be improved by extending the underlying model?

We have seen that the MBTI brilliantly measures four very important decisions but is unable to assess to what extent these contrasting types have been integrated *with* each other, as opposed to subordinated *to* each other. Might it be possible to *conserve* the best aspects of MBTI while inquiring about the extent to which introverted ideas have been extroverted, sense impressions have been intuited, feelings have been thought about and judgments formed on the basis of strong perceptions? And in this process of integration of opposites might we just find the key to creativity?

Given the millions of people who are interested in one way or another in MBTI profiles, it is important *not* to let all this measurement, coaching, mentoring and insight go to waste. We must, if possible, build on this famous instrument, not try to demolish it or replace it. This is what we have tried to do in our Integrated Type Indicator.

Our Integrated Type Indicator

If you are recruiting someone who has a slight preference for intuiting, what do you do if sensing is the organisation's preference for making a

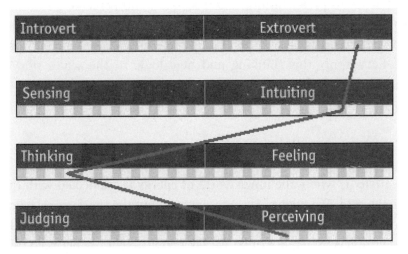

Fig 2.3 Classic MBTI – profile of a creative individual

successful career? And in an international company, can MBTI be of help in finding creative people to stimulate innovation?

Research has sought to correlate the MBTI scales with different job categories, functions and (national) cultures. There is evidence to suggest which dominant type best fits a marketing role, which type is found most often amongst successful managers and what is dominant in Asia versus the USA. And we have seen that considerable research has been focused on relating creativity to certain preferences on those MBTI categories.

However, since most of this research has been done in the USA, we are suddenly confronted with some interesting dilemmas that challenge this principle.

We have to remember that much of this type of research owes its origin to western thinking and research methodologies, even though it has been 'exported' across the world. When we begin to reflect on the philosophy of the underlying paradigms of inquiry and incorporate other types of logic, such as Yin Yang or Taoism, we soon realise that we have been restrictive in basing the profiling on bi-modal dimensions. We believe that the creative individual in the western world tends to start with thinking followed by feeling, intuiting followed by sensing, perceiving by judging and extroversion by introversion. In the Latin world, creativity tends to start with feeling, later checked by thinking, and in Asia there is a tendency to prefer intuition, introversion and perceiving followed by sensing, extroversion and judging. However, creativity exists in all environments; there is just a difference in preference about where to start.

Let's apply this thinking and new logic to the scales of Myers-Briggs.

Extroversion versus introversion

Creativity is where the inner world of energy is connected with the external world. We might have a preference, but the spark starts when the two 'energies' meet. So what we measure with the original MBTI type of question is preference only. We ask people to choose between two opposites. For example:

a)   Most of my personal energy comes from the people I meet and greet. It is as if an electric current between us has charged up my batteries.

b)   Most of my personal energy comes from ideas, feelings, and data generating sparks within me. I need to be alone and free from interruption to organise my ideas.

Obviously a) represents an extrovert and b) an introvert. But see what happens if we add the following two alternatives:

c)   Most of my personal energy comes from the people I meet and greet, but in quieter moments, what I experienced through them starts generating within me.

d)   Most of my personal energy comes from ideas, feelings and data generating sparks within me. But then comes the acid test, when I tell everyone what I have conceived. These four options tell us much more than the two initial ones. They allow subjects to:

1)   prefer extroversion to introversion
2)   prefer introversion to extroversion
3)   be extrovert before introverting

4) introvert and so invite extroversion to be given closure.

Our contention is that answers c) and d) select more integrated personalities and are more creative in the process. Answer c) puts extroversion first and then takes the results inside. Answer d) puts introversion first but in a way that communicates it to the outside world to share with others. We believe that people who select c) and d) are not only more creative, but *more able to deal with people of the opposite persuasion.*

The choices can be tabulated as follows.

Fig 2.4 Extroversion/Introversion

Choices a) and b) each exclude their opposites, but choice c) feels in a way inclusive of thinking, while choice d) thinks in a way inclusive of feeling. Both paths culminate in reflecting on vivid experience at top right. We believe that inclusive or integrated choices reveal leadership potential and predict more effective performances.

Note how the integrated answers move across the continuum, while the polarised ones stay put.

Who are the creative heroes who symbolise the integration of an extrovert mode with subsequent introversion? Donald Schön called these Reflective Practitioners[16]. They first practise in the real world and later reflect on that practice. Perhaps the world's first Reflective Practitioner was Hippocrates, a working physician in Athens whose experience culminated in the Hippocratic Oath, taken by doctors to this day and now over two thousand years old.

Note that the curve (c) starts with extroverted conduct, visiting patients in their homes, trying sometimes desperately to save lives. It then learns from and codifies this experience ex post facto.

Who are the creative leaders who symbolise the introverted style, which then acts boldly and decisively in an extroverted fashion? Western history's most illustrious example is probably Martin Luther. That he was initially introverted is in no doubt. He was a monk, much given to prayer, reflection and anguished confessions. He entered a monastery in 1505 and it was not until 1517 that he famously nailed his 95 theses to the church door in Wittenburg. We would have heard neither of Hippocrates nor of Luther had they not moved between types. In the case of Hippocrates, this was from extrovert practice to introvert codification; in the case of Martin Luther, it was from cloistered introversion to a famous act of extrovert defiance.

Thinking versus feeling

The MBTI tests for the relative dominance of thinking versus feeling by the following type of questions.

When I make a decision I think it is most important:

a)   to make sure that I test the opinions of others
b)   to reach a decisive conclusion.

The thinking personality marks b) and the feeling one a).

In all creative processes we combine logic and reason with what we believe to be right. We all use both modes for our innovations. Some start

---

16 Schön, D.A., *The Reflective Practitioner*, New York: Basic Books, 1983

with what they believe to be fair and correct by pre-defined rules. Others prefer to start in a subjective manner based on what they believe to be right within their own value systems.

To capture the essence of the creative process we added two more possibilities:

c)   to test the opinions of others before deciding.
d)   to be decisive and thereby elicit others' opinions.

These four questions tell us much more than the two initial ones. They allow subjects to:

1)   prefer feeling to thinking
2)   prefer thinking to feeling
3)   feel out opinions before thinking
4)   think and so invite feelings to be expressed.

Our contention is that answers c) and d) select more integrated personalities and are more creative in the process. Answer c) puts feelings first and then thinks about these. Answer d) puts thinking first but in a way that elicits feelings. We believe that individuals selecting c) and d) are not only more creative, but *more able to deal with persons of the opposite persuasion.*

The choices can be tabulated as follows (see over). Choices a) and b) each exclude their opposites, but choice c) feels in a way inclusive of thinking, while choice d) thinks in a way inclusive of feeling. Both paths culminate in *thoughtful sensibility* at top right. We believe that inclusive or integrated choices reveal leadership potential and predict more effective performances.

Sensing versus intuiting

These two types are contrasting ways of processing information. Sensing looks at discrete, empirical facts and records observations. Intuiting looks into a whole phenomenon, interpreting its meaning and significance. Here we ask: *Which* option best describes how you manage?

Fig 2.5 Feeling/Thinking

a) In solving problems I like to analyse the situation and look hard at the facts. I believe these speak for themselves, needing no window dressing.

b) In solving problems, I like to gain deep insights into the meaning of the issue. Once I have grasped this I test my supposition against all available facts.

c) In solving problems, I like to gain deep insights into the meaning of the issue. Facts are dependent on context. Once I grasp the context the facts fall into place.

d) In solving problems I like to analyse the situation and look hard at the facts, but then I start to draw inferences, until the meaning of this issue is clear.

The integrated answers are b) and d). The polarised answers are a) and c). In d), the person starts with sensed facts and develops intuitions. In b), the person starts with deep intuitions and tests these against the available facts.

The greatest scientific example of the sensing type was Sir Isaac Newton. He convinced three centuries of science to look first at the facts and only then to draw cautious inferences. The real world was neither what we wanted it to be, nor influenced in any way by our wishes. We must humbly reflect God-given realities on the pupils of our eyes and not let our beliefs or conceits stand in the way. Only after we have made sure

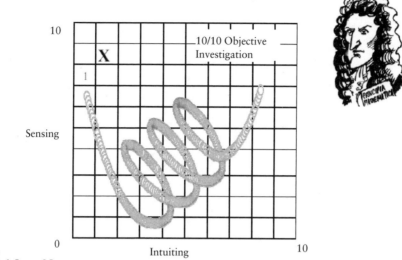

Fig 2.6 Isaac Newton

of all the facts should we start to draw inferences. This approach to the physical world is illustrated in in the anticlockwise spiral.

Yet science moves on, and theoretical physics is quite another challenge, needing intuition to disentangle its puzzling anomalies. Albert Einstein was famed for his intuitive powers and would cut himself shaving if an exciting intuition struck him. But none of this means that he ignored the available facts. Having gained his intuitions, he proceeded to test them – an example of how one type helps to verify the conjecture of another. The helix winding clockwise from intuition to sensing is illustrated in Fig 2.7.

Judging versus perceiving

A final example focuses on the preference between judging or perceiving. This is about how we perceive events and form judgments about them. Once you have made a judgment, this tends to foreclose further perceiving because you will probably act on that judgment. Some people judge very quickly; others always want more and more information. The perceiving preference leads to openness to experimentation and making mistakes, while a preference for judging leads to a need for structure and predictability.

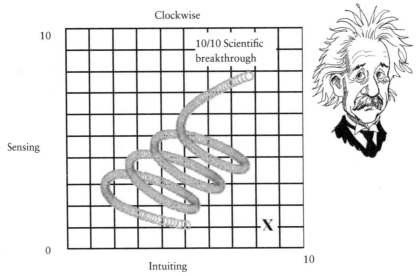

Fig 2.7 Einstein

Conventionally, instruments pose questions such as the following: *While* tackling an issue I prefer to work:

a)   in a structured and organised way
b)   flexibly and with the necessary improvisation.

In some cultural environments, such as Germanic cultures, there is a tendency to score higher on a), while b) would appeal more to the Latins. Thus in a team/group of both Germans **and** Latins, wouldn't the following be more effective to diagnose effective orientations?
While tackling an issue I prefer to work:

c)   in a structured way in order to stimulate improvisation within certain boundaries
d)   with the necessary improvisation, trying to develop the best procedures and organisation.

Here again c) and d) are the integrated answers and a) and b) are the polarised ones, in which judgment squashes perception and perception postpones judgment indefinitely.

The four choices can be tabulated as follows.

Fig 2.8 Perceiving/Judging

Choices a) and b) each exclude their opposites, but choice c) feels in a way inclusive of thinking, while choice d) thinks in a way inclusive of feeling. Both paths culminate in the error-correcting attitude at top right. We believe that inclusive or integrated choices reveal creativity potential and predict more innovative performances.

The Integrated Type Indicator model (ITI)

Let's summarise our conclusions. Like most social science instruments, MBTI-like scales attempt to measure object-like 'things'. The presence of extroversion, sensing, thinking and judging is thought to exclude introversion, intuiting, feeling and perceiving. In fact, all human minds contain both types – and they are not 'things' at all, but differences on a continuum along which we move continuously.

In our extended model of MBTI – the ITI – we use our own questions, which represent the two extreme opposing values for each conjugate pair. However, we also add two further choices that represent the clockwise and anticlockwise reconciliation of these extremes.

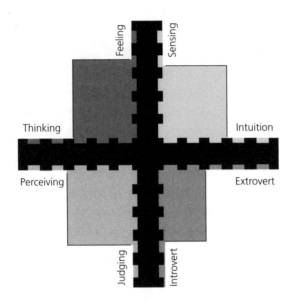

Fig 2.9 sample ITI profile

By combining the answers from a series of questions in this extended format, we can compute a profile that reveals the degree to which an individual seeks to integrate the extreme dimensions, and so shows that individual's potential for creativity.

From the relative shapes and sizes of the four blocks, you can tell the extent to which the ends of the four functions have been reconciled. Are candidates able to move from perceiving to making judgments, from generating introverted thoughts and ideas to expressing these openly to others in extrovert ways? This capacity to move to and fro on the four continua is much more valuable to the organisation than getting stuck at one end or the other: you can't usefully process information from a fixed position.

If each variable is scaled from 1 to 10, then we can attain an integration score for a whole group, department or company, like this:

(Introvert + Extrovert) + (Sensing + Intuiting) + (Thinking + Feeling) +
(Judging + Perceiving) ÷ 4 = Developing Creativity Potential

We have analysed responses to the web-based version of this ITI model. Taken by itself – that is, responses to this instrument alone – this model has already generated insights over and above the basic MBTI profile based on the traditional four linear scales. We have found that the instrument already has high validity and reliability – for example, design engineers in organisations such as the highly creative SatNav, TomTom and Siemens score above the mean on our index. However, the insights from our ITI are more usefully considered when combined (i.e. triangulated) with other measures we describe later.

Reconciliation: a new paradigm for creativity beyond cultural bias

Simply rejecting opposite orientations will get you nowhere. Abandoning your own extreme and adopting the other extreme is like trying to impress on your first date by acting out an unfamiliar role – and you'll soon be found out.

The integrated approach enables us to determine an individual's propensity for reconciling dilemmas, as a direct measure of creativity. We call this ability *innovative competence*. It transcends the single culture in which it may be measured and so provides a robust, generalisable model for all environments. Reconciliation is the real essence of the creative individual.

This ITI is different because it is underpinned by the recognition that, while managers work to accomplish this or that separate objective, creative leaders deal with *the dilemmas of seemingly 'opposed' objectives, which they continually seek to reconcile*. Given the importance of reconciling opposites, it is surprising that no instrument that measures this has been published before.

Published models of creativity tend to lack a coherent, underlying rationale or proposition that predicts effective innovative behaviours. These models tend to seek the same end, but through different approaches. Because of the methodology adopted, these are only prescriptive lists, like a series of ingredients for a recipe – you can only guess at what the dish is going to be. There is no underlying rationale or unifying theme that defines the holistic experience of the meal.

This creates considerable confusion for today's innovative leader. Which paradigm should s/he fit into? Which meanings should s/he espouse: his or her own or those of the foreign culture? Since most of our creativity theory comes from the USA and other English-speaking countries, there is a real danger of ethnocentrism. We do not know, for example, how the lists cited fare outside the USA, or how diverse conceptions of creativity may be. Do different cultures require different styles? Can we reasonably expect other cultures to follow a lead from outside those cultures?

We can see how creative leaders are able to reconcile opposites. Richard Branson can switch from being David in one business situation to Goliath in another. He reconciles the big player with the small player, so that the smaller player becomes big.

Our concern about applying any linear model across international boundaries might be explained by our own overdeveloped reconciliation profiles. But we insist that, with the combination of opposed orientations, today's leader can flourish in diversity. And no one has ever measured anything like that in us.

Please test yourself: www.ridingthewhirlwind.com

Learning styles revisited

Inspired by the work of Kurt Lewin[17], Kolb[18] provides one of the most useful descriptive models of the adult learning process available.
Kolb's model suggests that there are four stages that follow from each other: *concrete experience* is followed by reflection on that experience (*reflective observation*) This may then be followed by the application of known theories or general rules (*abstract conceptualisation*), and then the modification of the next occurrence of the experience (*active experimentation*), leading in turn to the next concrete experience. This cycle may all happen in a flash, or over days, weeks or months, depending on the experience itself, and there may be a simultaneous 'wheels within wheels' process.

Concrete experience corresponds to 'knowledge by acquaintance', direct practical experience (or *apprehension*, in Kolb's terms), as opposed

17 Lewin, K., (1942) 'Field Theory and Learning' in Cartwright, D. (ed.), *Field Theory in Social Science: selected theoretical papers*, London: Social Science Paperbacks, 1951

18 Kolb, D., *Learning style inventory*, Boston, MA: McBer and Company, 1985

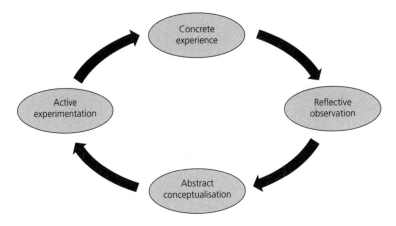

Fig 2.10 Kolb's learning styles

to 'knowledge about' something, which is theoretical, but perhaps more comprehensive (hence *comprehension*), represented by *abstract conceptualisation*. *Reflective observation* concentrates on what the experience means to the experiencer, (it is transformed by *intention*), while *active experimentation* transforms the theory of *abstract conceptualisation* by testing it in practice (by *extension*).

Kolb's model assumes that active experimentation and reflective observation are *opposite* modes, and that abstract conceptualisation and concrete experience are opposite modes, as described in Figure 2.10 and 2.11. By crossing or combining the four learning modes, four learning style types can be defined as follows.

- *Divergers – reflective observation combined with concrete experience*. Divergers have opposite characteristics to convergers. Their greatest strengths are creativity and imagination. A person with this learning style is brilliant at viewing situations from many perspectives and at generating ideas. Research shows that divergers are interested in people and tend to be imaginative and emotional. They tend to be interested in the arts and often have humanities or liberal arts backgrounds. Counsellors, organisational development specialists and personnel managers tend to be divergers.
- *Assimilators – reflective observation combined with abstract conceptualisation*. Assimilators understand and create theories. They excel at inductive reasoning and in synthesising ideas into an integrated whole. This person, like the converger, is less interested in

people and more concerned with abstract concepts, but is less concerned with the practical use of theories. For this person, it is more important that the theory should be logically sound and precise; in a situation where a theory or plan does not fit the 'facts', the assimilator would be likely to disregard or re-examine the facts. As a result, this learning style is more characteristic of the basic sciences and mathematics than the applied sciences. Assimilators often choose careers that involve research and planning.

- *Convergers – active experimentation combined with abstract conceptualisation.* Convergers' greatest strength is the practical application of ideas. They seem to do best in those situations where there is a single correct answer or solution to a question or problem, and where they can focus on specific problems or situations. Research on this style of learning shows that convergers are relatively unemotional, preferring to deal with things rather than people. They often choose to specialise in the physical sciences, engineering and computer sciences.

- *Accommodators – active experimentation combined with concrete experience.* Accommodators are polar opposites to assimilators. Their greatest strengths are executing plans and experiments and involving themselves in new experiences. They are risk-takers and excel in situations that require quick decisions and adaptations. In situations where a theory or plan does not fit the 'facts', they tend to discard it and try something else. They often solve problems in an intuitive trial-and-error manner, relying heavily on other people for information. Accommodators are at ease with people but may be seen as impatient and 'pushy'. Their educational background is often in practical fields such as business or education. They prefer 'action-oriented' jobs such as nursing, teaching, marketing or sales.

Convergent and divergent knowledge

This distinction was first made by Hudson[19] in terms of styles of thinking

---

19 Hudson, L., *Contrary Imaginations; a psychological study of the English Schoolboy*, Harmondsworth: Penguin, 1967

rather than forms of knowledge. Convergent knowledge brings a number of facts or principles to bear on a single topic: problems have 'right' and 'wrong' answers. Hudson believed that convergent learners tended to be more highly valued in school, because most assessment approaches focus on convergent skills. Examples include applied mathematics, engineering and some aspects of language. Convergent knowledge is located in the quadrant between abstract conceptualisation and active experimentation.

Divergent knowledge, on the other hand, is (very broadly) claimed to be more about creativity: it is about the generation of a number of accounts of experience, such as in literature, history or art. Judgment about the quality of divergent knowledge and skills is much more difficult, because these are private areas. It is generated in the quadrant between *concrete experience* and *reflective observation*.

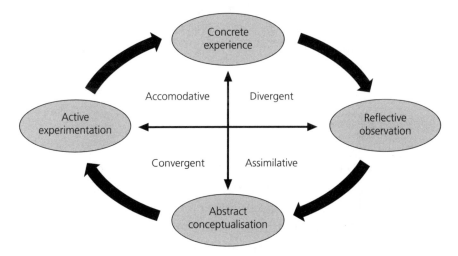

Fig 2.11 Four kinds of knowledge

Assimilation and accommodation

Hands up if you remember your Piaget! Assimilation and accommodation are, in his view, two dialectically related processes (i.e. opposing principles – *thesis* and *antithesis* – between which a *synthesis* has to be negotiated) that describe the (roughly) different relationships between knowledge of the outside world and knowledge already held in our heads.

Kolb's approach to integrating these Piagetian ideas within the cycle is generally less successful than his application of Hudson. The search for new rules (abstract conceptualisation) to formalise observations (reflective observation) may well be an accommodative exercise, and very often trial-and-error learning (active experimentation) consists of moving from one known rule to another in the hope that one of them fits, so it is has an important element of assimilation. Nevertheless, the approach does help to focus attention on the relationship between the general and the particular. Assimilation includes fitting particular instances into general categories; accommodation is about working from the general principle to the particular application

Broadly speaking, Kolb suggests that: practitioners of creative disciplines, such as the arts, are found in the *divergent* quadrant; pure scientists and mathematicians are in the *assimilative* quadrant; applied scientists and lawyers are in the *convergent* quadrant; and professionals who have to operate more intuitively, such as teachers, are in the *accommodative* quadrant. There are also differences in the location of specialists within the more general disciplines.

Learning styles and creativity

Kolb and Hudson took a useful step by integrating the extreme poles of their adjoining scales into new categorisations of personalities: respectively, the diverger, assimilator, converger and accommodator. However, our research indicates that the full creative process lies in the integration of the opposites, i.e. the reconciliation of active experimentation and reflective observation, and of concrete experience and abstract conceptualisation. Again, where opposites connect, the creative juices flow.

As mentioned earlier, Donald Schön referred to the reconciliation of theory and practice as The Reflective Practitioner[20]. Educators have become familiar with the concept of reflective practice through Schön's work[21]. This work has an historical foundation in a tradition of learning

---

20 Schön, D.A., *The Reflective Practitioner*, New York: Basic Books, 1983
21 Schön, D.A., *Educating The Reflective Practitioner*, San Francisco: Jossey-Bass, 1988

supported by Dewey, Lewin and Piaget, each of whom advocated that learning is dependent on the integration of experience with reflection and of theory with practice. Although each argued that experience underpins learning, they also maintained that learning can't take place without reflection.

Reflective practice is a mode that integrates action with reflection. It involves thinking about and critically analysing one's actions with the goal of improving one's professional practice.

But is this essential for creativity?

According to Schön, the stage is set for reflection when 'knowing-in-action' – the sort of knowledge that professionals come to depend on to perform their work spontaneously – produces an unexpected outcome or surprise.

This surprise can lead to one of two kinds of reflection:

- *reflection on action*, which occurs either following or by interrupting the activity, or
- *reflection in action*, which occurs during the activity (without interrupting it), by thinking about how to reshape the activity while it is underway.

Schön[22] says that, when reflecting in action, a professional becomes a researcher in the context of practice, freed from established theory and techniques and able to construct a new theory to fit the unique situation.

Before we can change professionals' theories or ideas about practice, we have to identify them. However, in skilful knowing-in-action, much of the 'skilful action reveals a knowing more than we can say', a tacit knowledge[23]. In other words, professionals are not able to describe what they do to accomplish an activity. However, reflective practice remains important as it develops the ability to articulate that tacit knowledge, in order to share professional skills and enhance the body of professional knowledge and practice.

---

22 Schön, D.A., *The Reflective Practitioner*, p.51, New York: Basic Books, 1983
23 Schön, D.A., *The Reflective Practitioner*, p.51, New York: Basic Books, 1983

Reflective practice has both advantages and disadvantages. It can positively affect professional growth and development by leading to greater self-awareness, to the development of new knowledge about professional practice, and to a broader understanding of the problems that confront practitioners. However, it is a time-consuming process and may involve personal risk, because the questioning of practice requires that practitioners be open to an examination of beliefs, values and feelings about which there may be great sensitivity.

Schön[24] suggests that professionals learn to reflect in action by first learning to recognise and apply standard practice rules and techniques, then to reason from general rules to problematic cases characteristic of the profession, and only then to develop and test new forms of understanding and action when familiar patterns of doing things fail.

So in short, the reflective practitioner, in reconciling active experimentation with reflective observation, needs also to integrate abstractions with concrete experiences in order to be creative and avoid making the same mistakes forever.

This complementary process leads to what Lakoff calls the conceptualising experience or experiential conceptualisation.

So, let's apply this logic of reconciliation to the full creative cycle, starting

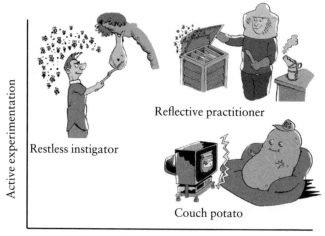

Fig 2.12 Reflective practitioner

---

24 Schön, D., *The Reflective Practitioner: How Professionals Think in Action*, Ashgate; New Ed edition (1991)

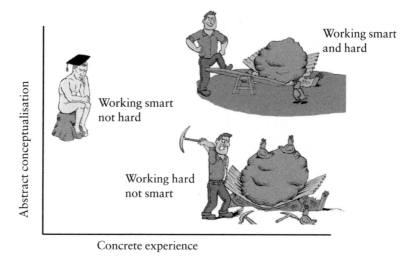

Fig 2.13 Abstract conceptualisation/Concrete experience

with a concrete experience, leading to all kinds of diverse possibilities (do they make sense in theory?), which are reflected upon through inductive assimilation.

Note that this also means that we have to ask different types of questions, to probe degrees of reconciliation, and abandon linear models.

Adaptors versus innovators

Kirton's KAI[25] measures individual styles of problem definition and solving. Style, in this case, refers to an adaptive, building or analogic problem-solving style versus an innovative or pioneering style. Kirton argues that:

> 'Adaptation-Innovation theory is located in the domain of cognitive function, specifically part of the strategic stable characteristic preferred style that people seek to bring about intended change … there is a sharp distinction between style and the capacity or level of cognition of which a person is capable, whether this is inherent or learned. The latter describes

25 Kirton, M.J. (ed.), *Adaptors and Innovators: styles of creativity and problem solving*, revised edition, New York: Routledge, 1994

the "power of the engine"; the former the "manner in which it is driven".'[26]

One way to look at the KAI is as a measure of an individual's relation to their problem-solving style, whereas the MBTI is more of a measure of an individual's relation to their problem-solving style and social environment. According to Kirton, it follows that style is unrelated to technique, as often discussed by Osborne or de Bono.

In the list above, Jack Hipple (et al.) summarises the two groups and how each group is viewed by its opposites[27].

Table 2.1: Characteristics of adaptors and innovators

Adaptor	Innovator
Efficient, thorough, adaptable, methodical, organised, precise, reliable, dependable	Ingenious, original, independent, unconventional
Accepts problem definition	Challenges problem definition
Does things better	Does things differently
Concerned with resolving problems rather than finding them	Discovers problems and avenues for their solutions
Seeks solutions to problems in tried and understood ways	Manipulates problems by questioning existing assumptions
Reduces problems by improvement and greater efficiency, while aiming at continuity and stability	Is catalyst to unsettled groups, irreverent of their consensual views
Seems impervious to boredom; able to maintain high accuracy in long spells of detailed work	Capable of routine work (system maintenance) for only short bursts; quick to delegate routine tasks
Is an authority within established structures	Tends to take control in unstructured situations

26 Lakoff, George and Johnson, Mark, *Metaphors We Live By*, Chicago: University of Chicago Press, 1980

27 Kirton, M.J. (ed.), *Adaptors and Innovators: styles of creativity and problem solving*, revised edition, New York: Routledge, 1994

How the 'other side' often sees extreme adaptors and innovators

Dogmatic, compliant, stuck in a rut, timid, conforming, and inflexible	Unsound, impraclical, abrasive, undisciplined, insensitive, and one who loves to create confusion

When collaborating with the 'other side'[28]:

Collaborating with innovators	Collaborating with adaptors
Supplies stability, order and continuity to the partnership	
Is sensitive to people, maintains group cohesion and co-operation	
Provides a safe base for the innovator's riskier operations	Supplies the task orientations, the break with the past and accepted theory
Appears insensitive to people, often threatens group cohesion and co-operation	
Provides dynamics to bring about radical change, without which institutions tend to ossify	

Kirton noted that some managers were able to initiate change that improved the current system, but were unable to identify opportunities outside the framework of the system[29]. Kirton calls this style 'adaptive'. Other managers were fluent at generating ideas that led to more radical change, but failed in getting their radical ideas accepted. Kirton termed this style 'innovative'. These observations gave rise to Kirton's hypothesis that there is a personality continuum called adaptor-innovator, which presumes two very different approaches to change[30]. The adaptor prefers to improve things while working within the given paradigm or structure. Adaptors are characterised by precision, reliability, efficiency, discipline, and conformity, and are safe and dependable in their work. The adaptor reduces problems by improvement and greater efficiency (see Table 2.1).

28 Hipple, Jack (et al.), 'Can corporate innovation champions survive?', *Chemical Innovation Magazine*, Vol. 31, No. 11, pp.14–22, November 2001

29 Kirton, M.J. (ed.), *Adaptors and Innovators: styles of creativity and problem solving*, revised edition, p.11, New York: Routledge, 1994

30 Kirton, M. J., *Management initiative*, London: Acton Society Trust, 1961

The innovator prefers to do things differently, to challenge the paradigm or structure. Innovators are sometimes seen as undisciplined, tangential thinkers who approach tasks from unexpected angles. The innovator solves problems by breaking down patterns and doing things differently. The descriptions of adaptors and innovators shown in Table 2.1 show the extreme characteristics.

Kirton believes these cognitive styles are found in everyone and that they play a role in creativity, problem solving, and decision making. He maintains that adaptors and innovators possess equal levels of creative potential. However, as Kirton says, 'Although both adaptors and innovators create in their own way, the literature on creativity has concentrated on describing the innovators.' Both styles of creativity are important and necessary for the development and growth of our organisations.

In Kirton's original KAI tool, a 32-item questionnaire was used to measure an individual's problem-solving style, on a scale from 32 to 160. A person with an adaptive style will usually score between 60 and 90, whereas a person with an innovative style will score between 110 and 140. In reality, whether an individual shows the characteristics of an adaptor or an innovator depends on context – where they are on the continuum relative to those with whom they interact. People with scores in the middle of a group, Kirton assumes, have some of both characteristics, and in some circumstances, they can function as 'bridgers'[31], people who are able to connect the strengths of innovators and adaptors.

The main weakness of Kirton's assumptions perhaps lies in their succinctness and precision. One of the main assumptions is that cognitive style, which underlies the KAI instrument, is conceptually independent of cognitive capacity, success, cognitive techniques and coping behaviour. We agree with this – but this all comes from an assumption that Kirton makes more implicitly: that the adaptor style and the innovator style are mutually exclusive and if you score in the middle you are a 'bridger'. This is shown well by the presentation of the scores of the KAI instrument as the scores on a balance, where a higher score on the adaptor side

---

31 Kirton, M. J., 'Adaptors and innovators: a description of a measure', *Journal of Applied Psychology 61*, pp.622–629, APA, Washington 1976

automatically results in a lower score on the innovator side[32]. Much as with the MBTI, the main focus is on the preferences that people have, as people have two hands but prefer to write with one.

Empirical evidence from our research

In order to provide empirical evidence for these bold conclusions, we asked some 250 managers from a variety of cultural backgrounds to complete our ITI and an adapted version of the KAI.

We found that creative people move more effectively *between* intuition and thinking, that innovators extrovertly publish their introverted calculation and constantly learn by oscillating *between* judging and perceiving, and finally check their feelings *through* thinking.

Moreover, certain individuals (mainly from north-west Europe and the USA) have a slight but significant preference for ISTJ, regardless of whether they were integrating or not, while most Asian started from INFP and most Latins from ENTP. The correlations between these preferences and the KAI scores were much less strong than between KAI and the reconciliation between the extreme orientations described by Jung.

At any one moment, you are being *either* introvert *or* extrovert, intuiting *or* thinking, but wasn't Einstein's brilliance that he thought (later) *about* his intuitions? Suppose we took a whole minute of time. Might not some of us choose to place our individuality at the service of the community? In doing so, might we become *more* individual, yet also *more* communal? Isn't the question at least worth asking?

The important finding is that culture often determines the side that respondents start from. So we are not saying that one culture is more creative than another; only that their starting point for looking at a problem is different.

Not combining opposite logics shows an absence of creativity. Clapping with one hand makes little noise.

---

32 Kirton, M. J., *Applied Psychology, 61,* pp.622–629, 1980. Kirton, M. J., *Long Range Planning (UK),* 17 (2), pp.137–143, 1984

Revisiting definitions of innovation and creativity

But do innovation and creativity really work like this? Our evidence suggests not. Isn't creativity closer to clapping two hands than writing with one? Look at the description of the innovator. We think that a better term would be 'inventor'. The innovator in you takes the inventions and implements them through adaptation. So again, innovation is the reconciliation of invention and adaptation. The inventor in you redefines the problem, and the adaptor implements the solution. When the inventor comes up with a breakthrough idea, the adaptor checks if it can work. Indeed, individual creativity and innovation shouldn't be measured on the KAI scale, but on one that measures the propensity of people to integrate the characteristics of inventor and adaptor.

So, instead of questions from Kirton's original KAI that are based on linear (Likert) scales, our 'integrated innovation indicator' asks questions like the following.

Q1 Which of the following four options best describes how you most frequently behave?
a) I am efficient, thorough, adaptable, methodical, organised, precise, reliable and dependable. (5 score in invention, 0 score in adaptation, 0 score in innovation)
b) I am ingenious, original, independent, unconventional and unpredictable. (0 score in invention, 5 score in adaptation, 0 score in innovation)
c) I am continuously checking in an organised and methodical manner whether my original ideas do work in practice. (5 score in invention, 0 score in adaptation, 8 score in innovation)
d) I am methodical and organised first, to set the basis to launch my unconventional ideas. (0 score in invention, 5 score in adaptation, 5 score in innovation)

Q2 Which of the following four options best describes you?
a) I tend to be concerned with resolving problems rather than finding them. (5 score in invention, 0 score in adaptation, 0 score in innovation)

b) I tend to discover problems and avenues for their solutions. (0 score in invention, 5 score in adaptation, 0 score in innovation)

c) I tend to look for redefining problems by trial and error after I have tried to solve the existing problems first. (5 score in invention, 0 score in adaptation, 5 score in innovation)

d) I tend to look for conventional methods of solving problems only after I have discovered all the possible problems and avenues for their solutions. (0 score in invention, 5 score in adaptation, 8 score in innovation)

Our research reveals that the traditional choice between invention and adaptation shows our preference for either one, while the reconciliations as described by options c) and d) score high on the innovation index. We can illustrate the main dilemma of the innovative style as the reconciliation between the adaptor and inventive styles as shown.

Is the creative individual the basis for innovation?

It is obviously a good start to have some creative talent in your organisation, but this is far from being the guarantee of an innovative team. It is a necessary but not a sufficient condition.

Research has demonstrated that individuals of various styles possess different creative strengths and weaknesses (Bloomberg, 1967; Kirton, 1976; Spotts and Mackler, 1967; and Zilewicz, 1986). Utilising the styles and strengths which various individuals bring to a group will empower the group to function more effectively and efficiently. Kirton (1977) believes that a team that is heterogeneous (in terms of styles) will be better prepared to meet all contingencies than a team that is homogeneous. Understanding and appreciating individual differences can be very beneficial for organisations. Instead of valuing one style, the organisation should respect and value the adaptive and innovative styles of creativity. Individuals within an organisation can work more effectively together by capitalising on each other's strengths, rather than punishing each other because of individual differences. If an atmosphere of openness and trust prevails in the organisation, the adaptors and innovators will be able to join their creative talents to propel the organisation to success.

Creativity + Business Discipline = Higher Profits Faster from New Product Development

Stevens (et al.) conducted a study among 69 analysts, evaluating 267 early-stage new product development (NPD) projects in a major global chemical company over a 10-year time span. This study found positive correlations between profits resulting from NPD project analyses and the degree of creativity of the analysts evaluating those projects[33].

Analysts with creativity indices above the median for the group identified opportunities that provided 12 to 13 times more profit than those with creativity indices below the median, when both groups were rigorously trained and coached in 'stage-gate' business analysis methods.

NPD requires breakthrough creativity because the first ideas for commercialisation are almost never commercially viable until they have been substantially revised through a particular thought process. It is therefore most productive to preselect innovative, creative people for the early stages of NPD, then to teach this group the business discipline required in stage-gate NPD processes.

The results show that, by utilising these principles, both the overall speed and the productivity of typical NPD processes can be increased approximately nine-fold, an order of magnitude when compared to today's typical linear stage-gate processes.

From humour to creativity:

Many of us fall into the same trap when we go hunting for brilliant new ideas. We roll up our sleeves and say, 'It's time to get to work'. A look at the creative process, however, suggests the opposite and that instead we should roll up our sleeves and say, 'It's time to go and play'.

As Koestler has shown, humour is built on bi-sociation – the ability mentally and emotionally to traverse both paths of a bifurcating line of thought, the recognition of which provokes laughter. Bi-sociation through humour allows managers a more complex view of their organi-

33 Stevens, Greg, Burley, James and Divine, Richard, 'Creativity + Business Discipline = Higher Profits Faster from New Product Development', *Journal of Product Innovation Management* 16 (5), pp.455–468, 1999

sation: it offers an and … and rather than an either/or orientation to the contradictions of managing and organising. The evidence from our work shows that this cannot be achieved with linear thinking and an a priori need to avoid mistakes. If we respect the diversity of the human species and its cultures, the (business) world we are living in starts to be loaded with dilemmas that cannot be pushed aside by making linear choices. An alternative, non-linear approach is needed to reconcile these dilemmas. Humour is just one powerful way of approaching dilemmas effectively.

Here are just some of the reasons why humour and/or play can lead to creative thinking:

1   Both humour and creativity involve playing with ideas and changing our mental perspectives.
2   Play uses other part of our brains – literally providing an energising experience that gets the neurons charged up and ready for action (laughing increases the level of adrenaline and oxygen going to the brain).
3   Play lowers our inhibitions, so we become less likely to suppress truly novel ideas.
4   Humour in a workplace fosters a culture of risk taking – an essential ingredient
5   Humour challenges our basic assumptions and rules.
6   Play encourages spontaneity – another key to generating creative ideas.
7   Humour keeps people focused on solutions rather than problems (brainstorming vs. 'blame-storming').

Creativity and humour are identical. They both involve bringing together two items which do not have an obvious connection and creating a relationship. We can elicit this underlying dichotomy in some examples from the better known comedies.

'Everyone's a winner'
Only Fools and Horses grew to become one of the very best British sit-coms of all time and has been shown repeatedly throughout the world for some 20 years. The sublime comic adventures of the Trotter brothers, Del and Rodney, follow a series of dilemmas as they duck and dive through

the streets of south London, trying to make a living. Writer John Sullivan was a master at creating whole episodes from placing the lead characters in a dilemma as the source of the humour.

In one storyline, the main character Del got to hear that the local pub needed to be redecorated, for which the brewery (as owner/land-lord) would pay. One of Del's best friends, Charlie, was the local builder and decorator and usually did this work. On the one hand Del wanted the chance to earn some easy money by quoting his services to paint the pub but on the other hand not upset his relationship with his friend. His friend said he would do it for £1000.

After some tortuous to and fro between the extremes of the dilemma played out during the episode, Del finally persuaded the pub manager to accept a business proposal on behalf of the brewery that Del's 'company' would do the work for £3000. When asked by the manager to justify the cost, Del explained that he would take £1000 profit himself for master-minding the business deal and he would give the manager £1000 bonus. 'But who will do the actual work?' demanded the pub manager. 'Why my mate Charlie will do it for £1000 – that's all he wanted in the first place,' said Del. "The brewery can afford it with all the beer I have bought in here."

Del proclaimed that everyone wins because his mate Charlie gets paid for doing his job, the manager gets a bonus, Del himself makes a fast buck and the brewery win because they get the pub redecorated and then Del and Charlie will spend their cash on even more beer.

'It's prime time TV'

The Simpsons revolves around 'the normal American family in all its beauty and all its horror,' as executive producer James L. Brooks once described it. While from time to time Homer, the lead character, may not feel understood, he finally always becomes aware of his failures and eventually manages to show his love, affection and even desperation: 'Marge, I need you more than anyone else on this entire planet could possibly ever need you. I need you to take care of me, to put up with me, and most of all, I need you to love me, because I love you.' Homer is more human than any human, always yearning for any kind of indulgence, but at the same moment loving and desperate to be loved.

Many scenes play out dilemmas as the source of the humour without the viewer necessarily identifying the dilemma or even recognising an underlying dilemma. In Episode 812, Mountain of Madness, Homer has brought his family along on a business team-building exercise in the woods, and his son Bart is standing in front of a Smokey the Bear statue, which has an electronic voice and a little 'quiz' to administer. Bart and Smokey have the following exchange:

> Smokey: (electronic intonation) 'Who is the only one who can stop forest fires?'
> (Bart examines response panel, which has two buttons, marked 'you' and 'me'. He presses 'you'.)
> Smokey: (electronic intonation) 'You pressed YOU, meaning me. This is incorrect. You should have pressed ME, meaning you.'

In Episode 203, Treehouse of Horror, the Simpsons are abducted and Kang is addressing them for the first time. Marge says, 'You speak English!' Kang says, 'Actually, I'm speaking Rigelian, but by an amazing coincidence, the two languages are exactly the same.'

This bi-sociation shows the power of creating a new reality by combining opposites. How this relates to creativity is even more evident by the following storyline:

An African man in his early fifties is fishing at the border of a lake when an expatriate sits next to him.

'So who are you sir?' asks the African. 'Oh I am an expatriate working hard.' 'Why so hard, sir?' 'Then I can keep my house here and go back to the UK.' 'And then?' 'Then I am going to work even harder to get promoted.' 'And then?' 'I'll buy another home and so on.' 'But why are you doing all this?' 'So I can sell all my houses when I am in my fifties.' 'So what?' 'Then I have enough money to retire early and do my hobbies.' 'What's your hobby sir?' 'I love fishing.'

A story or narrative only proves popular if it grabs our interest. It does this by negotiating crisis after crisis or, as we would say, dilemma after dilemma. Here we analyse 'The Builders', one episode in the *Fawlty Towers* series, starring John Cleese, Connie Booth and Prunella Scales. The protagonist in this series is Basil Fawlty, co-proprietor with his wife, Sybil, of a Torquay hotel, Fawlty Towers. It is upon poor Basil that our dilemmas bite.

A word should be said about the background to this whole series. Britain is moving from a much more traditional, straight-laced society towards the permissive norms that arose in the late '60s. Hotels in the '50s and '60s barred co-habiting couples from occupying the same room; hotels which allowed this were considered sleazy and not respectable.

Basil has some character defects too. He is a snob, resenting those he regards as 'riff-raff' occupying his hotel. The hotel itself is an extended satire on levels of poor service in the British hotel trade, aided and abetted by underpaid, foreign hotel workers, who rarely understand a word you say.

In *The Act of Creation*, Arthur Koestler saw humour as the embryo of creativity. In humour there is an unfolding logic which we can all follow, which collides with and is demolished by another line of logic, which cuts across it. Hence a man makes overtures to a young woman, who demurs. 'My heart is not free,' she tells him. 'I wasn't aiming that high,' replies the man. Here the word 'high' refers both to the nobility of the sentiment and the young woman's anatomy. There is a *collision between* these two concepts – a double meaning – so that in the funny story we only laugh if the punch line takes us by surprise.

For humour to extend to creativity, the fusion between two frames of reference must do more than collide and make us laugh – a mere gag can do that. It must *fuse into a larger meaning*. We'll see that 'The Psychiatrist' manages to create such larger meanings, and includes considerable insight into the human condition and into persons who prefer to 'uphold morality'. John Cleese's interest in psychology is crucial here. The hang-ups Basil suffers are dissected with a keen blade. It is vital that the audience does not sympathise with Basil; his misfortunes are self-inflicted and we rather rejoice that his killjoy antics end in defeat. Basil is fighting a rearguard action against the breaking down of class barriers, the acceptance of eroticism, the tolerance of bad service and the growing culture of what, today, we call 'spin.'

A dilemma analysis of 'The Builders' episode of *Fawlty Towers*

This is a review of 'The Builders' episode from *Fawlty Towers*, considered from the perspective of the core philosophy of this book. This story explores how humour 'works' to hold human conduct up to ridicule and thereby purge us of our misconduct. Comedy is 'first aid' for foolishness. Tragedy is what happens to people who cannot laugh at themselves and who persist in folly. Both on their own and in the extreme are forms of 'negative feedback.'

Both are forms of human 'play' when we pretend we can smoke out error before it destroys us. To err while playing can be entertaining. To err in reality may be fatal. The earliest comedies and tragedies were forms of moral teaching staged by the Cult of Dionysus in Ancient Athens. They were all expressions of *sophrosyne*, the maxim 'Nothing to Excess'. Comedy is excess that is funny. Tragedy is excess that is catastrophic. When presented, the bodies of the audience literally *convulsed* with laughter or with cathartic grief.

'The Builders' episode was acted by John Cleese and written in collaboration with his ex-wife, Connie Booth. It relates to those who manage businesses because it deals with the contracting out of services. Although the antics of the principals are hilarious, they deal with serious dilemmas facing most managers. Watching the errors of Basil Fawlty, the chief character, is an entertaining way to learn.

Basil and his wife have the weekend off and have left Polly, their manager, in charge. She is probably the hotel's most stable and competent employee, but she had a bad night and is looking for a much-needed sleep, so that Manuel, the Spanish waiter, is the person who in practice will be left in charge.

Anyone familiar with the series will know that Basil believes in cheap labour, the cheaper the better and he also prefers subservience. Having saved money on their hire, he manages them in a very directive manner, which does not shrink from physical assault if they misunderstand his often agitated orders.

As Basil and his wife are leaving, Polly is warned that some builders are coming around to re-position the door from Reception to the Dining Room and it will *not* be Mr Stubbs, their faithful and reliable contractor, but Mr O'Reilly, a cut-price incompetent, whose only virtue is that he is cheap. He is already two months late erecting a garden wall. Basil has countermanded his wife's orders and aims to make savings behind her back. He swears Polly to secrecy.

This introduces to the audience what is probably the most venerable dilemma in the history of business strategy. Do you go for the Low Cost Solution, pricing your product at a level which will drive your competitors out of business, while still making a profit, or do you offer Premium Service, such an enjoyable stay that your guests gladly pay extra to enjoy it. It is clear that Basil Fawlty is an advocate of the first strategy and his wife is much closer to the second. Manuel and O'Reilly give him a 'cost advantage', or so he hopes!

The dilemma looks like this:

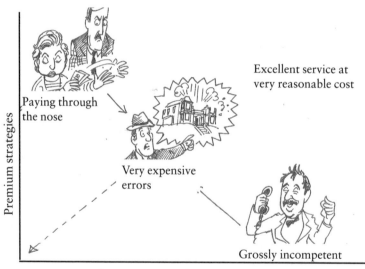

Figure 2.14 Retain excellent service

In the meantime a delivery man has carried a garden gnome into Reception. It is to play its part.

Basil tells Polly to supervise O'Reilly's workers when they arrive. But she wants to take a rest and sleep and tells Manuel to wake her up when the workers arrive. He promises to do so, but when the workmen

Figure 2.15 Including diverse persons

arrive he cannot wake her and, proud of being left 'in charge', decides to instruct them personally, with disastrous consequences.

'Are you men?' he asks them, and, believing their masculinity is being called into question, they become pugnacious. Basil calls in to make sure they have the right instructions, but when he says he's Basil Fawlty, Manuel tells him Basil is away and hangs up. This happens three times and finally enraged Basil tells Manuel to give a message to one of the workers, the one with a beard, to say that he's 'a hideous orang-utan'. Poor Manuel repeats the message and is duly punched out. A revenged Basil forgets the purpose of his call, an oversight which will prove fatal. The workmen remove the door, completely walling off Reception from the Dining Room. Here the dilemma is one of Diversity–Inclusion.

The world is becoming ever more diverse and Manuel and O'Reilly are just two symptoms of this fact, as are the superior management skills of Mrs Fawlty and Polly, both far more effective managers than Basil, the male proprietor.

Basil's main means of 'including' employees who misunderstand him is to lay his hands on them or curse them. But he cannot have it both ways. If he chooses to employ cut-price foreign labour he needs to invest time and money to help them and train them. He needs to explain himself clearly and patiently, but he does none of these things. It is Polly who speaks a little Spanish who most helps Manuel. Indeed the women are the reconcilers in this episode, while the men are the buffoons, oscillating from top-left to bottom-right on the dilemma charts. Like many contemporary employers, Basil must confront diversity, which includes the Spanish, the Irish, the female and in other episodes, Germans, a deaf woman, an amorous French lady and his *béte noir* guests of working-class origin.

A worried Basil now returns after lunch to make sure everything is all right! He is beside himself with rage at the disappearance of the dining room door and the solid wall confronting him. He picks up Manuel bodily and shouts 'Where is the door?' holding his face to the wallpaper, while Manuel echoes in surprise 'Door gone!'

Basil storms upstairs to where Polly is still sleeping. He blames Manuel. He blames her. Her curses and he shouts. Then she reminds him that the mistake was made by O'Reilly's men, which he, Basil chose to do the work. Basil explodes:

'Here I was thinking it was Manuel's fault for giving the wrong instructions. Then I thought perhaps it was *your* fault because I left you in charge and you went to sleep. Now I realise it is MY fault! I must be

Figure 2.16 Whose fault?

punished, naughty, naughty, naughty!' And he frenziedly smacks his own behind in a fit of fury.

The dilemma is one of Personal Fault versus Systemic Error. In a sense everything that goes wrong *can* be blamed on somebody, typically the person closest to the mistake when it happened. Yet punishing this person may avail you nothing if the real fault is in how the organisational system has been designed. The series is not called *Fawlty* (i.e faulty) *Towers* for nothing! Among the system's faults is the hiring of diverse persons without adequate supervision. An inability to communicate with Manuel, which is as much management's responsibility as it is his, and a husband-wife conflict over which contractors to hire, has led to outright deception and resulting confusion.

The dilemma is exacerbated by the fact that Basil refuses to take responsibility for the system he has himself designed and then mocks this insight by spanking himself. With employees/contractors like these his vacation is quite unaffordable.

One of the more amusing characteristics of Basil is that he is a *radfharen*, literally a (racing) bicyclist, who bows his head to authority and stamps on the people beneath him. The expression is German and is used for supervisors of his type. While blustering and shouting at everyone it becomes clear that what he most dreads is his wife's anger. He is desper-

Figure 2.17 Authoritarian conduct vs cringing deference

ate for her not to discover his subversion of her authority. 'We are all dead!' he wails at the prospect of his wife finding him out.

It is not just his wife he defers to. In other episodes it is a con-man pretending to be a lord, two doctors, a suspected hotel inspector and a disgruntled American guest who wants a late dinner and for whose benefit Basil is pretending to lecture a non-existent chef. All these episodes follow the same pattern. He even takes a swing at the peer-turned-villain.

Driven by fear of Mrs Fawlty he gets on the telephone to Mr O'Reilly.

'This is Basil Fawlty, the poor sod you work for.' He goes on to complain that the unfinished garden wall is still not complete, and is taking 'longer than Hadrian's Wall', but this is 'Nothing that you can't be sued for.' He wants his dining room door restored forthwith or 'I will insert a large garden gnome into your person... My wife will be back here in four hours!'

In a Responsibility Hierarchy, we both give orders *and* defer to those who know more than we do, see top-right of diagram.

Mr O'Reilly comes around but is in a jocular mood. 'You worry too much Mr Fawlty. The Good Lord intended us to enjoy ourselves.'

Figure 2.18 Panic vs denial

'My wife is the one who enjoys herself. I worry!' Basil tells him.

'The Good Lord will see us all through…' O'Reilly is waxing philosophical.

'If the Good Lord is mentioned once more…' snarls Basil, 'I will move you closer to him.' There is humorous counterpoint here between O'Reilly's relaxed and fatalistic attitude and Basil's gnawing panic at Mrs. Fawlty's pending appearance. Basil finds himself incapable of convincing O'Reilly that they are *both* in trouble! The first is too sanguine, the second too agitated and they are not communicating. We can call this panic versus denial (see Figure 2.18).

Doubtless O'Reilly believes he is calming Basil down, soothing him with wise reflections. But then his social skills are on a par with his professional skills and he is making Basil *worse* not better. We are spiralling downwards to disaster. While they might have helped each other to see sense (see top right of diagram) they are instead becoming ever more panicked and ever more self-satisfied, each provoking the other's excuses to greater extreme.

It is at this point that Mrs Fawlty comes back to the hotel having forgotten something she needed for her weekend. Basil orders O'Reilly

The more panicked Basil becomes …

… the more O'Reilly tries to soothe him …

… which only makes Basil panic more because …

… the idiot does not see the danger, so …

to hide himself in the bar. Since the door to the dining room has plainly disappeared Basil tries to blame it all on Mr Stubbs.

'There's Stubbs for you,' he exclaims, clicking his tongue, 'a reputable builder!'

'Where is Mr O'Reilly?' demands Mrs Fawlty.

'You never cease to amaze me,' bluffs Basil. Just because a mistake has been made, you ASSUME that Mr O'Reilly...

'His van is in the driveway.'

Basil immediately deepens his deception.

'Well he's here *now*, to clean up the mess...'

But Mrs Fawlty points out that if Mr Stubbs made the mistake then Mr Stubbs should put it right and moves towards the telephone. Basil desperately distracts her before she can reach it. He's just tried Mr Stubbs. He is out.

At that moment the telephone rings. It is Polly, holding her nose to make her voice sound deep and pretending to be Mr Stubbs. But Mrs Fawlty is not fooled. 'You deal with this,' she tells Basil and goes in search of Polly, finding her in the office behind Reception.

'Well done, Polly!' gasps Basil down the telephone. 'Where are you?'

'She's in here with me, Basil,' says Mrs Fawlty ominously. 'I am going to make you *so sorry* for this!'

'Fair enough,' Basil says miserably.

'You thought I'd believe your *pathetic lies* that this was done by a professional builder? Why did I trust you? We've used O'Reilly three times and three times he's failed us. The last time we had no water for a week! You use him because he's CHEAP. But you ignore the fact that he's NO GOOD. He belongs in a zoo! He's a thick Irish joke!'

It is at this moment that O'Reilly decides to cease hiding in the bar and 'calm things down'. He will defuse the situation with a little light banter.

'Oh dear, oh dear', he says cheerfully. 'What have I done *now*?' He decides unwisely to show gallantry towards 'the little woman' and treat her as if they were emotionally intimate.

'I like a woman with *spirit!*' he tells Mrs. Fawlty.

'You do?' she queries, eyes narrowing in rage.

'I do, I do!' he cries sticking out his scrawny chest like a bantam cock. Basil groans with horror. He knows how his wife will react. She picks up the broom and starts to belabour O'Reilly.

'I've seen better things than you crawl out of the garden pond. You're lazy, incompetent, useless…' and she sets about him while he jumps around protesting.

Clearly Mr O'Reilly is a complete stranger to gender equality in the workplace. He has not only infuriated her by doing an incompetent job, he now undermines her authority as the co-owner of the hotel by treating her anger as attractive and sexy, a tactic he clearly believes will 'charm' her. Such conduct puts business women in the bedroom not the board-room and understandably raises their ire. O'Reilly has heaped insult on incompetence.

No one denies that you need more than technical skills to survive in business. Skills of social engagement are vital. But trying to 'charm' a female boss when you have been utterly incompetent is a recipe for disaster. Mr O'Reilly is not just making light of his errors, he is trying to substitute for his incompetence with seductive overtures. The vicious circle reads as follows.

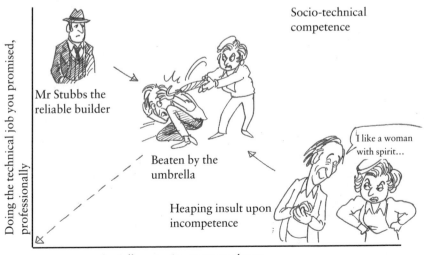

Figure 2.19 Technical and social skills

We have another downward spiral to disaster which happens to be very funny since those involved richly deserve their fate. Comedy has to be fair for us to laugh.

Mrs Fawlty now goes over to the telephone and arranges for Mr Stubbs to put things right first thing Monday morning. She then leaves to return to her vacation. The garden gnome delivered earlier is still in Reception. After instructing Basil she says, 'On second thoughts why don't we leave this in charge (the garden gnome). He'd do a better job.' Basil seethes.

An extremely chastised Mr O'Reilly is packing up his things ready to go home, but with his wife gone Basil is once more in domineering form. 'Are you going to take that from her?' He demands 'We'll show her! You are going to do the best day's job of your whole life!' Once again we get an insight into the employees Basil prefers, those he can completely make or break. O'Reilly goes to work.

We fade into the next morning. It is 9.00am. The door to the Dining Room has been restored and Basil is looking triumphant as Mrs Fawlty and Mr Stubbs enter the hotel together. There is nothing left for the (expensive) Mr Stubbs to do. Basil's faith in Mr O'Reilly has been

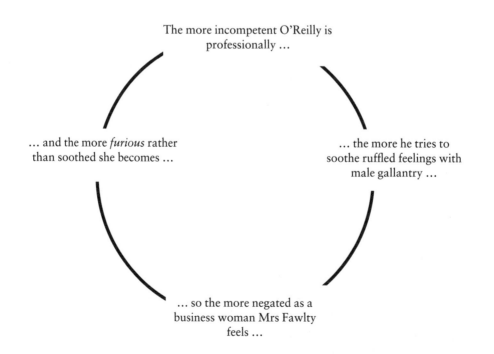

The more incompetent O'Reilly is professionally …

… the more he tries to soothe ruffled feelings with male gallantry …

… so the more negated as a business woman Mrs Fawlty feels …

… and the more *furious* rather than soothed she becomes …

vindicated. His money-saving motives *were* astute after all. Mrs Fawlty is clearly perplexed. 'I'm afraid this is rather embarrassing,' she begins. "I wanted you to do this job but the work appears to have been done already... I can't tell whether it is really a good job...'

'Looks pretty good to me,' says Stubbs.

'You see dear,' it says Basil delightedly. 'The opinion of a professional builder...'

'Of course, you used a jade lintel,' pursued Stubbs. 'Or was it a concrete lintel?' Basil opens and then shuts his mouth in confusion. Stubbs has realised on inspection that there is no lintel at all.

'But this is a supporting wall!' he explains. 'The whole building could come down at any moment... Cowboys!' And he goes hastily to work.

'BASIL!' shrieks Mrs. Fawlty. But Basil is striding down the street the garden gnome under his arm like a battering ram. Its pointed cap is sticking ominously upward. 'I'm on my way to see Mr. O'Reilly!' he announces.

Figure 2.20 Two forms of leadership

Our final dilemma is about two styles of leadership. Delegating your Authority to responsible persons and Making your own Decisions.

When we lead we need to delegate some decisions to experts. Neither Basil nor O'Reilly know what a lintel is! Mrs Fawlty has delegate wisely to the person who ultimately saves the hotel from collapse. In the meantime Basil, who trusts only himself, hires incompetents and then shouts frenzied orders at them, which only makes things worse, is chasing after O'Reilly with the garden gnome.

Humour teaches by indirection. It does not tell you what is right. It tells you what is ridiculous and hence wrong. It points out the Rock on the one side and the Whirlpool on the other and leaves us free to steer somewhere in between the two. In one sense *Fawlty Towers* is 'dated'. It is so full of political incorrectness that it could probably not be made today. We regard this as a pity, because the best way to rid ourselves of stupid prejudices to which Basil is so prone is to LAUGH at them. Condemnation is far less effective. Many people will settle for being considered wrong or immoral but to be laughed at – that is the surest remedy! We can reprove each other without getting nasty.

There are always two opposite ways of messing up. We must just laugh and try again.

NLP – Neuro-linguistic programming

Is there one universal way of being creative or are people creative in different ways?

Originally, advocates of Neuro-linguistic programming (NLP) taught that most people had an internal preferred representational system (PRS) and preferred to process information primarily using one of the senses.

Some people have a predominance for the visual and explain how they 'saw' and idea in their head. Others are auditory and describe noises or whispers they 'heard' in their head that gave them the new idea. Some are primarily kinesthetic and can 'feel' or 'touch' an idea. There are even the gustatory who get a taste in their mouth when creating, and some can literally 'smell' (olfactory) an idea. NLP practitioners have long observed that different people use their senses in different ways in displaying their creativity but this may not mean that they use their senses in a hair brain mode. While the loss of Beethoven's hearing prevented him from playing the piano properly, it did not limit his creativity. Between 1800 and 1824 Beethoven wrote nine symphonies, many of which are considered to be perfect. He went completely deaf in 1804, around the time he completed his third symphony, the Eroica.

NLP practitioners believe that you should observe the person with whom you are interacting and try to determine their preference. And then abandon your own preferred orientation and adopt the preferences of your business counterpart. However, we believe that this is like trying to impress someone on your first date by acting in an unfamiliar style. Creativity based on the integration and combination of all the senses is far more powerful.

Cerebral Dominance and HBDI

Ned Hermann 'began developing the HBDI™ and Whole Brain Thinking in the 1970s. It is well established that the human brain is highly specialised. His whole brain theory allocates the brain's specialised modes into one or more of these four physiological structures. This allocation of specialised modes is the basis of the four quadrant model. Since dominance can only occur between paired structures, we now have the basis of a much more sophisticated and useful model comprising not only the left and right modes, but also the cerebral and limbic modes. The cerebral modes are made up of the two interconnected cerebral hemispheres and the limbic mode is comprised of the two interconnected halves of the limbic system. Extensive data has shown that there are an equal number of people whose mental preferences are primarily cerebral or limbic as those that are primarily left or right.

Therefore, the four quadrant whole brain model (HBDI profile) allows us to differentiate between not only the more popular notions of left brain/right brain, but also the more sophisticated notions of cognitive/intellectual, which describes the cerebral preference, and visceral, structured and emotional which describes the limbic preferences. Hermann claims that once an individual or group has their HBDI profile, they are better able to successfully apply not only their understanding of their thinking style, but also their preferred learning, communicating and problem-solving styles, and hence become more creative and effective. However, no one HBDI profile appears to correlate with the capacity to be creative.

But again we argue that it is the integration of the cognitive and limbic, and the rational analytic with the more emotional quadrants that as a whole and in the end results in creativity. People may have different starting points in terms of preferences or orientations, but it is how well they make connections between these orientations that generates new thinking.

Developing creativity: some suggestions for professional practice

Is Anything Really New?
But is anything ever truly invented from scratch? Just as physically we can only change and rearrange existing matter, there is an argument that the same limitation applies mentally. Can we ever have truly original thoughts? Or do we simply rearrange what is already in our mind to 'create' something new?

If so then creativity becomes much less mysterious and we have the possibility of analysing the process. If we can pinpoint certain techniques we use without even realising it then we can potentially learn to increase our creativity.

Of course, we would encourage all readers to develop their creativity and to find for themselves the atmosphere or environment that boosts it. Some like peace and quiet; some like music in the background; some like walking the dog; and some lying in the bath. Try to think back to when and where you had your best ideas, so you can exploit what works best for you.

But, following the logic of this book, we encourage you to try approaching problems from an entirely opposite perspective. Forcing yourself to think about opposites will help develop your propensity to reconcile them.

For example, what if you can't get a (damaged) cork out of a bottle of wine? Can you push it *into* the bottle? Your real aim is to drink the wine, not to get the cork out of the bottle.

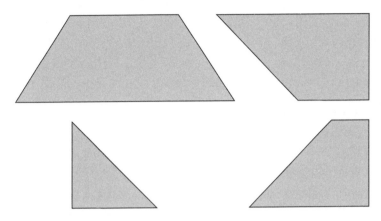

Fig 2.21 T pieces

Look at this puzzle. The aim is to put the pieces together so that they form the letter 'T'.

Why is this difficult? Because your assumptions force you to try to line up the straight edges. Because you become fixated on the idea of the straight edges need to be edges of the letter T so you need to re-centre your ideas around component sections of the letter T. Thinking of the opposite approach offers new insights and leads to the solution.

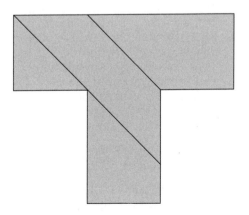

Fig 2.22 T answer

And with our inherent interest in culture, we would also follow the advice of Maddux[34]. His findings imply that companies can get the most out of their teams by rotating employees to new regions or by emphasizing foreign-living experiences in the hiring process. It is also likely that immersion in different cultures, not necessarily different nations, is the important factor; the more diverse the culture, the better. 'If you think of culture as a continuum,' Maddux asserts, 'the farther you get from your own particular culture, the more creative you're more likely to get.'

Table 2.2 Techniques for developing your creativity.[35]

Absence Thinking	Think about what you are thinking about, and then think about what you are not thinking about. When you are looking at something (or otherwise sensing), notice what is not there. Watch people and notice what they do not do.
Assumption Busting.	Surfacing and challenging unconscious assumptions.
Attribute Listing	Listing attributes of objects and then challenging them.
Brainstorming	The classic creative method.
Breakdown	Careful decomposition to explore the whole system.
Challenge	Challenge any part of a problem.
Chunking	Take a higher or more detailed view.
Crawford Slip Method	Getting ideas from a large audience.
Doodling	Let your subconscious do the drawing.
Essence	Look elsewhere whilst retaining essential qualities.
Forced Conflict	Using conflict to stimulate the subconscious.
Force-field Analysis	Exploring forces for and against an idea.
Guided Imagery	Letting your subconscious give you a message.
Head, Heart and Hands	Get all three systems of motivation engaged.
How-How Diagram	Break down problem by asking 'how'
How to	Frame statements as 'How to' to trigger focused thinking.
Incubation	Letting the subconscious do the work.
Is – Is Not	To scope out boundary of problems.
Lateral Thinking	Thinking sideways to create new ideas.
Lotus Blossom	Unfold the flower of extended ideas.
Morphological Analysis	Forcing combinations of attribute values.
Negative Selection	Sort out the 'definitely nots' first.
Pause	Think more deeply for a minute
Positives, Negatives	Look at both problems and benefits.
Problem Statement	Getting a clear statement of what you are trying to achieve.
Provocation	Shake up the session by going off-piste.
PSI	Problem + Stimulus = Idea!
Purposing	Finding the real purpose of what you are doing.

(Continued.)

34 Maddux, William W. and Galinsky, Adam D., 'Cultural Barriers and Mental Borders: Multicultural Learning Experiences Facilitate Creativity' (working paper, 2006)

35 Adapted from www.creatingminds.org

Random Words	Using a random word as a stimulus.
Remembrance	Remembering solutions not yet discovered.
Reversal	Looking at the problem backwards.
Reverse Brainstorming	Seek first to prevent your problem from happening.
Reverse Planning	Working backwards from a perfect future.
Role-play	Become other people. Let them solve the problem.
Rubber-ducking	Get someone else to listen to your talk.
Six Thinking Hats	Think in different ways about the problem.

Hat	Headline	Usage
White	Information	Asking for information from others.
Black	Judgement	Playing devil's advocate. Explaining why something won't work.
Green	Creativity	Offering possibilities, ideas.
Red	Intuition	Explaining hunches, feelings, gut senses.
Yellow	Optimism	Being positive, enthusiastic, supportive.
Blue	Thinking	Using rationalism, logic, intellect.

Storyboarding	Creating a visual story to explore or explain.
Swap Sort	Sorting a short list by priority swapping.
Take a Break	When creativity is fading.
Talk Streaming	Just talk and talk and talk until you unblock.
Unfolding	Gradually unfolding the real problem from the outside.
Visioning	Creating a motivating view of the future.
Why Not?	Challenge objections and assumptions.
Wishing	State ideas as wishes to expand thinking.
Write Streaming	Write and write and write until you unblock.

Concluding comment:

We have tried to show that with even the plethora of models and frameworks for exploring individual creativity, the emphasis is still on reductionism likely as a result of too much Western (Cartesian) based thinking and research.

The creative process is essentially a process where different logics are united and as such create a new reality. If we look at the Japanese garden we see it is an invitation to accumulate different viewpoints so that every tour is a creative act. And if we walk together it connects your-point-of-view with my-point-of view. Follow this journey in the rest of this book.

THE COMPONENTS AND OPERATION OF SUCCESSFUL AND CREATIVE TEAMS

Creative individuals in teams

The first part of this book was concerned with offering insights to help you understand the fundamentals of individual creativity and how it might be developed. But does this individual creativity guarantee teams and organisations that are more innovative, when these individuals work together?

The answer is very open to interpretation, but research consistently shows that, for a team to be innovative, diversity is crucial. Unfortunately, for many reasons, team leaders often don't start with an innate belief in the importance of this diversity.

The top reasons cited by Human Resources executives for increased diversity in the workplace include not just better utilisation of talent and understanding of the marketplace, but also enhanced creativity and problem-solving ability[1].

However, if you review almost 50 years of social science research on diversity in teams, the reality appears much less clear cut. Elizabeth Mannix and Margaret Lean[2] have attempted to disentangle what researchers have learned over the last 50 years and conclude that visible differences – such as those of race/ethnicity, gender or age – are more likely to have

---

1   Robinson and Dechant, 1997 *Building a business case for diversity* G Robinson, K Dechant – Academy of Management Executive, 1997 – faculty.washington.edu

2   Mannix, E. and Lean, M., 'Diverse Teams in Organizations', *Psychological Science in the Public Interest*, Volume 6 - Number 2, American Psychological Society, 2005

negative effects on a group's ability to function effectively. By contrast, underlying differences – such as differences in functional background, education or personality – tend to lead to performance improvement. In particular, underlying differences can facilitate creativity or group problem solving – but again, only when the group process is carefully supported.

In some early studies, Hoffman indicated that, for complex decision-making problems, heterogeneous groups produced higher-quality solutions than homogeneous groups. He suggested that diverse groups of individuals should be expected to have a broader range of knowledge, expertise and perspectives than homogeneous groups of like-minded individuals. These factors should facilitate more effective group performance, especially when the task is cognitively complex or requires multiple perspectives[3]. Conversely, other studies conclude that the business case for diversity (in terms of demonstrable 'black and white' financial results) remains hard to support[4]. However, these latter studies have all been based on generic research, without taking a holistic or medium- to longer-term perspective.

So what conclusions can we draw about how to make a team innovative?

Innovation and teams

In short, successfully innovative teams combine three main factors:

1   They are diverse.
2   They are inclusive and share knowledge and experience.
3   They take care of the basic enabling processes, especially leadership.

---

3   Hoffman, L. Richard, and Maier, Norman R. F., 'Quality and Acceptance of Problem Solutions by Members of Homogeneous and Heterogeneous Groups', *Journal of Abnormal and Social Psychology* 62 (2), pp.401–7, 1961

4   Kochan, T., Bezrukova, K., Ely, R., Jackson, S., Joshi, A., Jehn, K., Leonard, J., Levine, D. and Thomas, D., 'The Effects of Diversity on Business Performance: Report of the Diversity Research Network', *Human resource management*, vol. 42, no. 1, p. 3, 2003

An early stream of research into diversity and problem solving was carried out by Triandis and colleagues. They argued specifically that heterogeneity was most beneficial for challenging tasks requiring creativity[5]. Indeed, as in Hoffman's findings, teams with heterogeneous attitudes generated more creative solutions to problems than teams with more homogeneous attitudes. According to Singh (et al.)[6], such diversity can represent a fundamental strategic lever to improve business performance and support the process of continuous innovation. Implementing a diversity strategy will provide employees with new skills and contrasting perspectives, and thereby both promote a more flexible working environment and enhance innovations. It gives the organisation a better understanding of its customers' needs. A well-managed, diverse workforce offers a more efficient working environment through increased flexibility, because diversity promotes relationships between people with different sets of contacts, skills, information and experiences.

When you look more closely at what type of diversity leads to creativity in teams, you find that the invisible characteristics dominate. In particular, functional differences in skills, information and expertise have been shown to improve performance because they give rise to a stimulating debate, and this leads to creativity and improved problem solving. These findings fuel the view that diversity in teams creates a positive environment of constructive conflict – an environment in which ideas synergistically resolve into higher-level outcomes than would be achievable in more homogeneous teams. In the conceptual framework of this book, we describe this phenomenon as the reconciliation of dilemmas created by different points of view. The tensions deriving from these dilemmas is the main source of creativity; the reconciliation of these dilemmas is the essential challenge and is thus the competence required of a team leader[7].

---

5   Triandis, HC, Hall, ER and Ewen, RB, Human Relations, 1965 Member heterogeneity and dyadic creativity.

6   Singh, V., Vinnicombe, S., Schiuma, G., Kennerley, M., Neely, A., *Diversity Management: Practices, Strategy and Measurement*, Cranfield School of Management, Cranfield University, 2002

7   Bunderson, JS, and Sutcliffe, KM, Research on Managing Groups and Teams, 2002 See also Bunderson and Sutcliffe, 2002; Carpenter, 2002; Pitcher and Smith, 2000

So, diverse teams should be more creative and perform better than homogeneous teams, right? After all, it's intuitively obvious that diverse teams can exploit a variety of perspectives and skills. On the other hand, it's also obvious that 'birds of a feather flock together', for many reasons. They get along well, there will be less tension (and therefore less time wasted on arguments), and the like-minded team can come to a decision more quickly.

So should a leader assemble a diverse team or a homogeneous team? And then what can s/he do to maximise its performance?

Mannix and Lean[8] offer three suggestions.

- First they indicate that diverse teams are especially appropriate for tasks requiring innovation and the exploration of new opportunities, whereas homogeneous teams are better for exploitation and implementation of what is already known. Thus adapters (who we met in Chapter 1) thrive better in homogeneous groups and innovators better in diverse groups.
- Second, you must make a special effort to reduce any innate process-problems in diverse teams, particularly by helping the team develop a super-ordinate identity, shared goals and values.
- Third, you should take steps to ensure that minority opinions are heard and not suppressed.

A broader point is that organisational leaders should develop open organisational cultures that encourage and reward learning and change. Team leaders play a key role in implementing such cultures, or at least creating them within the team.

In conclusion, the creative output of a team is increased by the team being diverse. However, the raw materials of diversity are not sufficient; as much attention should be given to what the team members share through the elicitation of common goals, values and corporate identity.

Why some teams emphasize learning more than others: Evidence from business unit management teams.

8   Mannix, E. and Lean, M., 'Diverse Teams in Organizations', *Psychological Science in the Public Interest*, Volume 6 – No.2, p.35, American Psychological Society, 2005

And, ultimately, it is the leader who is responsible for the process that reconciles these differences.

In the next section, we focus first on how the diversity of team roles and cultural values can lead to more creative teams, if the differences are reconciled in practice.

Team role diversity and innovation

This section explores how teams can advance, support and facilitate innovation. We focus on how important it is to engage and resolve some important tensions between fundamental team roles.

Margaret Mead once said: 'Small groups have changed the world. Indeed nothing else ever has.' The qualities of the leader and of the team, and the interaction between all team members, are the most important factors in an organisation's success.

One of the most original thinkers on management teams is, of course, the British author and consultant, Meredith Belbin. In his first book[9], he describes how one Apollo Team of highly talented people achieved significantly less than a second Apollo Team comprised of people who were far less gifted, but who co-operated better. For Belbin, an effective team is a group of people that aims for a shared goal while progressing through four phases: forming, storming, norming and performing.

In this section, we take an unconventional view of Belbin's work. We try to build a general theory that team innovation comes from the tensions between the key roles. If any of these roles is missing or is poorly served, this hampers the process of moving from ideas to finished projects or products. We go beyond the focus on one particular role – that of 'the Plant' or creative ideas generator – within the group, as we did in our previous work. Here we focus on situations where the Plant's ideas receive broad support from other roles – and as a result we expect the team to be highly effective in its innovation[10].

---

9 Belbin, Meredith, *Management Teams – Why they succeed or fail*, Butterworth Heinemann, 1981 (2nd ed. 1993)

10 Trompenaars, Fons and Woolliams, Peter, *Business Across Cultures*, London: Wiley, 2005

In the case of entrepreneurship, the single founder of a company must either play all necessary roles him/herself or find colleagues to play these roles. In any event, the founder has to take responsibility for ensuring that these roles are played, or risk the failure of the entire enterprise.

Belbin's original team role model

Team members identify these themselves by completing a diagnostic questionnaire, which highlights their primary and other roles. Here are some of the role types Belbin employs.

The Plant

This is the ideas-generator and originator of the team's creative potential. S/he "thinks out of the box", is creative, imaginative, and unorthodox. Solves difficult problems. The vital spark! The Plant tends to ignore incidentals and is often too pre-occupied to communicate effectively.

The Shaper

The Shaper gets people to shape up around the new idea and drives the idea through. S/he is sometimes called the Product Champion and puts momentum behind the idea. S/he is challenging, dynamic, thrives on pressure. The drive and courage to overcome obstacles.
The Shaper is prone to provocation and tends to offend people's feelings.

Resource investigator

This is a person whose role is to spot opportunities, as well as mobilise the resources necessary to carrying through the project. The Resource Investigator is the networker for the group. Being highly driven to make connections with people, the Resource Investigator may appear to be flighty and inconstant, but their ability to call on their connections is highly useful to the team.

Co-ordinator

The responsibility of this role is to "open the gate" allowing the ideas into the team, co-ordinating and repairing the team as it digests the new ideas. New ideas are potentially disintegrative so restoring team cohesion can be vital. The Chairman/Co-ordinator ensures that all members of the team are able to contribute to discussions and decisions of the team. Their concern is for fairness and equity among team members.

The Specialist

This is the expert in some key discipline essential to the project/product e.g. the electronics engineer or tool-maker. The Specialist tends to be single-minded, self-starting and dedicated. Provides knowledge and skills in rare supply. The Specialist tends to contribute only on a narrow front and dwells on technicalities.

Monitor–Evaluator

This is the role of critic, who kills ideas that are wasting the team's time, but constructively improves ideas and implementations which require further work and elaboration.
The Monitor-Evaluator tends to be sober, strategic and often discerning. Sees all options and judges accurately. Often lacks drive and ability to inspire others.

The Implementer

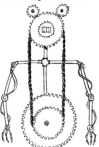

The Implementer is the person who gives the idea its embodiment as a product or services, who makes an ideal real and gives to some vision a practical utility. Being strongly rooted in the real world, they may frustrate other team members by their perceived lack of enthusiasm for inspiring visions and radical thinking, but their ability to turn those radical ideas into workable solutions is important.

The Completer–Finisher

This role "edits" the finished project/product and refines it for customer use. The C/F is a "detail person" and takes infinite pains to get the whole system user friendly. Team members who have less preference for detail work may be frustrated by their analytical and meticulous approach, but the work of the Completer Finisher ensures the quality and timeliness of the output of the team.

The Teamworker

This role is for the socio-emotional specialist who maintains the morale and the cohesion of the team by healing any hurts. S/he encourages participation, facilitates team processes and may even do running repairs on gaps or splits in the team. They are sensitive to atmospheres and may be the first to approach another team member who feels slighted, excluded or otherwise attacked but has not expressed their discomfort. The Team Worker's concern with people factors can frustrate those who are keen to move quickly, but their skills ensure long-term cohesion within the team.

Fig 3.1 Belbin's main role types

Exploring the link between dilemma theory and team roles

Dilemma theory is distinctly different from role theory. Dilemma theory sees the world as essentially uncertain and paradoxical, and focuses on values not as objects, but as *differences*. For example, the value of a traffic light signal lies in neither its greenness nor its redness. If it were to lock on to either colour, the traffic would come to a halt, accidents would happen and the whole system would be rendered worse than useless! The value of the traffic signal is in the *difference* between red and green, between stop and go.

Table 3.1

Role theory	Dilemma theory
A cluster of traits	Differences among components
Resembles an object	Resembles a relationship
Is unitary	Is binary
Relatively stable	Relatively dynamic
Providing continuity	Providing variability
Strengthening human identity	Expanding human identity

Role theories like Belbin's are neither better nor worse than our theory, but simply different. We've observed that most of the models that describe the characteristics of different roles in a team focus on complementary differences, and they are not wrong. But we argue that, to become creative as a team, you have to take advantage of the tensions *between* the roles – and this is where things can often go wrong.

Although dilemma theory provides new ways of elucidating role theory, it in no sense negates or invalidates it; rather it builds upon it and tries to enrich its meaning and significance.

Since a multiplicity of roles is vital to any and all innovative team working, we can understand why a team is, or is not, effective at innovation by studying *the tensions between team roles*. We can also 'map' these tensions so that teams can diagnose where they stand and, if stuck, take corrective action by strengthening the roles that are underperforming.

Team role tensions and phases of innovation

There has never been a greater need for lean, rapid and profitable new product development. Product life cycles are shorter, competition is more

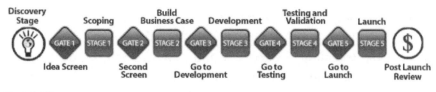

Fig 3.2 The stage-gate process

intense and customers are more demanding. Companies that fail to in-novate face a grim future[11].

Some leading companies have overhauled their new product proc-esses, incorporating what they have discovered through best-practice re-search in the form of a 'stage-gate' process for new products.

A stage-gate system is a conceptual and operational 'road map', used for moving a new-product project from idea to launch. It segments the effort into distinct stages separated by critical management-decision points, called 'gates'. Teams must successfully complete a prescribed set of related activities in each stage before getting management approval to proceed through the gate.

According to a Product Development and Management Association (PDMA) study of best practice, almost 70% of leading American prod-uct developers now use some type of stage-gate process[12].

To manage innovation in a team, it is not sufficient just to have the roles played in different intensities at different stages, but you also need to reconcile the dilemmas between the team roles. Below we take you through five typical key stages of a new-product project, and the dilemmas between different roles that these raise. Obviously, there are many other combinations of crucial encounters between roles in the total process, but these give some examples of the way such dilemmas can be addressed, stage by stage and gate by gate.

Five key stages

- **Stage 1: Scoping** A quick and inexpensive assessment of the technical merits of the project and its market prospects.

---

11   www.stage-gate.com
12   ibid.

- **Stage 2: Build business case** This is the critical homework stage – the one that makes or breaks the project. Technical marketing and business feasibility are accessed resulting in a business case with three main components: product and project definition; project justification; and project plan.
- **Stage 3: Development** Business case plans are translated into concrete deliverables. The product is developed, the manufacturing or operations plan is mapped out, the marketing launch and operating plans are developed, and the test plans for the next stage are defined.
- **Stage 4: Testing and validation** This validates the entire project: the product itself, the production process, customer acceptance, and the economics of the project.
- **Stage 5: Launch** Full commercialisation of the product – the beginning of full production and commercial launch.

Here we draw attention to just five of the most common dilemmas or tensions between the roles that are crucial to getting what has been 'sown' to the point of harvesting. While there are other crucial tensions, these five illustrate our main point.

Five common tensions or dilemmas

1. *Scoping* — Plant ——————— Monitor/Evaluator
(or Creative Ideas versus Critical Appraisal)

2. *Build business case* — Shaper ——————— Resource Investigator
(or Real versus Window of Opportunity)

3. *Development* — Specialist ——————— Co-ordinator
(or Disciplines versus Final Alignment)

4. *Testing and validation* — Team Worker ——————— Completer-Finisher
(or Consensus versus Mature)

5. *Launch* — Resource Investigator ——————— Implementer
(or Capturing Resources versus Practical Embodiment)

These five 'crises' are crucial tensions at the gates involved in the innovative process. The challenge is to ensure that each role engages successfully with its opposing role. When all these crises are resolved, successful innovation will follow.

We will now explore these dilemmas, describing:

a) the issue
b) mapping three forms of failure, and
c) mapping the (successful) reconciliation.

Stage 1 Scoping: Creative Ideas versus Critical Appraisal

> A quick and inexpensive assessment of the technical merits of the project and its market prospects.

The Plant or creative person must be present within the team, although there is scant evidence that several Plants are better than one or two. As with all roles, the team needs diversity. It needs all or most of the roles to be covered, otherwise major weaknesses occur. To have three, four or five persons spouting ideas with no one listening or taking them on board is a recipe for team sterility, however imaginative its talk. But having only Plants will lead to ideas that don't get tested: they need to be evaluated so that the merits of the project can be assessed.

The issue
Almost nothing is more crucial to innovation than the relationship between creation and criticism. Criticism can improve creativity, so that excellence emerges from the 'purging fires'. Yet the critic gets a bad press: 'No statue was ever erected to a critic.' Brilliant artists are depicted as starving in garrets because critics can't or won't acknowledge their genius.

Mapping the three forms of failure
Take a look at Dilemma Grid 1. On the horizontal axis, we have Creative Ideas, without which innovation is impossible. On the vertical axis, we have Critical Appraisal, without which endless time would be wasted on

half-baked notions. Creativity that resists or escapes criticism is mostly Blue Sky (grid reference 1/10) – so speculative, so long-term, so pie-in-the-sky that no one is tempted to engage critically with it. If it is *only* an idea, why bother?

But when critics go on the rampage, or the team is full of Monitor-Evaluators, many ideas are Strangled at Birth (10/1). The Monitor-Evaluator is often very intelligent, and what better way to display your critical faculties than to take an embryonic idea and shred it? Simply enumerating all the barriers to its realisation should be enough. It has barely popped out of the ground and you throttle it.

Grudging Acceptance (5/5) is unsatisfactory too.

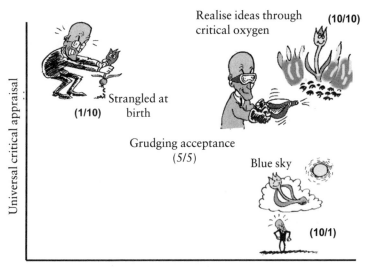

Fig 3.3 Dilemma Grid 1: Realise ideas through critical oxygen

Mapping the reconciliation

The supply of ideas soon dries up. Even when critics are less destructive, ideas may still have a Short Life (5/5). If they do not succumb at once, they may die in development, manufacturing, marketing, etc., especially if saddled with all the costs of distribution through new channels. EMI won a Nobel Prize for its Magnetic Resonance Scanner, but lost $300 million marketing it to hospitals, instead of music shops. Less than 10%

of registered patents actually make money. Perhaps there is too little criticism (not too much!). What is new to science may not interest customers; what is new to customers may use only routine science.

The way to achieve innovation is to improve ideas without destroying them (although some ideas *are* non-viable, for unforeseeable reasons). Criticism must be constructive, offered in the spirit of improving something or someone you admire. The Plant makes errors and needs corrective feedback just like anyone else. In fact, doing something new is *more* prone to error, and negative feedback from a friendly source is invaluable. Great ages of creativity have seen the *interstimulation of like minds*, with artists, patrons, critics, sponsors and sophisticated audiences all involved. The Dada artists not only challenged the conventional art of their predecessors, but criticised members of their own movement even more – always with the intent to improve.

On the 'map', we follow the path of the Creative Idea from an initial point (2/8), through a period of Critical Appraisal, back to an improved product, then as it is plunged once again into Critical Appraisal, until it emerges from the Refiner's Fire Constructively Improved.

Making it part of the team process
The logic and power of positive criticism is beyond doubt, as it increases the chances that bad ideas will eventually be killed and potentially good ideas will be supported. But how can we implant such a spirit into the team?

Synetics developed a very powerful approach. When someone comes up with an idea, anyone who wants to react must start by mentioning at least three good aspects of the idea, before any possible criticism. Criticisms then have to be formulated as follows: 'How can we overcome the handicap I see in achieving this innovation?' So instead of an idea being raised and immediately killed by the Monitor-Evaluator, the response might be:

> 'I like the idea a lot because it has the potential to open our market to a new segment of clients. It also shows that we have another high-quality product, and it would work in our existing distribution channel. How can we find the additional resources and budget to sponsor the market research, and how

can we test the reliability of this potential new product as economically as possible?'

And not:

'Interesting idea, but I think it will overstretch our budget and drain our scarce resources, plus I doubt that the product is reliable enough.'

End of idea.

In fact, positive criticism lifts the idea's potential and sharpens your response to its potential weaknesses. As a result, the idea gains focus. Criticism acts as oxygen to the fire of the team's innovative spirit.

Stage 2 Build business case: The Real versus Windows of Opportunity

This is the critical homework stage – and one that makes or breaks the project. Technical marketing and business feasibility are accessed resulting in a business case that has three main components: product and project definition; project justification; and project plan.

Now that the initial idea has survived the first criticisms, it is time to create a solid business case. All roles need to contribute, but it is imperative that there are sufficient resources. Here the Resource Investigator and the Shaper come into the picture. They can make or break the project by securing the various type of resource available.

The issue

Ideas have already been generated and provisionally accepted within the team. What's needed now is an exploration of the extent to which these ideas can be shaped and pushed through the organisation, to become realities. In this second stage, business feasibility is checked and project plans are shaped. The Shaper and the Resource Investigator need to reconcile the tension between the Shaper's realism and the Resource Investigator's opportunism, to create a solid business case.

Mapping three forms of failures

Have a look at Dilemma Grid 2. The Opportunity is shown on the vertical axis and Shaping the business case on the horizontal. The team fails when its opportunities prove unrealisable (10/1): perhaps they were never practicable. The resources needed to carry through the project are mobilised. Windows of Opportunity may only open briefly and you must dart through them. As the group's networker, the Resource Investigator can provide physical, financial or human resources, along with political support, information or ideas.

The Shaper gets people to 'shape up' around the new idea and drives the idea through by making a business case. This Product Champion puts momentum behind the team and tries to overcome obstacles.

But beware: the Shaper is easily provoked and tends to offend people's feelings, and so often closes the Windows of Opportunity that have been opened by the Resource Investigator.

The team fails when the Window is Closed at 10/1 and when there is No Response to the Opportunity (1/10). It also fails when Trying to Squeeze Through (5/5) with difficulty and pain: too little, too late.

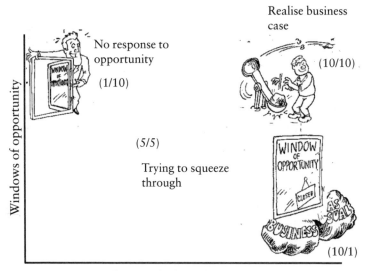

Fig 3.4 Dilemma Grid 2

Mapping the reconciliation

Only the top-right corner of the map shows the two values reconciled.

Here the team's *opportunities are fulfilled in action*. Team members have not just generated opportunities, but turned them into a product/project that makes a real difference to real people. Resources are assembled to give the project a solid business case.

Stage 3 Development: Rival Disciplines versus Alignment into Business Plan

> Business case plans are translated into concrete deliverables. The product development activities occur, the manufacturing or operations plan is mapped out, the marketing launch and operating plans are developed, and the test plans for the next stage are defined.

Now that the initial idea has passed the first tests, and the general business idea has been born, it is time to translate this into a business plan with concrete deliverables. Again, every role makes a contribution, but the reconciliation of one key dilemma is vital at this stage. This dilemma demands the integration of the deliverables of the product with the deliverables of the project surrounding the product. This dilemma involves the roles of the Specialist and the Co-ordinator.

Specialist ——————————————— Co-ordinator

The Specialist is the expert in some key discipline that is essential to the project/product. However, the Specialist tends to contribute only on a narrow front and dwells on technicalities, often unhindered by the need for practical utility. The Co-ordinator however is responsible for 'opening the gate', allowing ideas into the team, co-ordinating and integrating the diverse specialisms into one project. The challenge is to reconcile these different orientations so that the strengths from both roles contribute and synergise without frustrating team members.

The issue
Can the team ensure that there are creative inter-connections *between*

disciplines or intra-connections between a discipline *and* what business and customers desire?

Most creative breakthroughs occur *between* disciplines, like biology and medicine ('biomed') mechanical engineering and electronics ('mechatronics'). Yet the Specialist is typically beholden to his/her professional discipline and is reluctant to stray beyond its boundaries, where his/her expertise is no longer acknowledged. When faced with creative ideas, it is not simply the structure of the organisation and team which can feel subverted, but the structure of the profession itself. Specialists have to be persuaded to listen to *other* specialists and/or to people who wish to make the product saleable and profitable, all of which transcends the specialism itself. is

What is needed is a Co-ordinator, who can help specialisms to connect and can rebuild the team around the new idea, adding new members and specialisms and dropping others as required. The Co-ordinator creates an open-minded spirit, to give the idea a full hearing and, from there, a place in the full business offering.

Mapping the three forms of failure

Look at Dilemma Grid 3. Creative Connections are shown on the vertical axis with Specialist Disciplines on the horizontal. It was George Bernard Shaw who said: 'All professions are a conspiracy against the laity.' The Co-ordinator's main responsibility at this stage of the project is to breach the walls of the specialist professions, by joining them to other professions or to 'commerce', where professionals sell their souls for money.

Most Specialists do not *wish* to be joined to other Specialists by means of a creative idea or product. The mastery of one specialism is difficult enough! What is the point of specialisation if you don't stick to it?

So the relationship between Co-ordinator and Specialist is typically a troubled one. Even if most creative breakthroughs are between disciplines, such work is usually 'applied' science – less prestigious than the individual disciplines, and with less pure motives than those of each Specialist.

If Co-ordinators have their way, won't Interdisciplinary Studies meet their usual fate (10/1)? If the Specialists have *their* way, won't we be faced with Containerised Cargo kills Communication (1/10)? Here all individual ideas and initiatives are in separate 'boxes' separated from all others, killing Communication between them.

Even if the discipline is not utterly disgraced, its relationship with another discipline, or with commercialisation, may result in a Horrid Hybrid (5/5).

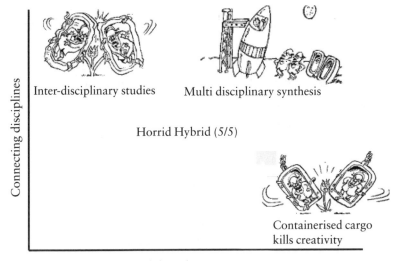

Fig 3.5 Dilemma Grid 3: multi-disciplinary synthesis

Mapping the reconciliation

Reconciliation accepts the need to break down the structures supporting the older system of ideas, but quickly builds up team support for the newer system of ideas. At the same time, it recognises that the organisation may have to change, just as the team microcosm of that organisation is changing.

The Co-ordinator fulfils his/her function by reorganising people and resources to create a structural rebuilding around the new idea, where disciplines are joined and functions integrated. This results in a Breakthrough Product as Multi-disciplinary Synthesis (10/10). Here, at least two disciplines (and hence two Specialists) have, by concerted efforts, joined with a Co-ordinator to create a novel synthesis and a breakthrough product or project – perhaps a lunar landing craft of the kind NASA designed, a feat that required more than one hundred engineering specialisms.

If we assume that the Co-ordinator has upset the Specialists by threatening to dissolve their disciplines (7/2), then the team needs to re-assure both Specialists that their professional skills are needed, but that they can contribute their respective strengths without weakening either. Technical skill is indispensable.

Stage 4 Testing and Validation: Consensus versus Mature Product

The purpose of this stage is to provide validation of the entire project: the product itself, the production process, customer acceptance, and the economics of the project.

Team Worker ———————————————————— Completer–Finisher

Now that the plans have been made by connecting disciplines, it is time to validate the entire project. The whole team needs to get aligned, on both the social and the technical level. To get through this gate, some major tensions need to be resolved. This dilemma involves the roles of the Team Worker, who takes care of the social side, and the Completer-Finisher, who dots the technical 'i's.

The Completer-Finisher 'brings conscientiousness' to the project/product and refines it for customer use. The Completer-Finisher is a 'details person' and takes infinite pains to get the whole system user friendly. S/he has a great eye for spotting flaws and gaps and for knowing exactly where the team is in relation to its schedule. The work of the Completer-Finisher ensures the quality and timeliness of the output of the team.

Team members who have less preference for 'detail' work may be frustrated by the Completer-Finisher's analytical and meticulous approach, and may feel that it threatens the project's next stage. So the Team Worker is called in. This role is for the socio-emotional specialist who maintains the morale and cohesion of the team by healing any hurts. S/he is mild and perceptive and as such encourages participation, facilitates team processes and may even do running repairs on gaps or splits in the team. The best Team Workers sense any incompleteness and supply the needed roles. They are sensitive to atmospheres and may be the first to approach another team member who feels slighted, excluded or otherwise attacked but has not expressed their discomfort. The Team Worker's concern with people factors can frustrate the Completer-Finisher, but their skills ensure long-term cohesion within the team.

The issue

The team is inspired by the fact that they are developing an innovative idea, but for innovation to occur, this idea must culminate in a Mature Product. What the Plant, Monitor/Evaluator, Specialist, Resource Investigator and Shaper have begun, the Completer-Finisher in the team must complete. S/he must make sure that the team's product (which could be just a feasibility study) is properly prepared, proof-read and bound for presentation, in a way that will gain the customer's acceptance.

As we saw earlier, this process is full of frustrations and irritations, so there is a risk that the team will dissolve into chaos. Can teams and those working divergently within teams support the converging contributions of Completer-Finishers? Can the team reorganise itself around new ideas, to propel and promote them? For this, the Team Worker is essential.

Mapping three forms of failure

Now look at Dilemma Grid 4. On the vertical axis, we show the Seminal Respected Inputs around which the product will finally take shape. On the horizontal axis is the Mature Product, made ready for customers to use by testing, refinement and perfection. The saying goes that true creativity is 10% inspiration and 90% perspiration. The long journey from idea to finishing touches accounts for the perspiration! The Plant, Monitor-Evaluator, Shaper and Resource Investigator may have started it, but without proper completion, who will want to buy it?

Two forms of orientation are competing here.

One identifies finished goods with finished people. A fashionable young woman in society can work in Harrods selling expensive perfume, but would not be caught dead in a factory or even a lab. This is frequently countered by the Team Workers marginalising and sanctioning the disruptive influence of a variety of independent roles. They are accused of being inconsiderate of others' feelings, of being a 'maverick', 'cowboy', 'trouble maker', etc. Having created a consensus with some difficulty, the team is reluctant to let go of it and does not want to go to the trouble of forging new agreements stimulated by the Completer-Finisher. A compromise is reached when one is Tolerated but Not Encouraged (5/5).

Because Plants, Specialists, Shapers and Resource Investigators are seen as trouble makers, subversives, tunnel visionaries, nerds and malcontents (top left), efforts to contain them and shut them up often succeed (bottom right). Not all teams are willing to reorganise their processes to facilitate innovation. Some teams regard their existing consensus as infinitely precious: only an insensitive clod would disturb it.

So we can't go on forever redesigning, adding new features or revising the product. But we have to ensure that we don't stop too early with the current prototype, because of the demands of closure. A further loop to remodel the current version may add much more. Without reconciliation, both these orientations combine to militate against innovation.

Worship of the originator leads to Consensus for Half-baked Products (1/10). Worship of finished goods leads to Polishing Antiques, in which no spark of novelty remains. There is also a potential 'No Man's Land' between a project's birth and the launch of the finished product, in which mere producers who use their hands get despised for their humdrum abilities. Into this abyss fall the Shaper, the Specialist, the Resource

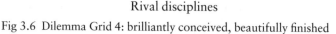

Fig 3.6 Dilemma Grid 4: brilliantly conceived, beautifully finished

Investigator and others concerned with the practical details of getting the product made or getting the project off the ground.

Mapping the reconciliation
This tension resolves itself in Brilliantly Conceived, Beautifully Finished (10/10).

What actually delights the customer is the finished product, not the agreed conception and harmonious co-operation behind the product! What makes an organisation accept the unanimous recommendation of a team is the final, polished presentation of its solution, which describes the route from an Emphasis on the Seminal Idea (9/1) to the Finished Emphasis on the Product (10/10). Many people decry this 'finishing' of a product or project as mere window dressing. It is nothing of the sort.

The Completer-Finisher makes sure that novelty is recognised by bringing out all its more familiar aspects. S/he is the impresario of a great performance, who can make us nostalgic for novelty. The Team Worker keeps the people together so that the team gets all the final details resolved without painlessly.

Stage 5 Launch: Capturing Resources versus Final Alignment

Full commercialisation of the product – the beginning of full production and commercial launch.

When all the earlier dilemmas have been reconciled, the team is ready to pass through the last gate. The idea has been tested, given a business case, validated and transformed into deliverables. Now it is time to fully commercialise the product, produce it and launch it commercially.

The last major dilemma to reconcile, in order to give closure to the innovation process, is where the Team Workers' discipline needs to be achieved, while the Resource Investigator is called in again to use his/her opportunistic and optimistic approach to get everything funded. The tensions are obvious.

Resource Investigator ———————————— Implementer

The issue

At this stage, the Resource Investigator needs to go out of the meeting and get on the phone. The Resource Investigator needs to take advantage of his/her great negotiating skills, probing others for information and support, and developing the idea further. Though the Resource Investigator's sociability and enthusiasm are good for exploring resources outside the group, at this stage s/he tends to lose interest after initial fascination with the idea (and Resource Investigators are not usually the source of original ideas).

The Implementer, on the other hand, is the person who gives the idea its embodiment as a product or service – who makes an ideal real and gives it a practical utility. The Implementer's key strength is taking a problem and working out how it can be addressed in practice. Being strongly rooted in the real world, Implementers may frustrate other team members because of their perceived lack of enthusiasm for inspiring visions and radical thinking; but their ability to turn those radical ideas into workable solutions is important.

Mapping three forms of failure

Look at Dilemma Grid 5. On the vertical axis, you see how Divergent Opportunism Eludes Implementation. The Resource Investigator behaves as if his/her window of opportunity is so 'precious' that implementing would be impossible without it. The Resource Investigator may appear to the Implementer to be divergent and inconsistent, but the Resource Investigator's ability to call on his/her connections is highly valuable to the team.

On the horizontal axis, you see that Convergent Implementation Wrecks Opportunities. The idea has been spoiled. The product or service does not, in its practical application, fulfil the original dream of those who conceived it. Poor technical skill and lack of operational experience have doomed an otherwise excellent idea to mediocrity. The vital question has been posed, but no real solution found.

The stand off between Divergent Opportunity and Convergent Implementation is little better. The Leading Edge Blunted testifies to the fact that creativity has been compromised and technical skills have proved insufficient to meet the novelty of the challenge.

Both parties have settled for second best.

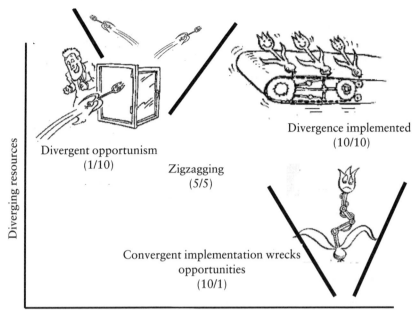

Fig 3.7 Dilemma Grid 5: Divergence implemented

Mapping the reconciliation

The tension between Divergent Opportunism and Convergent Implementation is resolved through Creativity Implemented. Here the new product or service has been given a practical expression worthy of its genius. Technical skill has combined with new vision to fashion a product of greatly enhanced value to customers. Remember: customers do not consume ideas or visions but what can be made out of these. The Implementer, like the midwife, brings something new and valuable into the world (10/10). The genius idea becomes not just real but available in multiple realisations – available to customers across the globe.

The builder, the engineer and the fabricating plant are all forms of implementation. Process innovation is creativity *applied to* the processes of production and may give the supplier an edge, not just in quality, but also in cost.

Research evidence: our web-based investigative model

We have repeated this extended team-role model with many client companies using an interactive, web-based system that captures the strategies that enable participants to work better with other team roles. From these assessments, we are now building a team-role dilemma database, which characterises all the combinations of primary and opposite team roles. This evolving database shows that these tensions are manifestations at the team level of the more generic dilemmas faced by organisations today. We also know from our work, where we measure the business impact of these reconciliations, that this analysis improves business performance at the bottom line through better team working.

Here are some examples of how respondents described how they would seek to reconcile their own primary team role orientation with their opposite roles – those roles where the orientation is a potential source of tension.

My principal team role:	The team role that is opposite to my own orientation:
Implementer	Completer-Finisher
I want to see my ideas finished and implemented	I get impatient – and want to force faster decisions
Give team members more empowerment and seek for more alternatives myself	
Shaper	Monitor-Evaluator
I get impatient with people who I feel spend too much time weighing up options	I spend too much time weighing up options
Be more patient and appreciate the value that comes from exploring all the options	
Monitor-Evaluator	Resource Investigator
I will not speak up for the sake of it, preferring only to contribute when I believe I have something of value to add	I need to recognise and learn from the skills and passion that this person will bring to the group
Be more patient (and get less frustrated) in meeting situations with any team members who is clearly a Resource Investigator. Be more vocal and volunteer information on a more regular basis	

Given the importance of reconciling opposites, we are surprised that no instrument has been devised to measure this – at least, not in published form. As we explained earlier, we recognised the limitations of our own cross-cultural instruments – which positioned people on bi-polar scales (the mutually exclusive extremes of seven dimensions) – and therefore we extended these instruments to evaluate how individuals reconcile cultural differences.

Alongside this extended team role models, we have produced an extended version of MBTI (we call it the Integrated Type Indicator) and the Integrated Scorecard, which extends Kaplan/Norton's Balanced Scorecard.

Our concern about applying any linear model across international boundaries might be explained by our own overdeveloped reconciliation profiles. However, we insist that, with the combination of seemingly opposed orientations, a team can flourish in diversity. Yes, all team roles need to be present and played out, but it is the reconciliation between them that makes the team excel. And no one has ever measured anything like this before.

The Chair: Big Chief Reconciler

In models such as Belbin, we should appreciate the implicit values associated with the diverse roles. In most theoretical frameworks for team roles, characteristics are often a straightforward addition of the roles, as if they are stable and independent. In reality, however, the effectiveness and innovative power of a team depends on how it takes advantage of the *differences* in roles, in which the dynamic of complementarities is essential. In particular, in the transitions between each of the five phases, the differences between the roles become even clearer, and the reconciliation of the different orientations becomes essential.

A leader needs to focus on reconciling the key dilemmas created between the various team roles, and on organising the relationship between the roles to this end. In this new *modus operandum*, the basic requirements of the team's success are secure, based on a strong underlying foundation, and are ready to be nurtured.

Dilemmas between people have to be played out, and it is the job of the Chair to provide an environment in the organisation in which such dilemmas can be reconciled. At the meta-level, the Chair's overall task is to reconcile the tension between the nomothetic (organisational perspective) and the ideographic (individual perspective of each employee) – what matters for the organisation and what matters for the team members.

So the Chair can create an atmosphere of questioning ideas. In a 'culture of creativity' there is no such thing as a mistake. If somebody is weak, then it stimulates a cascade so that others show their ideas. People need to build on each other. And further, the Chair should create a humorous atmosphere. As the Dalai Lama said, 'I love laughter because then people can have new ideas.'

Note that the stereotypical team roles we discuss are being applied to the *roles people play*, not the people themselves. People can take on many roles, and are far more flexible and complex than this typological framework implies.

In Figure 3.8, you see a female executive capable of playing *all* these roles, but such a paragon is rare. Most people *do* have role preferences, and much prefer certain roles to others. If there is any serious imbalance, like a team with too many Monitor-Evaluators or too many Specialists, then team performance deteriorates sharply. The Monitor-Evaluators cut each other down and the Specialists have difficulty communicating. There can even be too many Plants, producing verbal fireworks but no useful conclusions.

Belbin's research also infers a strong case for diversity. It is *because* diverse role-players are different that a team comprising them is effective. All the roles described are complementary, and authority should ideally shift as the process develops through various stages.

As innovation moves through the stages from accumulation and resolution of ideas (assimilation) to adoption, adaptation, acceptance, routinisation and infusion[13], all organisational actors (senior managers, middle/project managers, operational staff) are involved in the change process. To improve the capacity for absorbing innovation, Sherif and Menon[14] argue that all organisational actors must be engaged, though it is crucial that appropriate interventions are taken in each of the innovation-assimilation stages.

---

13   Cooper, R.B., and Zmud, R.W. 'Information Technology Implementation Research: A Technology Diffusion Approach', *Management Science* (36:2), 1990, pp 123–139.

14   Sherif and Menon, 'Managing technology and administration innovations: four case studies on software reuse', *Journal of the Association for Information Systems*. v5 i7. 247–281.

Fig 3.8 Nine roles, one personality

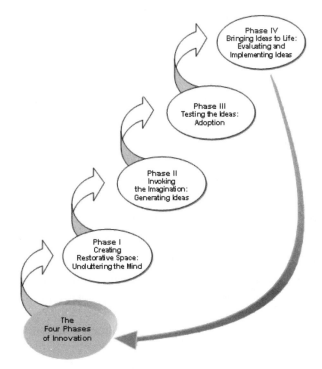

Fig 3.9 Phases of innovation

For innovation to become routine and infused in everyday working practices, a *culture change* must occur. New attitude and behavioural stances must be adopted, and employees must be ready to change[15].

To summarise, changes in strategy, process and culture must accompany innovation assimilation. Actors on various organisational levels are responsible for making these happen, resulting in faster and more successful innovation.

Cross-cultural teams

Earlier we have argued that one of the most significant sources of innovation is the internationalisation of the workforce because of the different points of view. Traditional idiosyncratic paradigms are challenged and multicultural diversity has become a great source of innovation to the team.

It is part of received wisdom that groups of executives or managers should learn to operate as effective teams. Getting everyone to think the same way is a tempting strategy, but our new research reveals that real innovative work comes when cultural opposites are integrated to work with each other.

As emphasised earlier, the importance of reconciling these opposites is a cornerstone of our work. As with MBTI, Kirton and other linear models, we have found there is too much one-dimensional thinking across too many of these frameworks and claimed solutions. Too many cultural analyses mark out people as either 'universalistic' or 'particularistic'. But why if you are a 'universalistic' person can you not act as a 'particularistic' person? And if you are 'individualistic', can you not also be 'collectivistic' and therefore work with others as a good team player?

The internationalisation of business has both brought standardization of business (MBA education, etc.) and an increased diversity of culture on the work floor. It is amazing how many creative breakthroughs have been accomplished by going international. Though many interna-

---

15 Leonard-Barton, D. and Deschamps, I, *Managerial influence in the implementation of new technology*. Management Science 1988 – JSTOR

tional teams resulting from mergers and acquisitions have failed, those that have succeeded have brought great innovative results.

But is international and intercultural team building that simple? If members of a team play different roles and have different cultural orientations, then the team is full of potential conflict and misunderstanding. Globally we have found the Anglo Saxon world of the USA and UK tends to be more individualistic, while Asians take to a more communal teamwork approach. So as long as the Americans remain in America managing all-American teams while, for example, the Chinese stay in China doing the same, then conflict and misunderstanding is at least on the local level. But in today's multicultural world, an American leader could be running a team of Thai, Chinese, French and English members. And furthermore, what if the senior management group already in place come with an imbalance of team roles?

When we begin to incorporate non-Western types of logic, such as Yin Yang or Taoism, we soon realise that we have all been restrictive in basing any profiling on bi-modal dimensions. We recognised these limitations in earlier versions of our own cross-cultural frameworks. For example, we were trying to place respondents along a scale with 'individualism' at one end and 'communitarianism' at the other. But in a multicultural environment, a highly individualised leader will agonise over the fact that many subordinates prefer to work with their team. Conversely, the group-oriented leader will fail because of an apparent lack of recognising the efforts of individuals. Thus we have a dilemma between the seemingly opposing orientations of individualism and communitarianism.

We have investigated how well organisations and their teams reconcile these seemingly opposing views by extending our own instruments to explore how well everyone works together in their team to help the organisation, but where teams encourage, stimulate, reward and celebrate individual contributions. And this is just one of the examples. Teams that are innovative reconcile the tensions that are created by the diversity of cultures from which its members come.

Seven intercultural dimensions of innovation

In approaching a model of competence for teams to become innovative by taking advantage of their diversity, we have applied our seven dimensional model of culture, which we've described more generically in earlier works. Each has contrasting value poles. These are selected because we have found that they best account for the major differences between national cultures.

> We have previously published exhaustive data mining our cross-culture database, using principal component and factor analysis that validates this framework. In the following pages, we give selected examples of 'scores' on these cultural dimensions. These should be seen as indicative and relative as, without a full consideration of matters of cultural convergence, multicultural societies, acculturation and generational differences, they do not embrace the full richness of this model.
>
> The reader is referred to our research monographs and other publications that give further detail[16]. Further information is available from www.creatingacultureofinnovation.com.

1. Rule making versus …

    (universalism)

    Exception finding

    (particularism)

2. Self-interest and personal fulfilment

    (individualism)

    Group interest and social concern

    (communitarianism)

3. Emotions Inhibited

    (neutral)

    Emotions expressed

    (affective)

4. Preference for precise, singular

    'hard' standards

    (specificity)

    Preference for pervasive, patterned

    and 'soft' processes

    (diffusion)

5. Control and effective direction

    comes from within

    (inner-directed)

    Control and effective direction

    comes from outside

    (outer-directed)

6. Status earned through success

    and track record

    (achievement)

    Status ascribed to person's potential,

    e.g. age, family, education

    (ascription)

7. Time is conceived of as a 'race'

    with passing increments

    (sequential)

    Time is conceived of as a 'dance'

    with circular iterations

    (synchronous)

---

16 Trompenaars, Fons and Woolliams, Peter, *The Measurement of Meaning*, Earlybrave Publications Ltd, June 1998

The seven dimensions are as follows.

Each of these seven dimensions can be polarised with each other, producing spectacular, amusing, and sometimes tragic contrasts; alternatively, all seven can be integrated and synergised, in which case we achieve team innovation.

We will now explore these seven dimensions in turn and consider their relevance to innovation.

For each we need to consider:

a)   the sophisticated stereotypes
b)   some typical misunderstandings
c)   what innovative leaders know and have learned, and
d)   how we measured transcultural competence.

Let us explain what is meant by 'sophisticated stereotypes'. We use this term to describe the stereotypes (or socio-types) of a culture that we have carefully researched and found to be valid and reliable. They are therefore not the product of prejudice or denigration, but remain nonetheless surface manifestations. We can't avoid stereotypes for several reasons, because cultures stereotype themselves – to sell popular culture, to sell tourism, to idealise themselves and to contrast themselves favourably with perceived enemies.

For twenty years or more, Geert Hofstede with his IBM samples and Charles Hampden-Turner and Fons Trompenaars, with their dilemma methodology, have classified respondents as belonging at one or the other end of various continua. Americans, for example, were individualist, not collectivist. The problem with sophisticated stereotypes is what they miss. How do Americans use groups, teams, communities? How do the Japanese create? Hiding beneath the stereotype there is a lot of crucial information.

We must therefore note the sophisticated stereotype, observe the trouble it causes and move beyond it. We will try to do this by delineating the competence of a team to become creative.

Dimension 1: rule making versus exception finding (universalism versus particularism)

What have the pizza, the Japanese car, Deming's Quality Management and Lego in common in becoming such successful products? There is a common thread that links these products and services. Year after year they have integrated the universal with the particular, the standard with the unique, the error with the correct. And they have done it through multicultural experiences and interactions. The American universalistic talent of sharing platforms to mass-produce was used by all the four examples mentioned above. But what made the products worldwide successes is the integration with the unique features. This needed the particularistic talent of the Italians for the toppings of their pizzas, and of the Japanese for customising their cars and adopting Deming's approach. It is mass customisation – the error-correcting system – that made the products and services unbeatable. Yes, the reconciliation of the universal with the particular is essential to the innovative process.

The sophisticated stereotype

Here the contrast is between the desire to make/discover/enforce rules of wide applicability – be they scientific, legal, moral, or industrial standards – and the desire to find what is, or to be, exceptional, unique, unprecedented, particular and one-of-a-kind.

As Figure 3.16 (p.120) shows, the USA, Finland, Canada, Denmark, and the UK are all high in their desire for universal rule making. In contrast, South Korea, China, Japan, Singapore and France are all relatively particularistic. One theme in universalism is Protestantism, which sees the Word of God encoded in the bible; a second is the common law tradition; a third is the whole concept of America as The New World, with rules designed to attract immigrants. That America has 22 times as many lawyers per capita as Japan is one consequence of the universalistic preference.

Is the USA an 'obvious' culture because it makes highly standardised 'universal' goods, e.g. Levi's, Big Macs and Coca Cola; or is France a 'snobbish' culture because it prefers products of high particularity, haute couture, haute cuisine and fine wines? Such arguments may entertain, but they are unfruitful[17].

Well-known manifestations of high universalism are scientific management, Fordism, formula fast foods, benchmarking, MBA education and platforms: '100% American', How to Win Friends and Influence People, and similar moral commandments. In contrast, a culture much higher in particularism is China.

Some typical misunderstandings

Note that both parties hung on tight to their conviction that jokes were/ were not appropriate. In her dealings with the world, America tends to

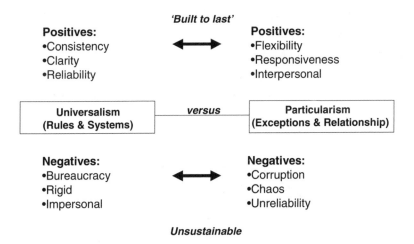

Fig 3.10 The sophisticated stereotype of Universalism and Particularism

see herself as the rule maker and global policeman. In her trade disputes with Japan, America tries to personify the rules of capitalism. 'Rice is a commodity. It must be freely traded.' The Japanese say: 'But we are different. Rice is the sacred symbol of our culture. Something very particular.'

A famous dispute about sugar prices broke out between Australia and Japan in the mid 70s. Japan signed a long-term contract to buy

17 Foucault, Michel, *The Order of Things,* Editions Gallimard, 1966

Australian sugar at below the world market price. Weeks later, the bottom fell out of the market. Japan wanted to renegotiate a new contract on the basis that their particular relationship with sugar exporters preceded contract terms. Australia wanted the original contract honoured as a universal obligation to keep one's word. Does particular partnership override the law? Or is legal conduct to be expected from true partners, however inconvenient?

What innovative teams know and have learned

As before, the secret of creativity and innovation lies not in the values of rule making and exception finding but between these. For, of course, these values are complementary. How else do you improve your rules except by noting each exception and revising your rules accordingly?

Either way, the innovative team can make a virtuous circle of rule making and exception finding, so:

Among famous examples of particularism integrated into universalism are Anglo-American case law, and even the case method at the

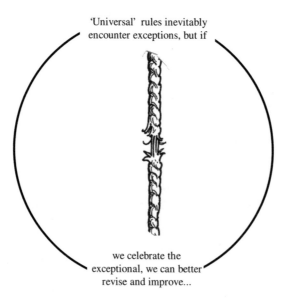

'Universal' rules inevitably encounter exceptions, but if

we celebrate the exceptional, we can better revise and improve...

Fig 3.11 Virtuous circle

Harvard Business School, which begins with particular cases before generalising.

Such virtuous circles are much easier to conceptualise than to put into effect. The fact is, it is often infuriating to promulgate a rule and then discover an exception. If you are a boss, you feel defied. If you are a scientist, you believe you have failed. If you are a moralist, you are aghast at such sinfulness. All too common, therefore, is the vicious circle.

Once again, 'the string has broken', the system is in freefall. Attempts to enforce rules escalate and escalate, as does deviance and defi-

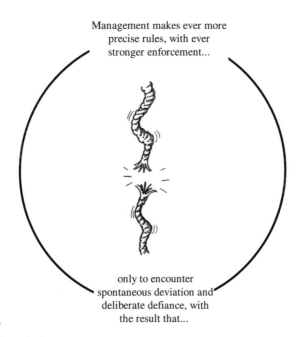

Management makes ever more
precise rules, with ever
stronger enforcement...

only to encounter
spontaneous deviation and
deliberate defiance, with
the result that...

Fig 3.12 Vicious circle

ance, which only intensifies rule enforcement, as 'the snake devours its own tail'.

There are several examples of innovative teams who have learned from exceptions how to improve rules. Richard Branson of Virgin, for example, shows how a large organisation, worth over $3 billion, with its own rules of operation, can nonetheless renew itself by spinning off numerous entrepreneurial ventures, each unique and particular. The trick is to let no unit grow too large, and quickly to divide those in teams who might do this.

Philippe Bourguignon and his successor Henri Giscard d'Estaing continue to protect the legacy that every Club Med vacation is a personal dream, a voyage into the discovery of an unfolding selfhood, with an *esprit* and an *ambience* that is unique and unrepeatable. Yet many of the elements going into that holiday can and must be standardised, globalised, systematised and generated in high volumes and at lowered costs -- all ingredients of a universal logic. You can create fresh scenarios of satisfaction *out of* standardised inputs. It is their combination that is unique, not the elements themselves.

With Lego, we've learned from the failure at the beginning of this century – where profitability dropped to unprecedented levels – that, if you disconnect the unique design of the end customer from the universal building block, the innovative business model disappears. Not only was the famous brick universalised, but also the end result was pre-coded. No choice was left to the creative end user; only one possible solution was correct – and sales plummeted as a result. Lego went back to the unique combination of universal parts that could be built into an infinite number of possible outcomes, through the creativity of the young player. Since 2006, Lego is thriving again.

At Applied Materials, rules have been global and exceptions local as they have set up a system of transcultural learning. In this system, a series of discoveries about local and exceptional circumstances is used to *test generalisations about universally applicable knowledge.* Does this principle apply in all places or only in some? How important are the exceptions? And *might one of these exceptions become a new global rule, replacing existing rules?* 'Global versus local' is transcended by 'Glocalism', the process of modifying global rules through examining local exceptions. And this company of highly innovative products, which makes machines for the semiconductor industry, is thriving on innovative teams making this possible.

The flea in the ear of Intel

Some ten years ago, Dr Martin Gillo, the Personnel Manager of Advanced Micro Devices (AMD) in Europe, approached Charles Hampden-Turner and me. AMD planned to open a new production facility in Dresden in former East Germany: 'The only way to continue competing with Intel is to combine the best of German and American culture,' stated Gillo. Intel was finding that the only way of keeping AMD at bay was continually to take them to court for 'patent infringement'. In the beginning of 2000, it became clear that the investment of 1.5 billion euros in the manufacturing of semiconductors was worth every penny: for the first time, AMD had beaten Intel by managing to introduce the first gigahertz chip more than two days earlier than the chip giant. Was it true, then, that cultural integration had created something that rose above the capacity of a single culture?

Both parties tried to form coalitions with the Americans just to spite each other. The Americans showed a slight preference for the entrepreneurial East Germans, as they tended to be good listeners and were more flexible. However, American-German misunderstandings were much more persistent.

The American semiconductor industry can attribute much of its success to the integration of individual creativity with teamwork, and to the successful completion of a long-term vision. AMD arrived in Dresden in typical American style; programmes were executed in a stereotypical American manner; videos, workshops, and pep talks done the 'Texan way' were combined in the pursuit of excellence.

Thoroughness seeking perfection versus risk taking

Dresden is the capital of Saxony and was the centre of the former East German microchip industry. Many highly trained East German engineers were contracted by AMD. It soon became clear that education-wise they were on the same level as their West German counterparts, but that their improvisation skills were much more developed. This is often seen in a catch-up economy, where many capable people suddenly get access to the means that allow them to experiment and ultimately manufacture a product. The final result in AMD was clear. The West Germans took care of the precise organisational structure in which the Americans could express their expertise and creativity. The vision was to become a reconciliation of a catch-up economy with market leadership.

It was interesting to see the role that the former East Germans played: they were the oil that kept the machine running. At crucial moments they were able, via improvisation, to widen the critical path in the technical as well as the political area. Martin Gillo was convinced that AMD could never have been a threat to an organisation such as Intel if the West Germans alone had been allied with the Americans.

Many cultural differences had to be reconciled between East and West Germans and Americans. Crucial for the innovative process, however, was the integration of the entrepreneurial spirit of both East Germans and Americans and the very systematic and structured approach of the West Germans. East Germans have been very active in Saxony in the former DDR. It was DDR's Silicon Valley, with one major flaw in the argument – there were hardly any resources available to set up expensive pilot plants, therefore their experimental attitude was developed to an extreme. And as regards the results and prices, AMD became the most respected firm. What happened?

'The Americans are can-do, pioneering, optimistic,' Dr Gillo says. 'They shoot first, aim later. The West Germans want to be absolutely thorough and correct, and sometimes they fall into "analysis paralysis". And then you have the East Germans. For 40 years, under communism, they smuggled their machine tools in from the West. When something broke, they couldn't call up for a spare part. They created brilliant solutions on their own, but they never learned how to take entrepreneurial risks because the official party lines did not like to see them fail. Now here we are, in our state-of-the-art plant, trying to build computer chips together.[18]'

When the Americans and West Germans arrived, it soon became clear that culture clashes could provide a real obstacle to success. Some Americans assumed that everyone would naturally want to follow the best universal practices brought from the USA. Some Germans perceived the Americans as condescending. There were West Germans who saw the plant as a

18 Kleiner, Art, 'Dilemma Doctors', *Strategy and Business*, second quarter, 2001

chance to help their East German brethren make up for the years of isolation, and East Germans who burned when they felt their unique talents for
ingenious solutions were being overlooked.

Dr Gillo credits the resulting multicultural style (and a similar effort
to bridge the gap between East and West Germans) with being the key
competitive advantage of the plant. After less than two years of operation,
the AMD Dresden factory was breaking production speed records; some
years ago it went through three generations of chip redesign without major
errors, compared to one redesign every 18 to 24 months for most plants.
'We caught up to one major delay within weeks,' Dr Gillo says, 'by having
people placed at the airport to pick up critical parts from America, driving
them into the factory, and getting them right into the machines without
delays. It reminded me of the women's relay team in the 1998 Olympics.
The American runners were faster individually, but the Germans beat them
by half a second because of the way the runners were attuned to each other
and handed over the baton.'

A salient role in the integration process was the introduction of the
'culture coach'. We trained this person in the facilitating of multicultural
teambuilding. In AMD, an organisation somewhat reliant on team meetings, this individual was responsible for guarding the cultural aspects of
interactions. It was taken in turns, and the culture coaches played a crucial
part in the enrichment of both the German and American cultures.

Gillo later labeled this approach 'systematic experimentation'. On the
one hand, the East Germans and Americans were the entrepreneurs who
took risks and quickly learned from their mistakes. The West Germans were
thorough, avoiding risks and looking for the systematic long-term approach
that avoided the little mistakes in the complex manufacturing process of
microprocessors. When we first talked to Gillo in 1995, AMD had a market
share of 5%. In 2007, it was close to 25%, with great future prospects
now that Dell had decided to put AMD processors in some of their key
machines. You can bet your bottom dollar that in the future Intel will again
feel someone on its heels.

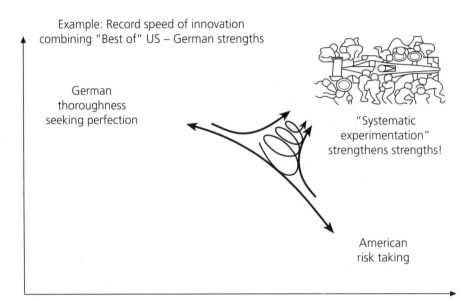

Fig 3.13 Combining Best of US – German strengths

In the process of innovation, we see that, if the universalistic codifications, standards and platforms are combined with the particularistic exceptions and unique combinations, the team becomes creative. With the pizza, we see that the uniform bottom is combined with the topping of choice and as such it becomes one of the top-selling products in the world. The Japanese car has combined the Japanese strength for customisation with the American talent of sharing standardised platforms, making for worldwide successes. And finally, with Deming's Quality Management, we see it needed the Japanese implementation process to make it popular in the USA. Now we see that errors are taken to be corrected, and the result is the worldwide success of the error-correcting system. The crucial element is that the team needs to combine the different cultural orientations to make it a successful innovation.

Measuring innovation competence

We should explain here that the thread of our main discussion and the conceptual framework we are offering has been developed and made more rigorous through our ongoing research. This itself has been a reconciliation between formal deductive research and our inductive learning from our consultancy. It is appropriate therefore to refer to some of the main sources of data that support our argument.

Results were first accumulated through our 'old' questionnaire. In these investigations, managers were given a straight choice between two conflicting values. For example, the issue of universalism versus particularism was measured by posing the following dilemma.

> You are riding in a car driven by a close friend. He hits a pedestrian. You know he was going at at least 50 mph in an area of the city where the speed limit is 30 mph. There are no witnesses. His lawyer says that, if you testify under oath that he was only travelling at 30 mph, it may save him from serious consequences.
>
> What right does your friend have to expect you to protect him?

Here the responding manager must either side with his friend or bear truthful witness in a court of law. Because the respondent is limited to these 'forced-choice' options only, there is no possibility of integrating opposites, no opportunity to display transcultural competence by reconciling this dilemma.

In our subsequent conversations with managers who had responded to this questionnaire, we kept encountering attempts to resolve the dilemma and some annoyance that we had pressed so stark a choice on them. So we designed a more discriminating questionnaire with five answers, not two. Two answers were the original polarised alternatives. One option was a compromise between the two values. The last two options were alternative integrations, one of which started with universalism and encompassed particularism, and the second of which started with particularism and encompassed universalism. These are set out below.

1   There is a general obligation to tell the truth as a witness. I will not perjure myself before the court. Nor should any real friend expect this from me.

2   There is a general obligation to tell the truth in court, and I will do so, but I owe my friend an explanation and all the social and financial support I can organise.
3   My friend in trouble always comes first. I am not going to desert him before a court of strangers based on some abstract principle.
4   My friend in trouble gets my support, whatever his testimony, yet I would urge him to find in our friendship the strength that allows us both to tell the truth.
5   I will testify that my friend was going a little faster than allowed and say that it was difficult to read the speedometer.

The logics behind these positions are as follows:

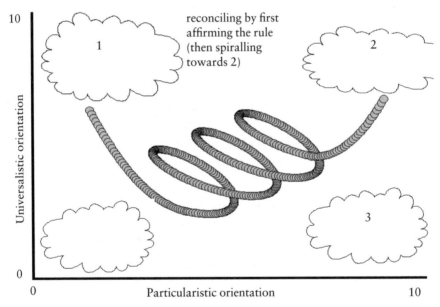

Fig 3.14 From law to friendship

1)   (1/10) is a polarised response in which the law is affirmed but the friend is rejected (universalism excludes particularism).
2)   (10/10) is an integrated response in which the rule is first affirmed and then everything possible is done for the friend (universalism joined to particularism).
3)   (10/1) is a polarised response in which the friend is affirmed as an exception to the rule, which is then rejected (particularism excludes universalism).

4) (10/10) is an integrated response in which exceptional friendship is affirmed and then joined to the rule of law (particularism joined to universalism).

5) (5/5) is a stand-off or fudge, in which both the rule of law and loyalty to friends are blunted (universalism compromised with particularism).

The underlying framework is this.

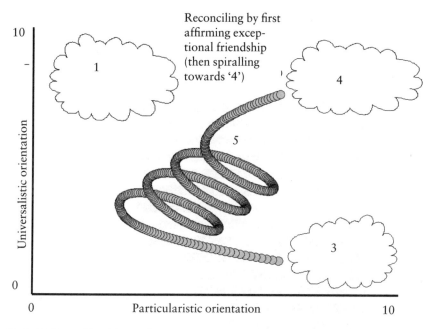

Fig 3.15 From friendship to law

- Integrated responses 2) and 4) show more transcultural competence than polarised responses 1) and 3), and than the compromised response 5).
- While American managers will typically put universalism first (adopting the anticlockwise spiral), and East Asian/Southern European managers will typically put particularism first (adopting the clockwise spiral), each can integrate his/her priority with its opposite.
- From this it follows that there are at least two paths to integrity, not 'one best way'.

- There are, however, better ways and worse ways.
- Transcultural competence will anticipate and explain success in overseas postings and correlates with 360° feedback ratings.

What we found

We used the questionnaire based on these types of questions with five options extensively. The results have been widely published as they have evolved over the years in the various editions of *Riding the Waves of Culture*. A small selection of the results are shown:

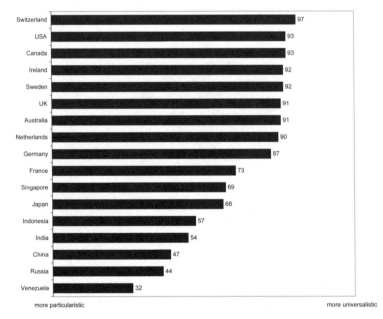

Fig 3.16 Country scores

Universalism versus particularism

Some cultures (such as North Americans and the Swiss) see morality as a matter of standard laws and rules, whereas other cultures (such as Koreans, Venezuelans and Eastern Europeans) see morality as variable, depending on particular loyalties and circumstances.

Dimension 2: Self-interest and personal fulfilment versus group interest and social concern (individualism versus communitarianism)

How is it that (former) communist countries lack any talent for innovation? How is it that a fully capitalist society with a free market like the USA has lost its consumer electronics industry? How is it that countries like Finland, Ireland, Sweden, Switzerland and the USA are among the countries that rank highest in terms of global innovation, according to new research[19].

It is because innovation is the reconciliation between individual invention and collective teamwork. An evaluation of 26 countries by Forrester Research found that taxpayers' money is being wasted because many politicians and bureaucrats confuse innovation with invention.

> 'National empowerment, power, wealth and well-being depend more on deployment of innovation than on the invention itself. The biggest flaw in most innovation agendas is that they look at nations as closed systems, as if nations must have all innovation capabilities in-house. It cannot be done … Nations must shed their inward-looking innovation attitudes to become successful in the end-to-end global innovation value network.'

Instead, the study sees an emerging global ecosystem of collaborative innovation among countries, companies, universities and other organisations. These 'innovation networks' involve countries identifying and assuming a specific role – inventor, transformer, financier and broker – to match their unique skill set.

As an example of what can be achieved, the USA semiconductor industry achieved global market dominance by fusing teams of creative individuals. Success for one of our clients came from not simply rewarding individuals for their creative ideas or teams for successful projects, but also rewarding the integration of these opposites. The key was to

---

19 Forrester Wave: *Forrester Research, Inc. All rights reserved. Forrester, Forrester Wave, Forrester's Ultimate Consumer Panel, WholeView 2, Technographics*

reward creative individuals for giving their findings to their team, and at the same time to reward teams for how they developed the creativity of their individuals.

Conventionally it has been difficult to relate these patterns to what creates effective collaboration in teams, especially across cultures – let alone between any individuals with different value systems. We thought that if we tried to extend existing team analysis tools to find a more subtle way of describing the range of behaviours employed by people in different situations, it would help in more effective collaboration in a team.

The sophisticated stereotype

Here the contrast is between the freedom of the individual – in which personal fulfilment, enrichment, expression, competition and self-development are championed above all – and the benefits accruing to the group, community or corporation. There can be no doubt where America, Australia and Canada stand. Their very populations are formed by those who left the only community they had known to seek their fortune in the New World. Isn't it interesting that the English language is one of the few languages where 'I' is written with a capital letter, and where people like to be called by their first name? When we go to more communitarian cultures such as the Chinese and Japanese, we find that you introduce yourself with your family name, and then mention your first name. Indeed Figure 3.21 shows that Canada, the USA, Denmark, Switzerland, the Netherlands, Australia and the UK head the national advocates of individualism, while India, Japan, Mexico, China, France, Brazil and Singapore head the advocates of communitarianism.

Did you ever see a Hollywood movie in which group opinion was proved right and the lone protagonist yielded to that view? Yet the superior judgement of he-who-stands-alone has been vindicated a thousand times! It was Hermann Melville who wrote:

'Take a single man alone, and he seems a triumph, a grandeur or a woe. But take mankind in the mass and they seem for the most part a mob of unnecessary duplicates.'

The communitarian attitudes of rice-growing regions should come as no surprise. With fewer than a dozen people co-operating, it is simply impossible to survive. The self-aggrandising schemes of warlords have brought China to starvation again and again. France has progressed historically only when angry groups surged into the streets and manned the barricades. The inspiration may have been individual, but the *force majeur* was communal. History shapes cultures.

Some typical misunderstandings

American plans to 'motivate' employees in foreign cultures typically fall foul of this crucial cultural difference. How many times has the 'Employee of the Month' called in sick, rather than face an envious peer group at work? Individual incentives can be unfair if other members of the group helped you to succeed or if you believe that your supervisor deserves the credit for briefing and mentoring you so well.

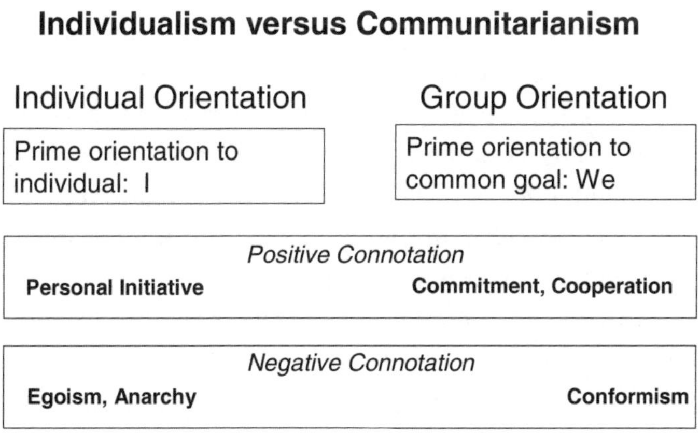

Individualism versus Communitarianism

Individual Orientation	Group Orientation
Prime orientation to individual: I	Prime orientation to common goal: We

Positive Connotation	
Personal Initiative	Commitment, Cooperation

Negative Connotation	
Egoism, Anarchy	Conformism

Fig 3.17 Cultures differ in putting 'I' or 'we' first

What innovative teams know and have learned

The real limitation of sophisticated stereotypes is at its most obvious here. Yes, of course, Americans are individualists, but they have also created groups for a wider variety of purposes than most other societies – the Town Meeting, the Community Chest, the Protest Group, the Training Group, team working, the Support Group, the Political Action Committee, and so on. The main purpose of this group may indeed be the advancement of personal interests, but it remains true that American individualism has important group expressions. For once again the wealth-generating solutions are not in values extolling groups or individuals, but in interactions between these values.

In this chapter, a large number of innovative teams have made artful combinations between individualism and communitarianism and between competitiveness and co-operation to create powerful and creative learning systems. As Virgin specialises in service organisations, Richard Branson looks first to the communities of his employees, who serve the communities of customers. By taking his company back into private hands, he is able to moderate the demands of shareholders (himself) and take his gains in terms of growth, not dividends. A similar strategy is pursued by Val Gooding of BUPA, Britain's premier private health insurer and provider. Without shareholders, she is able to invest all in staff, customer service and rapid growth. This can be a crucial advantage for 'caring organisations'.

We also witnessed how Suez Lyonnaise des Eaux captured an astonishing 52% of foreign-owned water and treatment systems. It did this by combining the energies released by privatisation with the social responsibility returned to the community through being given full ownership of their own municipal infrastructure after a 20–25 year overhaul. Rarely have private shareholder gain and responsibility for the integrity of a community been better combined.

Perhaps the boldest attempt to reconcile individualist and communitarian cultures – one that has been brilliantly successful – is by Jim Morgan, the retired founder and CEO of Applied Materials. Jim turned author to write a groundbreaking book on Japanese business culture in the 80s. The East Asian attitude to electronics, microchips (the rice of industry) and computers was essentially communitarian. These technologies, contributing as they did to the community's industrial infrastructure in general, could not be allowed to fail, and were accordingly nurtured by governments and banks. Jim realised early on that he had to give Applied Materials (Japan) the autonomy to locate itself at the heart of Japanese industrial policy, among the inner circles of industry itself.

He has followed this policy in Korea, China, Singapore and other major centres of communitarian consciousness. He has instituted an East-West dialogue at the apex of Applied Materials, in which the new freedoms of the electronic age converse with the priceless communitarian logics of accelerated learning for whole societies.

A group can make any one of its members feel like a million dollars. There may be nothing more satisfying in the world than being a heroine or hero to those who know you best. And who would grudge your subsequent promotion or pay rise, once you had steered your group to fame and fortune?

The cultural dimensions do not exist in isolation from each other. We get powerful insights into Russia's current predicament when we cross tabulate them as shown below.

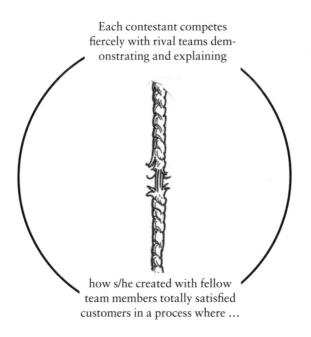

Fig 3.18 Virtuous circle

Russia's agony

What is clear from Russia's scores on our first and second dimension is that no viable system of social order currently exists. Civic order stems from two main influences: the combination of universalism with individualism, or 'The Legal Harness of Self-Interest', and the combination of particularism with communitarianism, or 'Special Deals for the Socially Responsible'. If we cross our first two axes, we find these two clusters.

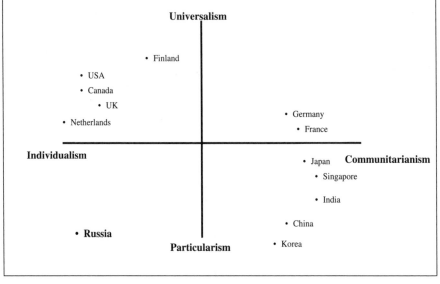

Co-opetition: compete for the best co-operation

The competent innovator knows that individualism-communitarianism is a false dichotomy. The real art is to nurture individuals and then get individuals to serve groups, a process which Adam M. Brandenberger and Barry J. Nalebuff have called co-opetition[20] (see below) .

An interesting example is Motorola's Total Customer Satisfaction competition. Teams that have 'totally satisfied' their customers in any part of the world gather together the evidence of their success and enter a worldwide competition in which they present their solution on stage, together with the results achieved. The contests teach all members how

---

20 Brandenburger, Adam, Nalebuff, Barry, *Co-Opetition : A Revolution Mindset That Combines Competition and Cooperation*, Currency; 1st edition (Dec 1997)

to compete fiercely – but note that this competition is about co-operating with customers and fellow team members. This is 'collaborative competing' or co-opetition.

Among the advantages of this competition is that 800 or so winning solutions surface, which can be studied and disseminated by Motorola University. Competing differentiates ideas; co-operating integrates them. Innovative executives have finely differentiated, well-integrated

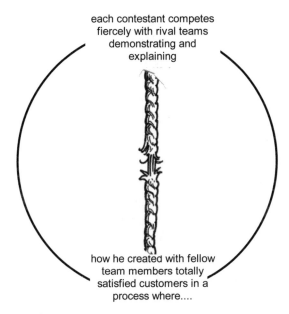

Fig 3.19 Virtuous circle

strategic maps of their terrains.

The term *co-opetition* has been coined to describe this type of co-operative competition. Cartels are well-known examples of companies working together in order to limit competition. In contrast, co-opetition focuses on co-operation between companies in imperfectly competitive markets. Examples of co-opetition include Apple and Microsoft building closer ties on software development, Sony and Philips setting the new standards for DVD players and Peugeot and Toyota co-operating on a new city car for Europe in 2005. Other examples are Free and Open Source Software companies: they all contribute to the production of a software pool that anyone can use as a base for their own business model.

The process of co-opetition is crucial in the creation of innovative teams. While individuals are the main source of invention, their autonomy and free thinking guarantees the stimulation of creativity. But if this goes unconnected to the larger environment – whether this is the team or the organisation – it remains an invention that will never be manufactured and launched onto the market. We have seen that formal and informal, material and immaterial reward systems unintentionally jeopardise the innovation process.

There is an assumption in most Western reward systems that one has to motivate the individual. We met an American HR manager who claimed that his company had developed a very interesting system of performance reward based on 50% variable pay, including options that would only materialise after three years of active service. Short- and long-term thinking were reconciled in this approach and people seemed to be highly motivated by the belief that their performance had a direct effect on the functioning of the organisation as a whole. He had to admit, however, that this approach had met with much resistance in Europe and Asia. In Europe, this was mainly because of tax constraints, but in Asia no clear reason could be provided. 'Could it be culture?' he asked.

Conversely, we see that in most communitarian cultures there is some immaterial pressure to conform to the larger team in which one plays, with the end result that no one dares to stick out their neck. With rewards, neither individual nor group orientations are good for the innovative powers of a team.

The solution is quite straightforward. If you are in America, you retain the individual reward system. In Asia, you motivate people by a team reward structure. In Europe, you do everything to avoid paying taxes. But there is a hidden problem. This decentralised approach works very well for a multi-local organisation. If, however, you grow into a transnational firm, characterised by many multicultural teams in which all sorts of different people with different motivations are united, the reward system needs to be adapted accordingly to make the team innovative.

With the reward system, it is optional to reward people for team spirit. People from Japan excel at this, but it often leads to collective mediocrity. The worst is the compromise: namely 'rewarding the small team'. Both the individualist and the team player feel demotivated. It makes a lot of sense that, in communitarian societies, so much attention has been given to 'creativity management', since individual excellence and creativity didn't come naturally at all.

But what is the (better) alternative?

It is all aimed at creative individuals forming teams that surpass themselves, as in the following examples.

At the end of the '80s we tried similar things at Shell. An experiment in the north of Amsterdam (2,000 staff in the research and development division of KSLA) was based on the joining together of creative individualistic researchers of different nationalities, mostly north-west Europeans, in a joint venture initiated by the Japanese counterpart. The Japanese partners started to complain that the reward process was based on individual excellence only: the best people were given bonuses after they were rank-ordered one-to-one. The Japanese saw this as jeopardising team spirit. In the space of a year, we evenly distributed 20% variable pay over individual and team bonuses. The individual bonus was given to the individual chosen by the team as the best team player; the team bonus went to the team that excelled in supporting individual creativity.

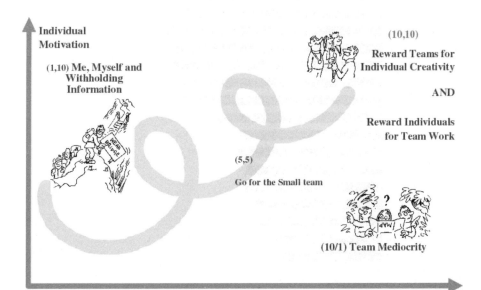

Fig 3.20 Co-opetition

The Shell researchers from Amsterdam competed for the best co-operation in teams and they worked together to compete better. And it made the cross-cultural joint venture into a very creative one.

What we found

A small sample from our database on this dimension is shown below:

Two people were discussing two extreme ways of increasing the quality of one's life. One said: 'It is obvious that if one has as much freedom as possible and the maximum opportunity to develop oneself, the quality of one's life would improve as a result.'

Another said: 'If the individual is continuously taking care of his or her fellows, then the quality of life for us all will improve, even if it obstructs individual freedom and individual development.'

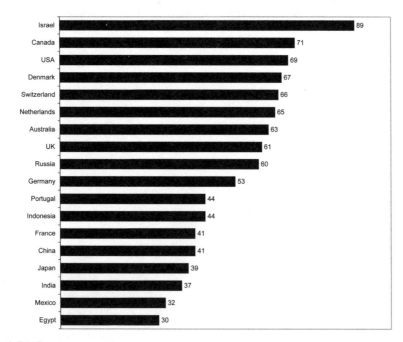

Fig 3.21 Country scores

Individualism versus communitarianism

Americans and Israelis (despite their kibbutz tradition) believe that success stems from individual achievement, while people from Japan, Egypt and India assign primary responsibility to the group. This dilemma often makes it difficult to establish viable performance assessments. An IBM sales team dealt with the problem by awarding bonuses to excellent groups (those that had nurtured individuals) and excellent individual performers (especially those who had been the best team players).

Measuring innovative competence: reconciling the individual and the group

We turn again to the measurement and strategic use of innovation competence and the results achieved so far. In our research, we repeatedly asked leaders to choose between five options. Two of these are unreconciled, one is a compromise, and two are reconciled answers.

Question: jobs in your organisation
Which of the following jobs is found most frequently in your organisation?

    a) A job that is part of an organisation where everybody works together and where you do not get individual credit.

    b) A job that allows everybody to work independently and where individual credit is received on the basis of individual performance.

    c) A job where everybody works together in teams and where the teams are constantly stimulating individual creativity.

    d) A job that allows everybody to work independently and where individual credit is given to the best team player.

    e) A job where there is neither too much individual creativity nor excessive 'groupthink'.

Answers a) and b) are unreconciled answers. Answer e) is a compromise. Answer c) is a reconciliation where we start with communitarianism and answer d) represents a reconciliation that starts with the beauties of individualism. Again, we found that leaders that chose these latter two options were significantly more effective than those who chose any of the others.

Dimension 3: emotions inhibited versus emotions expressed (neutral versus affective)

Football, cars and traffic are splendid expressions of a nation's culture, how it deals with emotions and how it leads to innovation. They also indicate what makes a team creative and a car a bestseller. How is it that one sports team has so much success while another struggles to stay within its league? The Dutch national football team symbolised the Dutch culture's ability to use cultural diversity in an amazing way. It was one of the first European teams to take advantage of its colonial past by combining the more neutral Dutch nature and the mostly Brazilian and Indonesian passion for creativity. Since good leadership was essential to make optimal use of this typical Dutch diversity, they were blessed with great coaches. Michels brought them two second places in the World Championships and one European title in the 80s. He was able to bring together the great passion and emotional play of Cruijff and Keizer in the 70s and van Basten and Gullit in the 80s and the solemn, controlled play of players like Neeskens, Krol and Rijkaard. In the intermediate years, leadership was lacking and so no successes were achieved, despite great talents mixing passion and control.

It is interesting to see how traffic behaviour and types of car, as well as football, are marvellous reflections of the bearers of a culture playing the game. Let's consider some examples. The German team plays in a way that is as dull and reliable as a Mercedes Diesel. It goes full speed ahead on the *autobahn* and often gets where it has to. If it breaks down, it is pretty hard to repair. The only time that the German team became WeltMeister was when the few exceptionally demonstrative and creative players like Netzer, Mattheus and Beckenbauer were put in team of a more reserved nature, with players like Vogts and Muller.

Portugal and Spain were interesting teams to follow. The Iberian Peninsula has shown that the heart is at the centre of national pride. Unfortunately, high individual skill, fed by passion, was never fully exploited for the group. Seat and Lopez also failed to make it to the final for the same reason: they lacked the integration with control. In the Latin arena, we find the Brazilian too. We know that Brazilians excel through individual creative heroes like Pele, Romario and Ronaldinho. For the Brazilians, the text is creativity while the context is control. A very disciplined way of playing has allowed their creative players to excel. And this is why they have been the most frequent World Champions: pure innovation through the combination of passion and control.

The sophisticated stereotype

It is well known that cultures display emotions to very varying degrees. The fury of the Frenchman when you nearly collide with his car and the way he uses his whole body to express his rage are legendary. In contrast, you can be forgiven for imagining that Japanese executives may have gone to sleep during your presentation. The posture of 'half-eye', with the eyelid half closed, can be very galling to those who do not understand 'respectful listening'. Equally unnerving are long silences following your statement. This may be read as 'boredom', when it is intended as evidence of thoughtful consideration. These contrasts are set out below (Figure 3.22), with the Japanese highly neutral and the French, Italians and Latin nations more volatile and affective.

But this particular dimension has more subtleties and variations than most others because, of course, there is strong disagreement about what one should be neutral or affective *about*. Americans, for example, show up as moderately affective, despite their Puritan origins of restraint in religious expression. They believe in showing enthusiasm for products, visions, missions and projects, but are less expressive to each other. They approve of positive emotion (enthusiasm) but not so much of negative emotion (anger or grief). They will talk *about* emotion ('I'm feeling angry') in a vaguely therapeutic manner, but rarely explode or show physical signs of anger.

The British use humour to release emotions and may begin a speech with a joke to relax the audience; Germans and the Swiss may see this as unserious and frivolous. The Japanese and Koreans reveal desires for intimacy by getting drunk together; Germans prefer to bare their souls and share their philosophies of life. The patterns are extremely complex.

Emotions: Neutral versus Affective

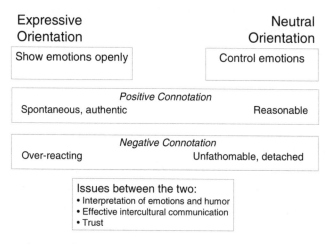

Fig 3.22 The sophisticated stereotype

Some typical misunderstandings

The Swiss can be quite serious, especially during work hours. Humour is for relaxing moments before or after the seminar. The Dutch presenter used a cartoon to 'break the ice'. Dead silence. He used a second cartoon. Again silence. Then a Swiss participant raised his hand. 'Can we get on with the seminar please?'

The Dutch presenter tried to make a joke of the intervention.

'You're a serious lot … Have you ever thought of going into banking?' Silence.

In the coffee break the senior Swiss manager approached the Dutch presenter.

'We didn't like to embarrass you, Dr Trompenaars, but in fact the Swiss have been in banking for some time.'

Note that both parties adhered to their national stereotype and conviction that jokes were not considered appropriate. Those who saw humour as inappropriate could not even recognise the attempt!

Often the same word triggers totally different associations. In a recent partnership negotiation, the Japanese and American sides both vowed that they would be 'sincere'. By this the Americans meant outspoken, unreserved, spontaneous – traits the Japanese found insulting. By 'sincere' the Japanese meant making genuine efforts to create a climate of politeness, good etiquette and gracious manners – a habit the Americans saw as 'bullshitting'. The meeting proved a disaster.

What innovative teams know and have learned

It is wise for a team to make the greatest possible use of its emotional range. There are wide variations in the fortunes of a company and it is appropriate to have a mood that fits the occasion. As Robert Whittington wrote of Sir Thomas More:

'Where should we find a man of such wit, affability and lowliness? As time requireth, a man of marvellous mirth and pastimes, and sometimes of as sad gravity, as who say: a man for all seasons.'

The innovative team operates in two contrasting realms: in calculated reasoning, which may require that emotions be temporarily suppressed; and in wisdom of the heart, which knows that emotional expression evokes a resonance that can heal, inspire, enthuse, comfort and calm those present.

A number of team leaders have managed neutrality-affectivity particularly well. Richard Branson regarded 'have fun' as the surest recipe for an organisation to serve its customers effectively. Good service should be a pleasure for those providing it, and in its absence something was wrong.

Lego put the switch from neutrality to exuberance and excitement to clever use by charging customers *before* they went into Legoland Parks, while the customers were still in a calculative mode. But the entrance fee gave families, and especially children, free access to all the attractions, so that they could let their excitement rip, without clawing desperately at mother's handbag for one more treat. There is a time to seek entrance, and a time to enjoy having done so; the first should be sober, and the second joyful.

BUPA's teams and Val Gooding had somehow to combine the cerebral calculations of a smart insurance company – which saw not people but trends, aggregates and numbers – with caring deeply about the one life that each customer had. When the customer calls for help, after years of contributions, whether the company is 'there' for him/her is a vital question. 'I'm sick, I need you,' says the customer and the voice at the end of that line will make or break that relationship by the swiftness, effectiveness and empathy of his or her response.

Technical excellence and the emotional climate

The last major challenge that Anders Knutsen saw himself as confronting was that of technical excellence and the emotional appeal of products. The latter was a subtle and diffuse concept. Beautiful audiovisual information had to be conveyed on instruments worthy of their content, in the same way that the instruments of an orchestra carry the spirit of the composer and express his or her feeling.

'Time is in our favour,' Knutsen believed. 'The world is flooded with discount junk products which strive to become classics. Products with emotional value will be strongly placed in our "throw away" culture.'

In the history of Bang and Olufsen, both technical excellence and emotional climate had been important – more so than sales or marketing – but even these leading values had not been reconciled or harmonised. First one was dominant and then the other, and their fight for dominance had made the resulting product unaffordable.

So Knutsen extended 'Idealand', a non-localised space where engineers, music lovers, designers and others – both within Research and Development and outside the company in the community of experts – could engage in an dialogue that would stimulate ideas, and balance them. Another balance is between the audio and the visual, which come together in digital sound pictures. Carl Henrik Jeppesen explained:

'We send development teams, usually to the USA, to study what sounds and sights are being made and consumed. They go to concerts, music studies, discotheques. You need someone to champion the original sound pictures and the emotions generated from them, and someone to champion the technologies of recording and playing those sound pictures. It is this creative clash between the artists and engineers that gives you optimal integration.

'In the old days, one competence would dominate the others, but no more. There came a day when Anders Knutsen and his team refused to sponsor a prototype product because the costs were out of line. That was a real shock for all of us. It had never happened here!

'With Break Point, the culture changed dramatically but values were retained and began to strengthen one another. In one sense, the Bang and Olufsen secret is integrated seamlessness – every part of the system has to work with every other part – and now this became true of our values as well.

'We now test our products with our customers and, if they like it, sales start at once with a projected product life of ten years. We position ourselves in the market in such a way that confirms or fails to confirm the hypotheses developed in Idealand. The latter is no private muse, but a testing laboratory for viable ideas, a set of hypotheses to which our customers say yes or no.'

We might also pause to consider ways in which emotions are mishandled, and players who are usually neutral may suddenly burst out with inappropriate emotion, uncontrollable anger and self-pity. It was the genius of Maradona that made the Argentinean football team win many matches. But he could also get out of control and was often sent off the field, leaving the team in despair. And who doesn't remember Zidane's head meeting the chest of the Italian provocateur? It left the French with only 10 players and unable to level with or even beat the Italians. This

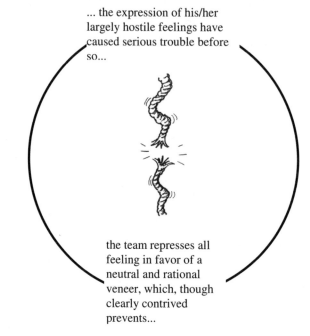

... the expression of his/her largely hostile feelings have caused serious trouble before so...

the team represses all feeling in favor of a neutral and rational veneer, which, though clearly contrived prevents...

Fig 3.24 Vicious circle

illustrates a vicious circle.

It is from such a player that one hesitates to buy a second-hand car and such a player is nicknamed 'Cowboy'.

What we found

Our diagnostic instruments include this question:

In retrospect, I quite frequently think that I have given away too much in my enthusiasm.

What is *your* position on this statement?

a) Strongly agree
b) Agree
c) Undecided
d) Disagree
e) Strongly disagree

Neutrality versus emotional temperament

To a Chinese person or a Northern European, a good leader never shows emotion and rarely (if ever) raises a voice or gestures excitedly; to a Kuwaiti or Italian, displays of emotion signify passion and commitment. Reconciling these cultural mismatches generally involves studied efforts to learn the other side's cues and to moderate your own.

Measuring innovative competence: reconciling neutrality with affectivity

We can measure the extent to which meanings and emotions have been reconciled by distinguishing two polarised strategies, two integrated strategies and a compromise.

Emotions can be so strong that they obliterate thinking. Thoughts can be so calculated that they repress genuine feelings. But to think first and then let out the emotions at the right time, or to feel first and then think hard about how to express this to the best effect, are both pathways to integration set out below. In the following question, we see some very innovative answers and some that make you choose between poles or compromise between them, leaving you with a sub-optimal result.

Question: performance or beauty

When designing a new product (or service), a number of trade-offs are required because of choices of materials, systems, size, strength, technical performance, etc. A group of managers were arguing about whether performance should lead or should follow design appeal.

Which of the following opinions that were expressed is closest to your orientation?

a) Design is always a compromise. In the end, one has to make the best trade-off to balance competing demands.

b) Technical performance must dominate. If the product doesn't work, then the customer has nothing. We can make the product attractive afterwards because of the wide range of shapes, materials and colourings available to us.

c) Unless the product looks attractive, whatever it is, the customer won't buy. We will always have enough technical competence to make sure it works, however it looks.

d) Whilst we start from a technical performance viewpoint, we can consider design and product appeal early.

e) We would start with a range of attractive designs with customer appeal but consider the technical feasibility of performance early.

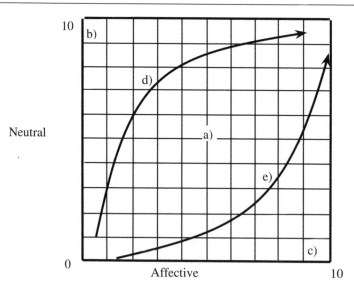

Fig 3.26 reconciling emotions with reason

If you look at all the innovative designs in the world, you see that those designs that reconcile the neutral technical performance and the affective appeal are the most successful. The iPod both is functionally technically brilliant *and* has designer appeal.

There are many ways for a team to position an innovative brand, for example. Censydiam, a leading market research agency, shows one of the better analyses on their internet site. Every year, Censydiam publishes their longitudinal study of the positioning of car brands. They use a two-by-two matrix, where on one axis plots the degree to which emotions are expressed, and the other axis the degree of social integration (see Figure 3.27). It is wonderful to see how the producers of these brands confirm their cultural preference.

Most of the French and Italian brands are represented on the expressive side. On the emotionally more neutral side you'll find British, Swedish and Japanese cars, with Opel and Ford. It will not surprise anybody that, on the side of social differentiation, Alfa-Romeo, BMW, Jaguar, Mercedes and Audi occupy the field, whereas on the social integration side, Fiat, Suzuki, Nissan, Citroën and Daewoo dominate the game.

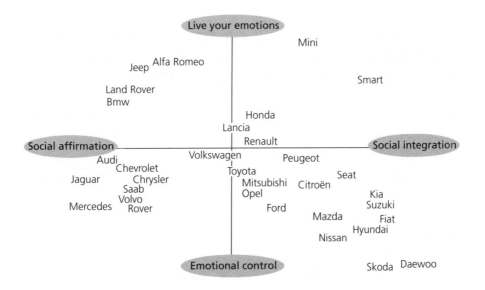

Fig 3.27 Living emotions in cars

Most innovative brands pose a problem, dilemma or anomaly and go on to claim that their product can resolve that dilemma. The more familiar the situation is and the more it engages our cultural archetypes or mental programs, the quicker the consumer will understand and bring his or her cultural ideas to bear on this issue.

For example, young children and babies are popular symbols of *innocence* trusting their caregivers to look after them. Any danger to a child evokes an immediate *protective* response from witnesses. There would be screams from the street, for example, were a child to be seen on a window ledge (hence the reaction to Michael Jackson).

It is striking that many successful brands refer to a tension between two values, and that they credibly claim that their product can reconcile this dilemma effectively. When Apple introduced the rainbow logo and a bite out of the apple at the beginning of the 70s, it was a clear reference to the tree of knowledge of good and evil. On the one side it referred to the attractiveness of the enormous knowledge and possibilities that the user was given, and on the other side it referred to the ability of the user to be able to easily master a computer and deal with enormous complexity. The reconciliation that Apple could offer was that it was possible to do both playfully.

Dimension 4: preference for precise, singular 'hard' standards and preference for pervasive, patterned 'soft' processes (specificity versus diffusion)

Which airline is the most successful? It's difficult to say. Airlines in America narrowly define their job as transportation: 'You're a piece of meat; we carry you,' says the typical flight attendant. They don't serve much food on short flights. Singapore Airlines, British Airways and most European airlines adopt a general, 'diffuse' sense of responsibility for passengers as guests. Naturally, they want to serve full meals, even on a 40-minute flight from London to Amsterdam, no matter how expensive or cumbersome that may be.

To reconcile this dilemma, former Scandinavian Airlines Systems CEO Jan Carlzon focused on 'moments of truth': SAS would concentrate only on those diffuse services – champagne on one flight, more attention to connections on another – that would make the most difference to customers.

The sophisticated stereotype

Here the contrast is between cultures that emphasise things, facts, statistics, units, atoms, analysis and 'hard' numbers, and cultures which emphasise relations, patterns configurations, connectedness, synthesis and 'soft' processes. These contrasting styles have been linked with the left and right brain hemispheres. We call them specificity versus diffusion.

America's exaggerated specificity manifests itself in many forms, such as 'keeping your word' (as if there were only one!), in 'bullet points', piecework incentives, straight-line forecasts, bottom lines, financial ratios and other attempted distillations of virtue. We urge each other 'to get to the point' and 'not beat about the bush'.

Specificity is increased when we argue with win-lose conflict that produces specific results and with debates between respective advocates.

Specific versus Diffuse

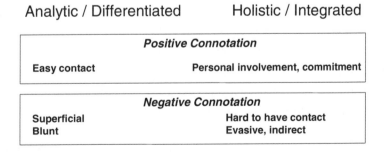

Fig 3.28 The sophisticated stereotype

Some typical misunderstandings

Alfie Kohn recently compiled a long, sad dossier of what goes wrong with Pay for Performance. Many managers recognise these problems, but are still reluctant to give up on the idea that, just as markets pull money and rewards towards successful enterprise, so should corporations. The problem with Pay for Performance is its exaggerated specificity. It assumes that superiors can know in advance how a task should be done and how difficult it is, and hence what pay should be attached to its performance.

But increasingly this is not possible. Work is too complex, too innovative, too subject to continuous improvement for superiors to know these things, much less construct an elaborate tariff. Markets certainly do pay for success – this is their genius – but they do not tell you in advance what you should do or how much you will gain by doing it! Markets are diffuse, chaotic processes with some very specific and measurable outcomes. Let's count, by all means, but let's not reduce reality only to what can be counted.

What the innovative teams know and have learned

The answer lies, as before, between the preferences of business cultures such as the USA and the Netherlands, with their predominant specificity, and the business cultures of Japan and Singapore, with their predominant diffuseness. While Americans like to begin with forecasts, budgets, checklists, etc. and then start a process to hit these targets, East Asians typically value harmonious processes *(wa)* and the spontaneous flow of work, and later subject these to detailed feedback on specific indicators.

Some famous American gurus, among them W. Edwards Deming and Joseph Scanlon, had their ideas picked over in America, but picked up and massively implemented in Japan and East Asia, and these have now been reimported to the USA. Why was this? Because both Deming and Scanlon placed spontaneous action and the free flow of ideas and industrial processes ahead of the feedback and specifics needed to monitor, guide and reward these. Deming's cycle of Act-Plan-Implement-Check starts with spontaneous action. The Scanlon Plan begins with the free flow of constructive ideas within work teams. Once implemented, the impact on the input-output ratio is calculated and specific gains from this process are shared among group members.

That employees are capable of self-organising to form teams with their own flow and momentum is by now a truism. It may begin with a challenge or problem definition by the sponsor of the team. Persons who care about this issue and have the skills and knowledge to address it select themselves and/or are selected by feedback from other volunteers. Note that the team is shaped by the problem profile and forms itself spontaneously to solve that problem.

Michael Dell of Dell Computers was one of the first to move beyond the supply of specific hardware or software to embrace process innovation via the internet. Dell starts with why you want computers, what you want them for and how you plan to mobilise information, and it helps you with that whole, diffuse process of knowledge management. Buying a computer from Dell is like being a gentleman attended by his personal tailor.

Chicago psychologist Mihaly Csikszentmihaly speaks of the flow experience in which teams or single competitors have so closely matched their skills with the attainment of their goals that the boundaries seem to dissolve. They are their challenge. The skier and the piste are one. The goal itself becomes a source of energy that speeds the team. Human beings and their teams, says Mihaly, are complex adaptive systems, capable of forming seamless, purposeful wholes.

In highly effective organisations, then, diffuse, 'chaotic', creative teams receive specific feedback on the success or otherwise of initiatives, managing, as it were, 'on the edge of chaos'.
Let's go back to Gillo's AMD to see how their teams got to be the leaders in innovation by creating the virtuous circle.

Holistische weltanschauungen and analytical bottom lines

The Americans often complained about the slowness and lack of creativity of the Germans. The Germans in turn stated that the Americans were too premature, throwing even the most undeveloped ideas into brainstorming sessions: the Americans had immediately jumped to the conclu-

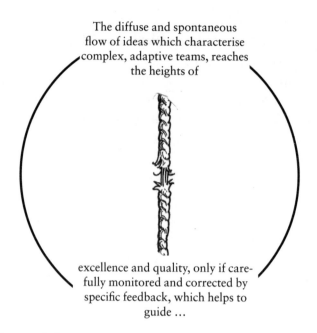

The diffuse and spontaneous flow of ideas which characterise complex, adaptive teams, reaches the heights of

excellence and quality, only if carefully monitored and corrected by specific feedback, which helps to guide ...

Fig 3.29 Virtuous circle

sion that nothing would work out, as the Germans showed no evidence of having the type of brain to storm with.

The solution seemed quite simple. 'Time-outs' were built into each meeting, and the Germans blossomed. In private, it was easier to swap ideas (in German) and to criticise them too. These ideas were then collated, put down on postcards and passed to the Americans. The Americans called this 'train storming' because they had noticed that many German trains had private coupés. There was all-round astonishment at the resulting German creativity.

The reconciliation of both cultures was found in a process where the Americans were asked to summarise the meetings and the Germans to set up the agenda on the basis of the minutes of the previous meeting. In a very implicit manner it came down to knowledge management. Americans were forced to share information and the Germans needed to become more specific.

Typically, these kinds of feelings can breed misunderstanding in even simple situations, such as figuring out how to conduct meetings. The American managers preferred freeform brainstorming sessions in English, where they could develop ideas openly and spontaneously in the group. The Germans, coming from a culture in which it is a breach of privacy to open someone else's refrigerator, typically did not want to present their thoughts unless they were well prepared. A conventional solution (for a typical American-owned company) would have been to force everyone to adopt Amercian informality. The AMD Dresden startup team rejected that approach, and considered alternating German-style formal meetings one week, and American give-and-take sessions the next.

Instead, in a series of meetings with the team, it was suggested that they could have it both ways, but not at the same time. To combine the strengths of their different perspectives, the Americans and the Germans would gradually have to build up their capabilities together. The Dresden team designed a meeting format that opened with American-style, free-wheeling brainstorming sessions, in which new ideas were encouraged from anyone, regardless of place in the hierarchy. But they also set up a formal reflective process – for summarising and thinking through the ideas between meetings, and then presenting them again, in improved form, during the next meeting. When appropriate during the brainstorming sessions, ideas were written down and posted on boards, to ensure that participants who weren't confident of their verbal skills could also add ideas easily. Although AMD's *lingua franca* was English, the meetings were held in both English and German; any member could switch to either language at any time to express an idea, without recrimination. The story seems, at first glance, like a compromise, as if each side magnanimously gave in to make the other feel important.

Measuring innovation competence: reconciling specificity and diffuseness

In our diagnostic instruments, our respondent managers considered five possible answers to the following idea to probe what the best work environment is.

Question: the best work environment

People have different opinions about how the work environment influences job performance.

Which of these alternatives best describes the work environment in your organisation?

a) People you work with know you personally and accept the way you are, both within and outside of the organisation.

b) Colleagues respect the work you do, even if they are not your friends.

c) Colleagues know you personally and use this wider knowledge to improve job performance.

d) Colleagues take some private circumstances into consideration, while disregarding others.

e) The people you work with respect the work you do and are therefore able to offer to help you in private matters.

Here we see that the most effective work environments e) and c) are those in which specific and diffuse sources of knowledge are combined – in

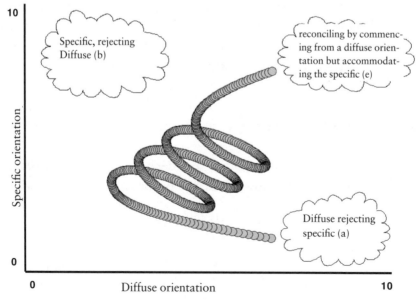

Fig 3.30 Reconciling from diffuse to specific

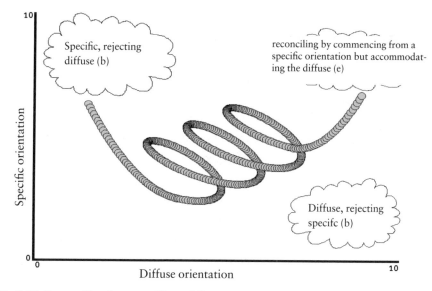

Fig 3.31 Reconciling from specific to diffuse

either order. In each case, the recognition of dilemmas and their reconciliation helped us and our leaders to create a wider and more inclusive 'integrity of values'.

Formal research investigative studies

More extensive triangulation studies, where we correlated reconciliation with bottom-line results, business unit performance and 360° peer review, have been subject to detailed statistical analysis by our internal research team and several of our University-based PhD students. We have accumulated strong evidence that this integrity or bridging of diverse perspectives is a vital aspect of creating wealth and sustainability.

What we found

This dimension was probed with the following question.

Question: the essence of an organisation

There are two extreme ways to consider an organisation.

Which of these two ways better represents the way you perceive the essence of an organisation?

a) An organisation is a system designed to perform functions and tasks in an efficient way. People are hired to fulfil these functions with the help of machines and other equipment. They are paid for the tasks they perform.

b) An organisation is a group of people working together. The people have a social relationship with other people and with the organisation. The functioning of the company depends on these relationships.

Dimension 5: status earned through success and track record versus status ascribed to a person's potential e.g. age, family (achievement versus ascription)

How is it that so much innovative work is coming from Asia? Singapore is one of the highest on the list of innovative countries. And how is it that the French are leading in the peaceful use of electricity generation through nuclear devices and in high speed trains (TGV)?

Highly ascriptive cultures, such as Asian and Latin cultures, have a tendency first to give a project status within which it is protected and expected to achieve. This is reconciled by eliciting potentials from all potentially innovative projects, thereby giving them the best chance of achieving – a self-fulfilling prophecy. This has led to the success of innovative projects like the Eiffel Tower, the TGV, the Malaysian Twin Towers, the hybrid car of Toyota and Concorde. Each started with a grand design with great status and a large budget, which motivated teams to live up to the expectations by delivering great creative performances.

And obviously there is the reverse helix that starts with achievements and gradually, step-by-step, leads to the status of the ascribed. This process is to be found in more achievement-oriented cultures like the USA, UK and north-west Europe. If you look at the innovation process

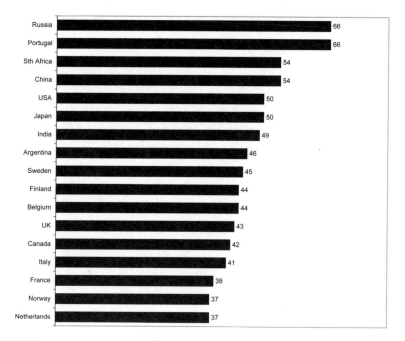

Russia	66
Portugal	66
Sth Africa	54
China	54
USA	50
Japan	50
India	49
Argentina	46
Sweden	45
Finland	44
Belgium	44
UK	43
Canada	42
Italy	41
France	38
Norway	37
Netherlands	37

Fig 3.32 Separate versus connected country scenes

at Microsoft, SAP, Intel and Dell computers, you see that ascribed status was achieved through incremental steps, from MS-DOS to Windows Vista, and from Pentium 1 to Pentium 4.

The sophisticated stereotype

Here the contrast is between being esteemed for what you do and being esteemed for what you are. Status can be conferred almost exclusively on your achievements. It can also be conferred on your being or potential. So we may expect more of males, of white people, of the college-educated (which includes past achievement), of older people, of well-connected people and of people of good family or class. People assigned to certain roles, e.g. electrical engineer, may have higher status because the business or nation anticipates that such jobs will be crucial to its future.

As we might have expected, Americans, Canadians, New Zealanders, Australians and all immigrant nations have strong preferences for achievement. When you immigrate, you leave class and family associations behind you. Few in the New World care that you came from a 'prominent family in Kent'[21]. But Norway, the Netherlands, Sweden, Ireland and the UK are also high in achievement orientation.

Among those ascribing status are cultures with formidable records of economic growth in the recent past: Japan, Korea, Hong Kong, Taiwan, China, France and Singapore. Are these against achievement? Surely not. They just approach achievement in a different way. They ascribe high status to those entrusted with 'catching up with the Americas', who are given prestigious posts within key innovative projects. The idea is that these people will achieve as a consequence of the trust placed in them.

Achievement orientations assume that what is being tried is *worth achieving*, but this is not always true. Rising to the top of a criminal conspiracy engaged in racketeering is a doubtful achievement.

Some typical misunderstandings

Societies that achieve status and societies that ascribe it are often at odds in first encounters. When Americans visit East Asia with a product or proposition, they usually 'put their cards on the table' and behave automatically, as they see it. This is the deal. These are the costs. This is the size of the likely opportunity. With profits on this scale, should we not sink our differences? All this is 'achievement talk'.

And of course, it is deeply offensive to cultures that ascribe status. What these cultures want to know is this: Who are you? With whom are you related and connected? What is your background? What family do you come from?

They also want to know if you are inherently gracious, polite and hospitable. By putting you in relaxed settings, they seek to establish trust. Many hours, even days may be spent on small talk, but the implications are not small. If you were pretending, you would not be able to keep up the pretence. The scattered impressions would not be coherent. What, after all, is five days in a partnership lasting five years or more?

---

21 Kent is a 'county' (small regional unit) in the south-east of the UK

Status: Achievement versus Ascription

What you do	Who you are
•Previous status ignored •Free market	•Previous status acknowledged •Strategic industry

Positive Connotation	
Focus on competence	Stability

Negative Connotation	
Past performance doesn't count No time for learning	Status quo not challenged Rigidity and steep hierarchy

Fig 3.33 Sophisticated stereotype

But if we look more closely at this misunderstanding, we see that it is really an issue of priorities. Once Americans have decided to do business with someone and feel that a deal is in the offing, then it is sensible to get to know them, deepen the relationship and check their references. Once a Chinese or Japanese executive has got to know an American and deepened the relationship, then it is time to turn to business. Each accidentally offends the other by getting this sequence wrong.

The reason it is so important to learn from other cultures is that 'pure achievement' or 'pure ascription' are both liable to fail. The British pensions industry faces a pensions mis-selling scandal in which tens of thousands of pensioners were induced to surrender their group pension plan for an individual portable pension, with significantly smaller benefits. The volume of this duplicity is a staggering £2 billion, with companies 'named and shamed' by government watchdogs until they repay the difference.

How could salespeople fan out across the country and talk luckless savers into pensions provisions worse than the ones they currently held? All too easily, we fear, because these sales staffs were being paid on commission only – on what they achieved only.

Most companies in the world, by a very large margin, are still family-owned. Even in publicly owned companies, family concepts survive. One thinks of the Japanese term *amai,* meaning indulgent affection between mentor and subordinate, and *sempae-gohal* (brother–younger brother relationship). Training your workforce and mentoring them is an investment in their potential, a form of ascribed status. That people who care for and respect each other go on to achieve is a natural consequence. The larger training expenses of several East Asian cultures speak for themselves. Japanese auto-assembly plants in the USA give new workers 225 hours of training in their first six months; American plants give just 42 hours.

What innovative teams know and have learned

Our research findings confirm that cultures putting ascribed status first are still capable of great innovative achievements. Even with East Asia's present troubles, its growth rates are the highest yet recorded in the history of economics. The reason for this is that ascribing status and achieving status are complementary. If you want someone to achieve, then show them initial respect.

In America, we keep stumbling over this fact, but too often 'lean and mean' management ignores it. In the original Hawthorne Experiment, Irish and Polish immigrant female workers were given the status of co-researchers with Elton Mayo and Fritz Roethlisberger from Harvard. Instead of just assembling telephone relays, they were invited to investigate how telephone relays might be better assembled – a totally transformed job description. The fact that they were withdrawn from the factory floor into a small group meant that they could affirm each other's identities.

Many innovative teams also showed great skill in handling the achieved–ascribed dimension and using it to learn with. Richard Branson starts with critiquing those industries in which he has decided to compete – that is, ascribing to them defective status and ascribing to himself the reputation of a reformer of those industries and an underdog in challenging them. Unlike many reformers, he then actually *achieves* superior levels of performance and so proves his original contention, using wide sympathy in the press and among customers to establish his case.

The issue is granting teams sufficient autonomy to *achieve*, without thereby diminishing the *ascribed* status of the senior manager who sponsors that team's efforts. Martin Gillo of AMD struggled with the need to have senior managers risk their senior positions in delegating resources and authority to problem-solving teams. Where these were successful, the sponsor's authority was actually enhanced, and the status ascribed to the team was used by it to achieve and thereby add to the sponsor's reputation.

Stan Shih of Acer had to make sure both that managers and employees achieved *and* that others were prepared to mentor that achievement: to describe, judge and celebrate excellence and in that respect rise above achievement to assure that its ends were worthwhile. You cannot have everyone achieve; some must judge and consecrate the goals of that achievement and some must ascribe status and be seen to symbolise the ends themselves.

Bombardier was another successful family company, which Laurent Beaudoin, son-in-law of the founder, took over some years after the latter's death. Although this might have the appearance of status ascribed by family membership, in fact family members had to work even harder than outsiders to justify their places in the hierarchy, and Beaudoin was not the nearest relative.

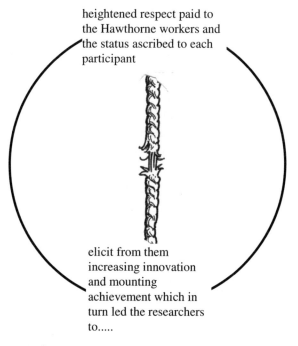

heightened respect paid to the Hawthorne workers and the status ascribed to each participant

elicit from them increasing innovation and mounting achievement which in turn led the researchers to.....

Fig 3.34 Virtuous circle

The company made very successful acquisitions and in each case the new company became a member of the 'family' and was studied with extraordinary care and respect by Beaudoin, the Scholar-Acquisitor. He took over and managed companies of far greater complexity than the one his father-in-law had founded – hence 'The Ski-mobile which took to the Skies'. By welcoming each new acquisition into the 'family', and giving it great importance, the company laid the groundwork for a succession of extraordinary innovations.

That this was no coincidence has been found many times since. Consultants who use interviews as a method of inquiry often find that executives have seldom had the experience of being listened to, and their morale and competence grows before your eyes. Royale Foote and colleagues tested the proposition that interviewing alone could boost productivity. In the Annheuser Busch's Fairmont plant they trained each level of supervision to interview the level below, from the top of the organisation to the very bottom, which was unionised by a tough Teamsters' local. Interviews were not focused on work issues specifically, but on whatever concerned the interviewee. There was no additional intervention.

In the eight years of the interviewing process, the Fairmont facility climbed from almost the worst plant in the network to by far the best, on a score of hard measures. Something as elementary as brewing, canning and trucking rests squarely on the status and respect ascribed to each member of the organisation.

No less a luminary than Douglas McGregor taught that the respect and confidence we have in one another fulfils itself in subsequent achievement. He called this Theory Y. As Bernard Shaw put it in Pygmalion: 'It's the way she's treated that makes her a lady.' No wonder the Pygmalion Effect has been found in the workplace and the classroom. When teachers are told that a child will 'spurt', the child does, although the 'spurters' were actually picked at random. It was the teacher's belief that spurred the child to achievement.

Measuring innovation competence: reconciling achieved with ascribed status

There are two roads to integrating these values. You could argue that you must first decide *who* you are (ascribed status) if you are to go on to achieve in a way consistent with this. Or you could decide that achieving at this and that is a good way of discovering who you are (ascribed) and what you were meant to stand for.

The five responses below were used to measure reconciliation versus polarisation.

Question: what is important?

Which one of the following best describes your values?

The most important thing in life is:

a) getting things done, because in the long run it serves you best to think and act in a way that is consistent with the way you really are

b) that you are able to do things at times and to relax at others

c) to think and act in a manner that is consistent with the way you really are, because in the long run you will achieve more

d) getting things done, even if it interferes with the way you really are

e) to think and act in a way consistent with the way you really are, even if you don't get things done.

We plot these answers on the grid below.

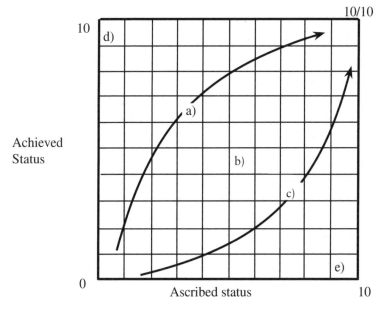

Fig 3.35 Reconciling achievement vs ascription

Achievement versus ascription

America's tradition of deriving status from a merit system (achievement) creates a culture of 'winners and losers' in which the 'losers' are often blue-collar people, shut out from decision making.

The alternative followed in many Asian nations (and in the British House of Lords, and most labour unions), in which status is hereditary or rooted in one's community, rewards mediocrity.

A trucking company bedevilled by safety problems resolved this dilemma by enlisting its unionised drivers as 'knights of the road', making them directly involved and respected participants in increasing highway safety.

3.17 Dimension 6: Control and effective direction comes from within versus control and effective direction comes from without (inner-directed versus outer-directed)

Car shunt

We all make mistakes in life. Some years ago, Fons asked his wife if he could borrow her car – a Mitsubishi Space Wagon – to get some loudspeakers from town. He was driving and had to stop at a pedestrian crossing. Just after coming to a stop, he heard a noise indicating that a car had hit from behind. He stepped out and saw that the length of their impressive Japanese car had diminished by at least 20%. Psychologically, Fons thought that the whole back of the car had disappeared in the crash. Virtually inside Fons' car was a Volvo 200 series, better known as 'the tank'. There wasn't a scratch to be seen on this vehicle, even when you looked closely. The driver came out with his head in one hand, covering a severe cut. He apologised almost casually. 'There is not much left of your car, sir,' he said, 'but are you ok?' Fons felt fine, because he had hardly felt the collision.

Isn't it interesting to see how cars have become safer and safer by joining different cultural logics into one new philosophy? The Swedish car, built according to 'inner-directed' values, was built strong, to withstand and dominate its environment. It wasn't dented, but its passenger was bruised. The Japanese car yielded on impact, responsive to its environment. Its fender crumpled, but the riders were unscathed. And the new generation of cars have reconciled the two approaches by internationalising safety. It has opted for very tough parts to allow other parts to be flexible. Intercultural encounters of this kind lead to innovation.

The sophisticated stereotype

Here the question is about the source of virtue and direction. Is it inside each of us, in our 'soul', conscience, integrity – or outside us in the beauty and harmonies of nature, in the needs of families, friends, customers? Is it virtuous 'to be your own man', or 'to respond to your environment?'

Americans tend to plan and then make those plans work, to rely on ability not luck, and prescribe taking control of their lives. The USA is joined in strong inner direction by Norway, New Zealand, Canada, Australia and France. The latter, we may note, combines communitarianism with inner direction, as in the group of fiercely convinced rebels seizing control of the nation's destiny. While inner direction is advocated by Judeo-Christian values, outer direction is sanctioned by Shintoism and Buddhism. Gods are believed to inhabit mountains, streams, storms, harvests and winds. You mollify the gods by shaping attractive containers they will wish to inhabit.

On this particular bifurcation, we cannot evade the truth that American popular culture celebrates and satirises itself. We have Superman vying with planes and bullets and overwhelming natural forces. We have Frank Sinatra 'doing it my way' and even small children bearing arms against each other in school. *Fortune* magazine celebrates 'America's Ten Toughest Bosses', despite their very brief tenures. Alf Dunlap dresses himself in battle fatigues and ammunition belts to impersonate Rambo. Unfortunately, there are real casualties. When life imitates art, all concerned can escalate to absurd extremes. The flaw in celebrating inner direction is that for every boss 'so tough he tells you when to go to the bathroom', there would have to be several American subordinates waiting to be told! It hardly improves effectiveness overall.

Internal versus External Control

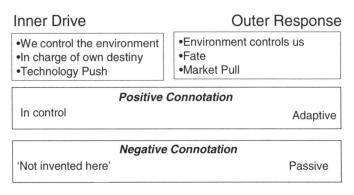

Fig 3.36 Sophisticated stereotype

Some typical misunderstandings

No concept has ever taken American management theory by storm as powerfully as strategy. The metaphor is, of course, military and conjures up Alexander the Great's conquest of the known world. No concept better reflects the grip of inner-directedness upon the American imagination. It is the genius and conviction of business leaders that justifies their multimillion dollar salaries.

Now it is true that strategy can make or break innovative business. People Express grew to be a $2 billion corporation when Don Burr slashed the costs of flying. He took out galleys, increased seats, sold tickets on board and had passengers lift their own baggage into larger lockers. This enabled him to slash prices and get loadings (occupancy) above 80%.

But strategy also defeated PE. American Airlines and United used statistical analysis to predict how full their flights would be on the day of travel and slashed fares to fill planes. Their flexible fare-cuts beat PE's rigid fare-cuts.

The problem with brilliant inner-directed strategies is that these are not confined to corporate HQ. Intelligence is widely distributed, and the closer you get to the interface with the customer, the better such strategies are informed. In his brilliant *Harvard Business Review* article, Henry

Mintzberg argued that strategies typically emerge from the grassroots of the corporation, where market changes begin.

The problem with strategy 'designed at the top' (or inner-directed strategy) is that top managers are typically furthest from the field and from customers.

The danger is that their strategy will be abstract and largely alien from the culture of the corporation. At worst, the strategy will command the impossible; at best, it will command something the grassroots of the organisation have been doing for years without recognition. Top-down strategy says in effect: 'I think, therefore you act.' It reserves for subordinates the role of putting their energies behind the superior thoughts of their leaders. In fact, nearly everyone has a strategy and all of us want to think.

This might help explain why outer-directed Japanese car makers still register 28 implemented suggestions per employee per year, while inner-directed Western corporations register 1.8 at best.

It is prestigious to be outer-directed in Japanese and most East Asian cultures, which is why superiors listen, while subordinates exercise initiatives, as hundreds of suggestions and strategies emerge. If you are really senior in a Japanese corporation, you hardly talk at all!

We are not, of course, claiming that outer direction is better. We do not even agree with Henry Mintzberg that emergent strategy obviates designed strategy or that it is worth holding debates between their respective advocates. We believe that top management can create grand strategies *out of* the initiatives emerging from the grass roots.

Push and pull
This core competence for today's innovative teams is the ability to connect the voice of the market with the technology the company has developed, and vice versa. This is not about technology push or market pull. The innovative team knows that the push of technology finally leads to the ultimate niche market, that part of the market without any clients. If you only choose for the market, your clients will be unsatisfied. Innovative teams are not adding value, because only simple values add up. Values are combined by creative groups: a car which is both fast and safe; high-quality food which is also easy to prepare. Nobody claims that combining values is easy; nevertheless, it *is* possible. A computer that

is capable of making extremely complex calculations can also be user friendly. The ever-expanding system of satisfaction of values will form the ultimate test for the leaders of this century.

What innovative teams know and have learned

The metaphor which best unites inner with outer direction is the jiu-jitsu artist. He/she carefully observes the outer-directed momentum that is lurching towards him/her and deflects that person in the direction of his/her own choosing. Much of China, Japan, and East Asia tells of the Monkey King who, unlike Superman, is physically weaker than other forces in his environment, but a lot more agile and clever. The trick is to harness your own aims to the external dynamisms and momentum of the market.

Michael Dell was extraordinarily innovative for having challenged the very categories of 'inside Dell' and 'outside Dell'. By using the internet, Dell's 'inner' deliberations were opened up to suppliers, sub-contractors, customers, etc. in ongoing dialogue. Interested parties at any point in the network could gain access, so that parts' suppliers could discover the company's inventory levels for themselves and take responsibility for making sure that customers never ran short, and were supplied 'just in time'. Instead of ordering compliance, you share knowledge and the other responds. Knowledge accumulates, whether its source is within Dell itself or from a partner.

Towards a 'Big Bang'

The creative power of multicultural teams is not just attained by putting different nationalities together. Cultural diversity can be attained by having different disciplines together – a must for the innovative spirit that is made to make surprising connections.

It is remarkable how little attention is paid to the cultural differences that can come into play within an organisation. Talk at random to any employee of an innovative organisation and you'll get confirmation that the relationship between Research and Development (R&D) and

Marketing is its Achilles' heel. Our 80,000 person plus cultural database also confirms that the orientations of both functional groups differ significantly.

The manifestations of this tense relationship are revealed in three main areas. First of all, researchers often complain that Marketing rarely allows them enough time to deliver an adequate piece of work: 'Marketing gives us too little time to develop, test and fine-tune a product. This frequently leads to discrepancies between the expectations of a client and the delivered goods. In these cases, most of the profits are lost in upgrading the product to the originally expected standard.' By contrast, marketeers often complain about the lack of flexibility and reaction speed of R&D. Research undertaken by Trompenaars Hampden-Turner into differences in time-horizons between the two functional groups shows that the time-horizon of the marketing function is significantly shorter than that of those working in R&D. Moreover, the R&D employee is much more universalistic than the marketeer, particularly than the salesperson. This last group seems to move from one exceptional situation to the next, which drives the researcher up the wall.

A second source of misunderstanding seems to be in the area of communication. Here too our research supports the view that R&D people often communicate in a direct, specialised and specific tone. Their language is to the point, but is only understood by a small group because of the jargon they often use. Marketeers tend to use rather flowery language, which is less to the point. As a result, the easiest solution seems to be to stop communication all together. Obviously, this leads to significant problems, in particular to researchers complaining that they are not involved enough in the marketing process.

Finally, the lack of understanding of each other's work and culture seems to be one of the main reasons for the tension in their relationship. Researchers attack: 'Marketing often doesn't do enough work to find out the full possibilities within a market ... a large portion of their time is given to the development of a market that ultimately doesn't exist.' And marketeers counterattack: 'If researchers had just a little more imagination and lived slightly less in their own world, we would have significantly fewer co-ordination problems.' Here too a fundamental cultural difference can be seen. Marketing people are inspired by the outside world;

the R&D people start from within and often lack a connection with the swiftly changing world around them.

But what needs to be done to take better advantage of these different orientations? The Marketing Science Institute (1994) conducted interesting research on how organisations can take advantage of this fundamental field of tension.

MSI's research

The exploration of cross-functional development groups. These so-called 'skunk' groups can achieve many successes when they integrate functions on-site and, further, when they are not too badly hindered by existing bureaucratic processes. In these groups physical, linguistic and cultural borders are very effectively overcome. However, a good deal of attention needs to be given to the quality of management in these groups.

Moving people between functions. Cross-functional moves between R&D and Marketing are not easy because of the specialised nature of their activities. Starting with the recruitment phase, one needs to work at attracting people who can be useful across functions and can be placed in a variety of environments. Moreover, focused internal development programmes need to support the mobility of staff.

The development of informal social systems. This aim is not easily achieved because it cannot be forced upon people, but recreational activities can encourage informal social interaction in a lighthearted way. Here too, much can be achieved by minimising the physical distance between the functions. Fruitful collaboration often occurs unexpectedly around central coffee points.

Changing the organisational design. GE and Philips have many co-ordination groups that bring together specialisations in a balanced way. With good management stimulating cross-fertilisation, many cultural and linguistic barriers can be crossed. Another option is the matrix organisation, in which functional specialists carry on reporting to their particular boss and have a 'dotted line' responsibility toward the project leader.

A more focused reward system. It appears that marketing staff often have a variable reward system linked to market share. Developers frequently receive their bonus on the basis of technological developments. A reward system that depends greatly on how much information is transferred across functions will have a very positive effect on the company's revenues and profitability.

Formal management processes such as project management can add greatly to the effectiveness of the integration between R&D and Marketing. This is how Mitsubishi, for example, developed the Quality Function Deployment (QFD) process whereby the client, via a programme called 'Qualityhouse', was given a co-ordinating role between Marketing and R&D. Such processes seem to decrease market uncertainties as well as having a positive effect on an organisation's innovative power. However, even if an organisation follows all of the above advice, ultimate success will depend on the quality of leadership and the organisational culture in which these processes need to unfold.

One company that has excelled in this is Bang & Olufsen. Is there any reader who hasn't looked at one of Bang & Olufsen's audio systems or television sets with great admiration? Only a few producers of consumer electronics make such an impressive impact on both the ear and the eye. Nevertheless, Bang & Olufsen once faced severe financial problems. Bang & Olufsen products were so perfect that fewer and fewer people could afford to buy them. Then, in 1991, Anders Knutsen assumed control. He managed to save a tradition of unequalled industrial design and audio technology from seemingly inescapable ruin.

What did management do during this turnaround period?

One thing is certain: the concept of integration of design and technology remained untouched. Closer analysis shows that three major dilemmas were reconciled brilliantly.

Firstly, Bang & Olufsen reconciled technology push and market pull in a remarkable way. Traditionally, Bang & Olufsen's products were a reflection of the brilliant insights of the technological creativity of Peter Bang and the extrovert sales guru, Bengt Olufsen. When the organisation was still small, the integration of brilliant products and sales to a market that was known in every detail was very natural. After the two pioneers retired, many of the functions were professionalised, with negative consequences. Like that, Bang & Olufsen suited

Philips, the Dutch giant, who became the majority shareholder. This led to a guaranteed demand by Bang & Olufsen for Philips components. All very well. The most beautiful designs, made by professional designers such as Jacob Jensen and David Lewis, were stuffed with the most advanced technological delights. There was a small problem, however. They had found the ultimate niche market: that part with no customers.

Bang & Olufsen introduced the 'butterfly model', with wings symbolising R&D, Marketing and Sales. The dilemma was reconciled by making Bang & Olufsen staff sensitive to sales figures without jeopardising their creative spirit. Moreover, an increasing number of Bang & Olufsen shops were now being established, focusing on selling their own products. Management had found out that Bang & Olufsen products were often used as window dressing, attracting clients to a shop they left an hour or so later carrying a Daewoo or Philips. This new approach led to a dialogue between customers and salespeople that proved to be extremely profitable.

Innovative teams we have measured can integrate outer and inner direction. The 'virtuous circle' is typical of their thinking. Mintzberg calls this 'crafting strategy', as when the clay rises spontaneously from the potter's wheel, and hands lightly shape it.

Measuring innovation competence: reconciling internal with external loci of control

We measure how inner-directed versus outer-directed a leader is by considering the relative merits of 'push' and 'pull' strategies. Should you allow the customer to *pull* you in an outer-directed fashion towards his or her wishes, even where those wishes change, or should you *push* terms, conditions and deliveries upon a customer in an inner-directed fashion and, having won his or her agreement, carry this through as promised? Below is the dilemma and responses.

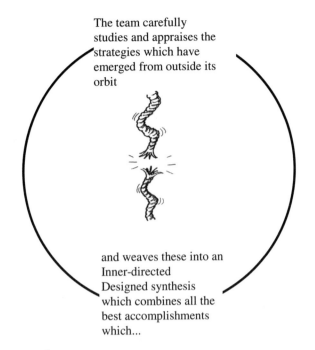

The team carefully studies and appraises the strategies which have emerged from outside its orbit

and weaves these into an Inner-directed Designed synthesis which combines all the best accomplishments which...

Fig 3.37 Vicious circle

Question: push or pull?

Several consultants were arguing that you achieved greater customer satisfaction and quicker delivery times by using a customer-focused pull strategy, and that push strategies were outmoded. Several consultants disagreed.
　　Which position is closest to your viewpoint?

a) A pull strategy is best, because it lets the customer reset the deadline and permits resources to converge upon the customer on cue. Remember customers get behind schedule too, and change their minds about the relative advantages of speed, quality, cost, etc.

b) A push strategy is best, because this commits the supplier and customer to a joint schedule with costs, quality and specifications agreed in advance. The customer may, of course, change his mind, but then the costs for altering the original schedule are calculable.

c) A combination of push and pull strategies is best, so that the customer helps us to decide when not to push our products and we tell the clients when we cannot meet their requests.

d) A push strategy is best, because this commits supplier and customer to a joint schedule with costs, quality and specifications agreed in advance. If you do as you promised and you do it in time, then you cannot be faulted and your record speaks for itself.

e) A pull strategy is best, because it lets the customer reset the deadlines and permits resources to converge upon the customer on cue. The customer wants it when he wants hit and pushing hard may get him too early and at needless expense.

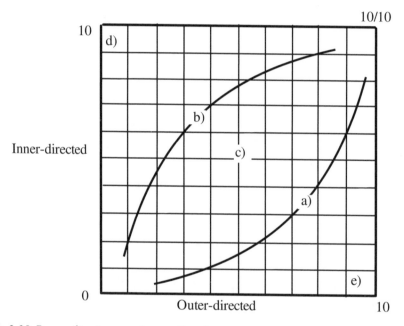

Fig 3.38 Reconciling inner and outer-direction

The five possible answers are scored as in Figure 3.38. Answers a) and b) are integrated with outer-directed pull put first in the sequence in the case of a), and inner-directed push put first in the sequence in the case of b). c) is a compromise, while d) and e) are inner-directed and outer-directed polarities, which brook no opposition from the conflicting principle. Answer d), for example, is concerned with the supplier not being 'faulted', not with satisfying the customer.

What we have found

Though much of our research has focused on national differences, our database allows us to look into functional differences as well. This shows another important source of cultural diversity that could be taken as a source for innovation.

Question: reality

Of the following two statements, which do you believe to be more in line with reality?

a) What happens to me is my own doing.
b) Sometimes I feel that I do not have enough control over the direction my life is taking.

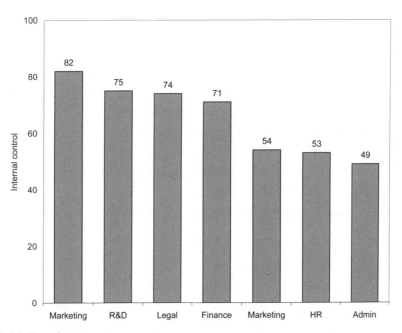

Fig 3.39 Function scores

Dimension 7: Time is conceived of as a 'race' with passing increments versus time is conceived of as a 'dance' with circular iterations (sequential versus synchronous)

The sophisticated stereotype

The contrast is between two alternative concepts of time. Since time cannot really be seen or touched, culture looms large in its definition. 'Time-as-a-race' sees time as a sequence of passing increments; an aim of life becomes doing as much as possible within time limits. 'Time-as-a-dance' concentrates on timing, or synchronisation, so that one moves in time with other people or processes.

Our data shows that American managers take a sequential approach to time, in common with Brazil, Ireland, Belgium, Italy and the Philippines. Japan and China take a mostly synchronous view, as do Hong Kong, Korea, Singapore, Sweden and France. Orientation to time is part of America's self-satire and stereotyped view of itself. There are 'time and motion' studies or 'racing against the clock' as workers sang in *The Pajama Game*. Benjamin Franklin said 'time is money', so no wonder Americans seek 'to make a quick buck'. Andrew Marvel, the Puritan poet, even chided his bashful mistress by saying that 'Time's wing-ed chariot' was overtaking the slow pace of their love life.

While America's time and motion studies made a priceless contribution to the efficiencies of mass-production, so too has the Japanese concept of 'just-in-time' and parallel processing. The former is clearly sequential, the latter synchronous.

Let's consider conflicts arising from the clash of expectations.

Some typical misunderstandings

One of us was buying a book at Singapore airport. The clerk took his credit card, wrapped the book and proceeded to serve the next customer, the card and the book both in her possession. When the purchaser objected, she explained, quite reasonably, that she was saving time. It would take several seconds for the credit card company to respond. When the credit had been cleared, she switched her attention back to the original purchaser.

In practice, few cultures are as well balanced between concepts of time as Singapore. A more usual experience is that sequential cultures regard synchronous cultures as 'rude', because they typically run late and then overstay to 'make it up to you'. Synchronous people dislike waiting in line for service and often form a scrum. They also interrupt your work and are themselves highly distractible, seemingly doing several things at the same time.

Synchronous cultures may regard sequential cultures as 'rude' because they respond not to you, but to some 'inner clock'. They stride hurriedly from one place to the next, occasionally waving at you but never stopping, and are so immersed in their work that they ignore people. They seem to want to stand behind you or in front of you, but never by your side. They refuse to abandon their plans in the face of unexpected meetings. Politeness makes them impatient.

Synchronous cultures have a logic of their own. You 'give time' to people important to you and if these abound, you will be delayed. Top people deserve more scope to synchronise their face-to-face engagements, so they enter the room last, after juniors have assembled. Synchronisation is often symbolised by bowing, nodding or making exclamations of assent. It is as if you were all on the same wavelength, practising the co-ordination of your inputs.

While pure sequentialism leads workers and employees to be machine-timed and dehumanised, purely synchronous cultures seem haphazard and inefficient, episodic and lacking purpose. Sequentialism is typically short-term, since deadlines need to be close by to have much effect. But synchronous cultures may or may not be long term. If they lack direction, there is no long-term goal.

What innovative teams know and have learned

We can identify innovation competence by giving respondents an opportunity to integrate sequential with synchronous views of time and seeing if they take this opportunity – because, of course, modern innovative practices must combine both concepts; neither is sufficient by itself.

It is self-evident that you will complete a process sooner if you speed it up. The gains from synchronous thinking are less immediately obvious. One source of considerable timesaving is to take a sequence 80 yards long, and divide this into four 20-yard sequences, work on these simultaneously and then assemble the four parallel processes. No wonder the workers at AMD sing 'Doing it Simultaneously'.

Historically, costly sacrifices have been made to continuous process machinery. Such machines symbolised speed. Sequential movement was what it was all about, so cheap workers doing simple operations were hired to keep the machines moving. Other sacrifices were just as serious. The machines had to be buffered by large inventories of supplies and work-in-process. In some plants, 80% of products were not being worked on, but remained in large piles, tied up in such inventories.

Enter Taichi Ohno and the Toyota Production System. If you think synchronously as well as sequentially, the huge inventories and the semi-trained workers doing dumb, repetitive tasks are suddenly seen as limitations. Inventories are cut to a fraction by JIT (Just In Time), and you need multiskilled workers of considerable intelligence to ensure smooth synchronisation among parallel processes. The West has known all this for a decade or more, but cultures are stubborn patterns to change.

In the case of Lego's turnaround, the teams were particularly concerned that every stream of ideas met their own 'window of opportunity'. The ideas themselves were neither right nor wrong: they had a rendez-vous which shaped their destiny. They either synchronised with the needs of the market, or the windows closed in their faces. It needed good timing to dart through the window.

Reconciling a sequential concept of time with a synchronous concept of time can give you the advantages of both and the limitations of neither. Each corrects for the potential excesses of the other. Ever-faster sequences with ever-finer synchronisation is what modern manufacturing is all about. The virtuous circle can be seen in Figure 3.40.

Roughly the same rules apply to reducing 'time market'. The traditional approach has been sequential, with 'progress chasing' and a push strategy to get projects through faster. Analog Devices even culled projects running behind schedule by more than the permitted margin, so that the remaining projects would 'run for their lives'.

The fast sequencing of industrial
processes saves considerable time, but
doing these in

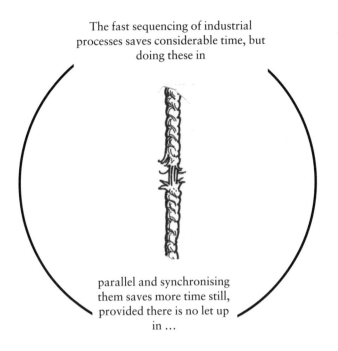

parallel and synchronising
them saves more time still,
provided there is no let up
in ...

Fig 3.40 Virtuous circle

A recent innovation at Motorola University substituted a synchronous 'pull strategy'. This adopts the deadline and the viewpoint of the customer and pulls resources, people and products into the development process in the volumes needed to make the rendezvous with the customer. More resources are needed for late projects, fewer for those ahead of schedule. Since the customer falls behind schedule himself, such delays can release resources needed elsewhere. Here, just-in-time means synchronisation with the customer's latest deadline.

Measuring innovation competence: reconciling sequential with synchronous time

In the dilemma below, a somewhat haphazard and synchronous fashion house is frustrating a sequential and time-conscious wholesaler.

Question: how to speed up latecomers

You, as a manager of a wholesale distributor of a fashion company, are getting very worried about late delivery times to your clients. The summer did not allow you to deliver high-priced goods within a week of the scheduled delivery date that is the accepted norm in the fashion industry. You have tried many ways of solving the problems of late delivery. You still have not made any progress. You are now also in conflict with the transport firm because a contract was signed and the fashion supplier denies any responsibility.

Which of the following most closely describes what you would do?

a) You need to explain your problem to the supplier while appreciating the excellent quality of the goods. This will most probably lead to better adherence to deadlines.

b) You need to order early and ask for the goods two or three weeks before you need to distribute them to the shops.

c) You need to recognise that the fashion business is highly dynamic, artistic and in constant turbulence, and to accept that sometimes goods will be early as well as late. What difference does another week make anyway?

d) Your partners have a flexible time mindset and you will not be able to change that. You need to talk to your clients in order to prepare them for a possible late delivery and give them a discount if it occurs. Separately you need to negotiate a premium for punctual delivery.

e) You need to know the suppliers personally. You should try to avoid problematic issues and during the visit emphasise how important it is for the clients to get on-time deliveries.

We classify the responses as integrated, d) and a) , as integrated, b) and c), as polarised, b) and c), and e) as compromise, as e).

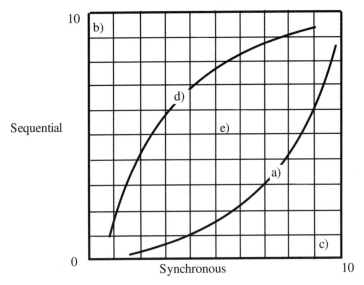

Fig 3.41 Reconciling sequential and synchrony

Clock time versus cyclical time

As well as considering the sequential versus synchronic aspects of time, we also found cultural differences arising from the relative concern for the past, present and future. In addition, 'time horizon' is another variable that differentiates the meaning that cultures give to time. How long ago was your past? Is the future next month's sales figures, your next financial year or the next stop-go economic cycle?

Value differences and innovation: a summary

The challenge for teams and their leaders to become successfully innovative is to integrate the value differences we have discussed. These tensions and their reconciliations are summarised as follows.

1   We first contrasted rule making and exception finding and argued that they are integratable. You use exceptions to improve rules and rules to recognise what is genuinely exceptional. We call this learning 'revising rules to accommodate exceptions'.

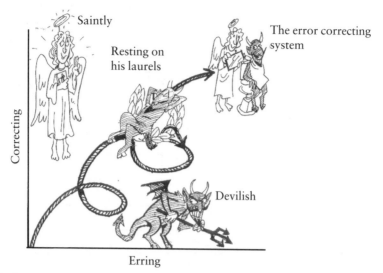

Fig 3.41 Continuous improvement

2   We then contrasted competitive individualism with the requirement that communities co-operate and argued that these were integratable. It is possible to compete at co-operating with customers and/ or within your team. It is possible for communities to develop and to celebrate their outstanding individual members. Competing helps us to differentiate best practices. Co-operating helps us disseminate and adopt the best. We called this learning 'co-opetition'.

3   We contrasted the preferences for analysing issues into specifics and synthesising, elaborating these into diffuse wholes, and argued that these were integratable. You have to allow self-organising knowledge, values and team processes flow diffusely, then supply detailed, specific feedback on their effectiveness. We call this learning 'co-evolution with corrective feedback'.

4   We contrasted neutral and rational with affective forms of expression, in which feelings are fully owned, and argued that these were integratable. You cannot think about your emotions unless these are owned, expressed and shared, but you also have to control yourself until the right moment and circumstances. We agree with Pascale that the heart has its reason.

5   We contrasted two sources of experienced control: that from inside us, inner-directed, and that from outside us, outer-directed. Strategy,

for example, could be designed from within top management, or it could emerge from the company's interface with customers, outside top management. We argued that these processes were integratable. Top management could use its inner resources to design and reshape the strategies emerging outside, which had already pleased customers. We called this 'crafted strategy', in honour of Henry Mintzberg, as when the clay rises spontaneously from the rotating potter's wheel.

6   We contrasted status earned through achievement with status ascribed to the person's potential, i.e. age, family, and argued that these were integratable. The more you respect a person's potential and the more you invest in training them, the more likely they are to reciprocate by achieving on behalf of the company. We called this 'mentored achievement'.

7   Finally, we contrasted a sequential view of time as some kind of race against the clock, with a synchronous view of time, as in a finely choreographed dance. We saw that these were integratable, as when by synchronising processes just-in-time you 'shorten the race-course' by way of parallel processing, before combining these in final assembly. We called this 'flexible manufacturing' or, in a market context, 'pull strategy'.

Not only do these seven integrations constitute transcultural competence, but they also represent a model for valuing in general, wherein the preferences and stereotypes of a culture are relative, while the need to integrate values is absolute and essential to civic society as well as to wealth creation. The danger of stereotyped cultural imagery is that it hides this necessity from us. It follows that foreign cultures may arouse what is latent in our own values: they may remind us that what is perhaps overemphasised in their culture is underemphasised in ours. We have the preferences of foreign cultures within our own, albeit in a weaker state.

Measuring innovation competence
We experimented with several questionnaires with different formats, but these were all based on the same underlying conceptual framework: to distinguish between rejecting opposite values, going for compromise, and reconciling by either starting from one's own perspective and accommodating the other or vice versa. We have researched a wide range of

organisation types and industry sectors and sought to correlate responses with innovation other business performance variables, such as profitability, costs, growth metrics, etc.

One example included the Intercultural Communications Institute summer school near Portland and to several European samples. The following trends are already evident.

There is a capacity to deal with and reconcile values in general. Respondents who reconcile dilemmas are likely to employ similar logics across the board, as do 'compromisers' and 'polarisers'.

Innovation competence, as measured by our conceptual framework, correlates strongly, consistently and significantly with:

a) extent of experience with international assignments
b) rating by superiors on 'suitability for' and 'success in' overseas postings and partnerships, and
c) high positive evaluations via 360° feedback.

This arguably reconciles equality versus hierarchy, since the verdicts of peers, superiors and subordinates are compared. But this is what surprised us. With the exception of Chinese 'high-flyers' recently influenced by American training, transcultural competents (TCs) do not put their own cultural stereotype ahead of foreign values in a logical sequence. For example, American TCs are as likely to argue that good communities and teams generate outstanding individuals as the reverse proposition. TCs can begin with the foreigner's socio-type and join this to their own.

This probably reveals skill at negotiating and entering dialogue, where you share understanding of the other's position in the hope of reciprocity. It may also reveal a case-by-case adoption of foreign methods where these are considered appropriate, along with curiosity about 'the road less travelled' by one's own culture.

Finally, we can conjecture that transcultural competence may only be the tip of the iceberg, representing the most visible manifestation of human diversity in general. The role of leaders and managers is increasingly to manage diversity per se, whatever its origins in culture, industry, discipline, socio-economic group or gender. If there is indeed a way of thinking that integrates values as opposed to 'adding value', the implications are far-reaching.

ORGANISATIONAL CREATIVITY AND INNOVATION

4

'When we talk about analytic versus intuitive decision making, neither is good or bad. What is bad if you use either of them in an inappropriate circumstance.'

Malcolm Gladwell in Blink

Creative people and teams: necessary but not sufficient

Your staff may follow all the advice in Chapter 2, *Individual creativity* and how they can contribute their creativity to their team as considered in Chapter 3, where we considered the 'inventive team'. Both creative individuals and inventive teams are necessary, but this is not sufficient to generate conditions for an organisation to be innovative.

In this chapter, we'll discuss the path that most organisations can take to turn creative individuals and inventive teams into sustainable innovations by creating an integrated corporate culture.

It's a bumpy path with many crossroads and many crises to be overcome. And the path never ends, because the culture of creativity needs to continuously integrate all the fundamental logics of an organisation into a culture of sustainable innovation. The dynamics and processes are quite different from those we've discussed for the individual and at the team level. But what they have in common is that many key (and frequently recurring) dilemmas have to be reconciled. And the methodologies that enable us to diagnose and provide routes to improvement for corporate culture need to evolve from a rather static snapshot picture to a dynamic process of reconciling competing values.

Historically, the path of creating an innovative culture frequently starts with the creative logic of the entrepreneur/founder establishing a 'person-oriented incubator' culture – but that soon leads to a crucial step-point in a crisis in leadership. As a consequence of the growth of the organization, innovation quickly becomes simply *invention*. The need for direction and *intention* becomes evident, and the next stage is best described as a 'family' culture: more business structure is established and authority is respected to streamline the operations and stabilise the innovations. This eventually leads to a crisis of autonomy, since a need develops for delegation and the decentralisation of operations, in order to get closer to the customer. The third transition is the typical task-oriented 'Guided Missile' culture where managers focus on *invasion* and are thus empowered. Ultimately, this results in a crisis of control. The organisation responds by morphing into a typical role-oriented 'Eiffel Tower' culture aimed at efficiency, prescriptive procedures and overt role descriptions to try to allow *implementation*. When taken too far, this culture hits yet another crisis of bureaucracy. It needs to reconcile its major strengths with the orientations that characterise the 'Incubator' culture, through the development of an 'Inquiring' culture. Only then is the ground laid for the last stage. Here all aspects of creativity, power, effectiveness and efficiency are integrated into the sustainable culture of *innovation*. This happens through the integration of outside sources as alternative business models and the co-creation of new markets through co-opetition with other organisations.

The importance of corporate culture

From the dearth of literature on corporate culture, it is becoming clear that any dominant organisational culture has its strengths and weaknesses. After twenty years of measuring corporate culture ourselves, we have identified that the large majority of organisations – such as those we discuss in our book *Riding the Waves of Culture* – have a single dominant corporate culture that struggles with less dominant orientations. We distinguished four corporate culture stereotypes, which we will summarise next.

Four corporate cultures

These four cultures derive from two dimensions. They are either rather egalitarian or rather hierarchical; and similarly rather oriented to people or oriented to tasks. But this does not mean that cultures with an elite hierarchy set no store by equality. There may have been recruitment examinations in which all entrants had an equal chance, but performed differently. Nor are task-oriented cultures completely dismissive of the people who do these tasks. In a very real sense, these four boxes are stereotypes, or 'archetypes', to give them a less opprobrious label. Yet we can't avoid such labels. They are woven into the mythology and symbolism of all cultures and loom large in the minds of members. Cultures, whether corporate or national, stereotype themselves. The Eiffel Tower, the Sydney Opera House, the Empire State Building … their images are flashed onto screens to enable audiences to locate the action.

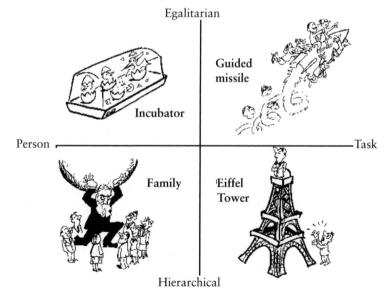

Fig 4.1 Four corporate cultures

We all form first impressions quickly. We would not be able to function effectively without doing so. It's part of our survival mechanism: are we being confronted by a friend or an enemy? The point is not to avoid stereotypes; these are everywhere. The point is to go beyond superficial impressions to see what lies deeper and half-submerged, and to use our understanding of stereotypes as a way to consider the complexities of real world cultures. This is what we will be doing with these four quadrants.

The Incubator

Let's first examine the quadrants, even if only as manifestations. The Incubator, top left, typical of Silicon Valley, is a culture that is both person-oriented and egalitarian. It is highly creative, 'incubating' new ideas. We're not referring to 'Business Incubators' *per se*, but using incubation as a metaphor for hatching creative ideas. Such organisations are egalitarian because anyone, at any moment, regardless of their status, may come up with a winning idea. They are person-oriented because the tasks necessary to making and distributing these new products are not yet defined. The Incubator has been given many labels including organic system, loosely-coupled system and temporary system, which Mintzberg referred to as an 'ad-hocracy'. Here people are not controlled but inspired. People are fully committed and love to be challenged. As an innovator, the manager is expected to facilitate adaptation and change. Uncertainty is limited by continuously scanning the environment for new trends. In this role, the manager is expected to be creative and intuitive, to envision innovations and make others excited by the sheer packaging of them. He manages by passion. The manager of the Incubator also needs to be a broker as he is continuously maintaining external legitimacy and obtaining external resources. So he also needs to be politically astute.[1]

Incubator culture is positively characterised by a person-oriented mindset, where people thrive on learning, passion and flexibility. The downside of this dominant culture is that, when it grows, it becomes too differentiated, leaderless and chaotic. Many growing Incubators have ei-

---

1 'Diagnosing and Changing Organizational Culture: Based on the Competing Values Framework', *Jossey-Bass Business & Management* p.41, Pfeiffer Wiley; revised edition, 2006

ther made the jump to Guided Missiles or Families or were sold to larger entities. *Homo apprendis* has its limitations in growing environments.

The Family

Family culture symbolises perhaps the oldest culture, since a large number of companies originate from family lifestyle or livelihood enterprises, even if they eventually go public. On a global scale, there are more family-owned companies than any other. But we are speaking of Family *culture*, not legal ownership. Family culture is hierarchical because the gap between 'parents' (owners) and 'children' (employees) is very wide. The 'old man' may be revered or feared. He – and it is often a 'he' – may regard his employees as members of his family, whose burdens he carries (see Figure 4.1). Mentoring and coaching are borrowed from the family ideal.

Family culture is person-oriented, because who you are looms larger than what you do. Family members may not be fully professional. Those most accomplished at tasks may be passed over in favour of the well connected. Insiders have advantages over outsiders. Such cultures are often warm, intimate and friendly, but their internal integration may be achieved at the price of poor external adaptation, and they can 'hug and kiss each other into bankruptcy'. Creative genius rarely passes down a dynasty, so the founder's vision may not get renewed in the generations that follow. It generally reflects a highly personalised organisation and is predominantly power-oriented. Employees in the Family seem to interact around the centralised power of the father or mother.

This power-oriented culture thrives on personal relationships that are loyal and trusted. But it often becomes dysfunctional itself because of an exaggeration in politics and an overly introverted outlook on organisational life. This monolithic model of the *homo socialis* can destroy itself if it doesn't overcome political battles and succession problems of who is taking the role of daddy.

The Guided Missile

In contrast, the Guided Missile is an egalitarian, task-oriented culture in which project groups steer towards the accomplishment of team tasks. They are typically multi-disciplinary, taking from the various functions of the organisation only those people essential for completing the set task. They are egalitarian because whose expertise is relevant to their shared problems is an ever-open question. NASA was probably the most famous culture of this kind. It took over 100 disciplines in science and engineering to land on the moon. The relative contributions of each had to be negotiated among equals. The only 'boss' was the task or mission itself. 'Getting the job done' with 'the right person in the right place' were favourite expressions.

Guided Missile culture is characterised by a task-oriented mindset, where members are motivated financially for the benefit of shareholders in a very effective way. However, this pure financial and instrumental view is much too limited to capture the quality of an organisation in swiftly changing environments. Return on Investment has been shown to be too one-sided. Short-term orientation puts dominant Guided Missile cultures under pressure, as does the treatment of its employees as pure one-sided instruments. Anonymous money-shufflers thought you could become rich without adding any value. And employees are now being judged on their contribution for corporate profit. A human organisation is more than just a collection of rational robots that need to operate in the most efficient way as a *homo economicus*.

The Eiffel Tower
Eiffel Tower culture is more like that described by Max Weber and assumed by Frederick Winslow Taylor and Henry Ford. In the case of a factory processing physical materials, it's highly structured; and in the case of a large bureaucracy it does precise, detailed and routine tasks without error. Everyone has a precise job description – be it only fixing a wing mirror to a succession of automobiles on an assembly line – and precise orders come from the top. The culture is stable, predictable, safe, routine and reliable. It is steep, stately and very robust. Control is exercised through systems of rules, legalistic procedures, assigned rights and responsibilities. Procedures for change tend to be cumbersome, and this role-orientated organisation is slow to adapt to change.

Eiffel Tower culture is characterised by a mindset of rules and procedures, where members are motivated by expertise for the benefit of the efficiency of the organisation. Here also we find the limitation of a dominance by this role-oriented culture dictated by formal definitions of roles and responsibilities. Once it was scientific management that reigned over organisation theory, but it committed suicide because of extremism. Similarly, we see that the Eiffel Tower is often sluggish and much too slow to adapt quickly to the ever-increasing speeds of the societies in which it operates. *Homo efficientis* looks very much at the means, and is not always very end- or goal-directed.

INCUBATOR	GUIDED MISSILE
A leaderless team in which people aim for personal growth. Individualisation is one of the most important features. The organisation exists only to serve the needs of its members. And its members are motivated by learning on the job for personal development.	'Getting the job done' with 'the right person in the right place' are favourite expressions. Organisational relationships are result-oriented, based on rational and instrumental considerations, and are limited to the specific functional aspects of the persons involved.
• Person-oriented • Power of the individual • Management-by-passion • Commitment to oneself • Professional recognition • Self-realisation	Achievement and effectiveness are weighed above the demands of authority, procedures, or people. Authority and responsibility are placed where the qualifications lie, and they may shift rapidly as the nature of the task changes. Everything is subordinate to delivering the encompassing goal(s).
Challenges for Innovation *Attract, Retain and Motivate talent*: Intuitive Recruitment, Self-realisation and continuous learning *Reward Staff*: learning *Evaluate Jobs*: people make jobs, no formal process *Develop Staff and Leaders*: on the job *Plan Staff*: where needed and short term *Main role*: Change Agent by facilitating transformation	• Task orientation • Power of knowledge/expertise • Management-by-objectives • Commitment to tasks • Effectiveness • Pay-for-performance
	Challenges for Innovation *Attract, Retain and Motivate talent*: Quantitative measurements, high material rewards and focused learning *Reward Staff*: high material pay *Evaluate Jobs*: task makes jobs (benchmarks) *Develop Staff and Leaders*: task focused and professional *Plan Staff*: middle term where task requests *Main role*: Strategic business partner through aligning HR with business strategy

FAMILY	EIFFEL TOWER
A highly personalised organisation predominantly power-oriented. Employees in the 'family' interact around the centralised power of the 'father' or 'mother'. The power of the organisation is based on an autocratic leader who - like a spider in a web - directs the organisation. There are few rules and thereby little bureaucracy.	Steep, stately, and very robust. Control is exercised through systems of rules, legalistic procedures, responsibilities, and assigned rights. Bureaucracy makes this organisation inflexible. Respect for authority is based on the respect for functional position and status. The bureau or desk has depersonalised authority. Expertise and related formal titles are much appreciated.
• Power orientation • Power of network • Personal relationships • Management-by-subjectives • Affinity/trust • Promotion	• Role orientation • Power of position/role • Management-by-job description/ evaluation • Rules and procedures • Order and predictability • Expertise
Challenges for Innovation *Attract, Retain and Motivate talent*: Fit with Political elite, loyalty programs *Reward Staff*: increased authority *Evaluate Jobs*: by management's discretion *Develop Staff and Leaders*: knowing the power elite *Plan Staff*: life time across the family *Main role*: Employee champion responding to employee needs	Challenges for Innovation *Attract, Retain and Motivate talent*: Fit with quantified job requirements, expertise and life time learning *Reward Staff*: education *Evaluate Jobs*: formal job classification systems *Develop Staff and Leaders*: expert training *Plan Staff*: apprenticeship *Main role*: Administrative specialist facilitating Re-engineering processes

The need for a new paradigm of corporate culture

In our 20 years of seeking to capture different corporate cultures in well over 100 organisations with very different signatures, we have observed that all four orientations exist to some degree in all organisations. However, one logic is normally dominant. This could partly be explained by the fact that within organisations all kind of sub-cultures emerge, with more of an Incubator for R&D, Family in manufacturing, Guided Missile in marketing/sales and Eiffel Tower in finance. When searching for correlations with performance, or innovative strength, or whatever other output variable we considered, there were no significant correlations. Families did as well or as badly as Incubators. Eiffel Towers showed no better performance than Guided Missiles. We infer either that corporate culture made no difference for an organisation's performance, or that we were missing an important variable.

The research of scholars such as Jim Collins and Robert Quinn[2] undoubtedly demonstrates the importance of corporate culture in creating a high performance organisation. We've also found that where organisations have established a sustainable culture of innovation (IBM, Dell, HP, Lego, Microsoft), this can't be explained purely by a Johari window-style cutting of organisational realities into four elegant paradigms. This doesn't have the requisite variety and is not sufficiently comprehensive. Four-quadrant models like this are just a snapshot photograph of a static model that persists in the current, as well as in the desired, culture.

Its attraction is that it appeals to the dominant type of linear thinking, where people make sense of the world by analytic, sequential, rational, discontinuous and verbal ways of reasoning. It is based on traditional (more Western) logic, looking at framing corporate cultures in such a way that you can describe at least four general perspectives on what 'good' organisations are and what 'good' leaders in those cultures do. This is true for all these types of framework, whether promulgated by Handy[3], Harrison[4] and Cameron or Quinn[5] and Dennison. They all combine two organisational perspectives, such as internal versus external focus with flexibility versus control, task- versus person-orientation and egalitarian versus hierarchical orientations, coming together in a two-by-two Johari window.

These models tend to thrive because of our bias in how we process information, and because we have a preference for living in certain kind of settings. Because these dominant orientations are so powerful, it is difficult to ignore them without being schismogenic[6]: in other words, it is

2 Collins, Jim, *From Good to Great*, Collins Publishers, 2001; Quinn, Robert, *Beyond Rational Management*, San Francisco: Jossey Bass, 1988

3 Handy, Charles, *Gods of Management*, The Changing Work of Organisations: Arrow Books Ltd; new edition 1995

4 Harrison, Roger, *Corporate Ideologies*, San Francisco, 1972

5 Cameron, K.S., and Quinn, R.E., *Diagnosing and changing organizational culture*, Reading, MAL: Addison-Wesley, 1999

6 The term *schismogenesis* ('creation of schisms') according to Bateson in *Nature*, 1979, refers to arguments, theories, or perspectives that are broke

difficult to recognise that there are weaknesses in our own perspective and advantages in opposing perspectives. And the diagnostic questionnaires used to measure those mutually exclusive realities invited the respondent to make a choice between them! Aren't we all used to 'forced-choice' questionnaires that contain traditional questions such as the following?

In this organisation…

a) one is open to the personal needs for learning and growth. (Incubator)
b) one has a clear division of functions and responsibilities. (Eiffel Tower)
c) one respects the judgment of those in authority. (Family)
d) one clearly allocates resources and expertise for the job at hand. (Guided Missile)

In this organisation…

a) criticism is aimed at the task, not at the person. (Guided Missile)
b) criticism is only given when asked for. (Eiffel Tower)
c) criticism is mainly negative and usually takes the form of blame. (Incubator)
d) criticism is usually avoided because people are afraid of hurting each other. (Family)

Unfortunately, the empirical foundations of traditional social science often stand in the way of attempts to build a better theory base, which can cope with more complex and realistic environments. Empiricism is primarily a rational-deductive perspective, designed to answer the question: 'What is?' It is constantly breaking things apart, looking for linear, cause-and-effect relationships. The observed is seen as 'molecules that don't talk back', as Alfred Schutz so eloquently said.

(schismo) at the outset (genesis). One of two opposing but connected values is chosen over another.

One way of exposing the limitations of stereotypical two-by-two culture frameworks is to take them to an extreme and see what pathologies they develop. Notice how cultures cooped up in one quadrant of our chart become, over time, half-crazed with the potentials of their vision. Each of the 'good' criteria can become overvalued by leadership and pursued in a one-dimensional fashion. In this perspective, Quinn notes: 'When this zealous pursuit of a single set of criteria takes place, a strange inversion can also result. Good things can mysteriously become bad things ... criteria of effectiveness, when pursued blindly, become criteria of ineffectiveness.'[7] In this case, the axes of egalitarian-hierarchical and person-task, which are initially conceived as neutral and only serve to categorise, acquire negative overtones as in anarchy (too much challenging authority) versus autocracy (too much respect for the status quo of leadership) and hedonism (too much attention to personal development) versus tunnel vision (blind focus on tasks and short-term end results).

Astute readers will recognise that these pathologies occur when the tensions reflected in the axes are not reconciled.

Ultimately the entrepreneurial Incubator culture leads itself to chaos since no authority is respected but one's own, and discussions about what to do go on forever and nobody decides the actions that need to be taken. Creativity is there for the sake of creativity and no effort is made to get it to market; emphasis on inventiveness and change turn into premature responsiveness and disastrous experimentation. So many organisations have come to an end where egalitarianism, flexibility and person orientation were taken to their limits into pure hedonism. And when the entrepreneur/founder left the organisation, it lacked the common unifying bond to survive.

For similar reasons, the stereotypical Family also dies in its own exaggeration. In organisational history, there are examples of Seagram and Vivendi type organisations, where the CEO gathered so many supporters around themselves that this grandeur soon led to catastrophe – particularly because no criticism was expressed and the organisations became too centralised and not responsive enough to react. The Family turns into an irresponsible 'country club' where human relationships and

---

7   Quinn, Robert, *Beyond Rational Management*, p.69, San Francisco: Jossey Bass, 1988

loyalty are emphasised to the point of encouraging laxity and negligence. In this pathology so many games are played for acquiring subordination that the Family starts to look like a political party, where the main game is gaining power and the task is all forgotten.

More recently, we see the pathologies of Guided Missile culture taken too far. In companies like Ahold, Worldcom and Enron, the short-term gain of the shareholder's overriding power has jeopardised the longer-term survival of the company. The Guided Missile was taken to an extreme and became an oppressive sweatshop. Short-term gain for the shareholder came at the cost of all other stakeholders: the employees, the client and supplier, and even society at large. Shareholder value became the value for people who never shared. In this pathology, effectiveness is rationalised to an extreme so that the processes of getting there are neglected. Staff become cogs in a machine, and the emphasis on short-term profit and shareholder value turns into perpetual exertion, human exhaustion and associated blind dogma.

And the Eiffel Tower that excludes elements of humanity, flexibility and equality will lead eventually to sheer, frozen bureaucracy and long waiting lists. Here, there is too much emphasis on internal processes through excessive measurement, documentation and red tape. Everything is done 'by the book' and individual tasks are just written down in stable job descriptions. As a result, anything new is killed from the outset under the argument that 'we have never done it in this way'.

Any experienced leader knows that, essentially, his or her role is to integrate the opposite logics that the organisation demands of them – even in cases where one culture paradigm is dominant. The entrepreneurial leader of the Incubator will at once seek to depersonalise his or her authority by introducing a more task-oriented approach, together with some loyalty of people surrounding him or her. The effective *pater familias* of the Family will try to find ways to define roles objectively to counterbalance the otherwise adherence to person-orientation. At the same time, s/he will try to find ways to decentralise operations to diffuse the focal points of unquestioned authority. The task-oriented CEO of the Guided Missile should try to introduce some internal control mechanisms that commit to longer-term interests, and seek to bind people accordingly. And finally, the leader of the role-oriented Eiffel Tower should feel the urgent need to humanise the workplace and try to get staff to orient themselves to the market outside.

Any good leader will always try to integrate cultural aspects that are not dominant in their own cultural logic. Only when this is realised effectively will true innovation be sustainable.

Towards the integral organisation

In this section we argue that a prerequisite for an innovative organisation is the reconciliation of the variety of organisational cultures, in order to face the challenging dynamic world in which it operates. In this way, it can overcome the limitations of the dominant culture into which it will otherwise tend to drift, looming from crisis to crisis.

Now we can see how and why that creativity works with destruction in successful entrepreneurship, just as human resources work with physical resources. In the Hawthorne Experiment, the Formal System works with the Informal System, Tasks were not connected with People. The Social System supported the Technical System, instead of trying to subvert it.

There is synergy among all our pairs of extreme cultures. It is this that distinguishes creative and productive cultures from stagnant and ineffective cultures taken to extremes. If Ruth Benedict hadn't looked between values rather than at them, she would not have understood the subtlety and power of culture.

We are now in a position to present our enhanced definition of culture, which seeks to overcome the limitations of earlier frameworks.

Culture is the pattern by which a group habitually mediates between value-contrasting differences, such as rules and exceptions, technology and people, conflict and consensus, etc. Cultures can learn to reconcile such differences from such values at ever-higher levels of attainment – for example, so that better rules are created from the study of numerous exceptions. From such reconciliations come health, wealth and, above all, true innovation. But cultures in which one value polarity dominates and militates against another will be stressful and stagnate.

Given this revised definition, the Four Corporate Cultures in Figure 4.1 may seem to break our own rules, for they are not only very different, but are polarised. Quite so, but polarity versus reconciliation must itself be synergised. Without any initial difference or diversity between people or cultures, there would be nothing to reconcile! Polarities – which 'is another way of saying 'diversity – are an essential part of processing information. We need to make distinctions and we need to combine them, so let's live with these polarities for a while to help us think through different scenarios.

Organisations that are truly innovative are continuously reconciling the major tensions that were facing them *between* their organisational (sub) cultures. We found many examples of 'Guided Incubators' and 'Family Missiles' among them.

Our traditional 'cookie cutter' model and the questionnaire derived from it couldn't do the job required any more. And so we developed a new type of questionnaire that could measure the different characteristics of the separate corporate cultures *and* the degree to which they were reconciled with alternative models. This is a new instrument that explores the reconciliation between the extremes. The 'forced-choice' questions were replaced by questions such as the following.

Please indicate how much you agree with this statement	++	+	–	– –	
Each person is given a clear definition of their responsibilities in the organisation.					Eiffel Tower
Information is shared widely so that everyone can get the information needed when required.					Family
We work in flexible networks in which personal development is key.					Incubator
There is an orientation to results and achievement to get the job done.					Guided Missile

The main difference in the earlier questionnaire (and similar instruments used by quoted authors) is that respondents were forced into one of the four quadrants, whereas now one can score (potentially) high on all elements. Moreover, questions are included that explore not only the positive aspects but also the negative side of each cultural stereotype. The latter we refer to as *cultural inertia.*

An overview of the characteristics of the cultures can be seen at http://www.businessacrosscultures.com

From invention to sustainable innovation: organisational growth cycles

Thorough analysis of the evidence from our research and consulting reveals an organisation becomes innovative when the dominant Incubator culture gives the context necessary to produce one innovation after the other. You put creative people in a playground, the lead entrepreneur's passion manages them, and things flow. However, our evidence confirms what others have said: that this type of culture alone is not sustainable once it grows. To make the culture sustainable while maintaining the spirit of long-term innovative capacity, the Incubator must reinvent itself without throwing away its creative powers.

When examining the problems associated with growth and the impact of change on corporate culture, the well-established model described by Larry E. Greiner[8] on how to develop an organisation as it grows is helpful. Greiner argues that growing organisations move through five periods of evolution, each of which ends with a period of crisis and revolution. In order to create a meta-level approach for a culture of sustainable innovation, we need to revisit these phases and how they interact.

This looks a lot like the stage-gate process we described in Chapter 2. According to Greiner, organisations tend to follow a pattern from evolution, to a crisis of management style and the problems they face, and then to revolution.

Creating invention: growth through creativity

We can call the first stage of organisational growth 'creativity', as illus-

---

8 Greiner, Larry E., 'Evolution and Revolution as Organizations Grow', *Harvard Business Review*, May-June, pp.55–68, 1998

trated below. This stage is dominated by the founders of the organisation, with an emphasis on creating both a product (or service) and a market. These founders are usually technically or entrepreneurially oriented, and they view management activities with disdain. Their physical and mental energies are absorbed entirely in making and selling a new product. At the birth and newborn stages, communication is frequent and informal. Long hours of work are rewarded with modest salaries and the promise of ownership benefit[9]. Decisions and motivations are highly sensitive to market feedback.

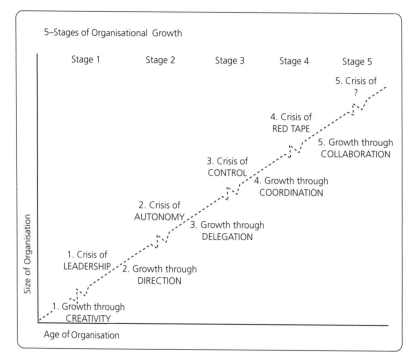

Fig 4.2 Stages of organisational growth

The prime resource of early capitalism, a resource that pre-dated machinery in the Industrial Revolution, was the entrepreneur. This word comes from the French, meaning 'to take a stand between'. The entrepreneur stood between the factors of production, land, labour and capital, and recombined these in ways that generated new wealth and value.

9   ibid, p.60

While the great nineteenth-century entrepreneurs still lived, a vital leader (often the founder) remained at the helm of the big companies into which they grew. No one spoke of human resources in those days, but they did speak of genius, innovation, creativity, and mobilisation of the greatest mass of resources the world had ever seen. It is these pre-bureaucratic manifestations of human enterprise that we need to revive. Yet as the nineteenth century ended, the great American and European entrepreneurs began to die off, and by the 1930s very few were left. This produced a crisis of legitimacy.

All growing Incubator corporations face a 'span of control' problem as their numbers increase beyond their founder's capacity to know employees personally. At this point rules, procedures and processes need to be invented. But what kind of substitutes are these for the founder's actual presence? How much of the original genius is lost? All the individualistic and creative activities are essential for a company to get off the ground. But as a company grows, those very activities become the problem. It was once an organisational culture where the inventions became innovations, and the company could find the resources to get these to market because of its smaller size and ease of internal person-to-person communication. With the growth of the organisation, more inventions froze at the level of creativity and never reached the market. This is because increasingly functional specialisation separates R&D from manufactur-

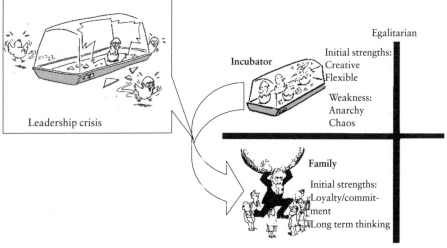

Leadership crisis

Incubator

Egalitarian

Initial strengths:
Creative
Flexible

Weakness:
Anarchy
Chaos

Family

Initial strengths:
Loyalty/commit-
ment
Long term thinking

Hierarchical

Fig 4.3 Crisis of leadership

ing and marketing, and the creative inventions fall between the walls – and communication becomes much more impersonal as a hierarchy of titles and positions grow. The result is a 'Crisis of Leadership', according to Greiner. Informal communication becomes infeasible as additional functions must be implemented. As the organisation grows, there are management problems that cannot be handled through informal communication and dedication. So the founders find themselves burdened with unwanted management responsibilities, and conflicts between the harried leaders grow more intense.

From invention to intention: growth through direction

As we've seen, Incubator culture that supports great inventions can't cope with growth too well. An increased feeling of lack of direction often results, and the Incubator gradually grows into its own pathology of anarchy. There's a growing feeling that the entrepreneur/leader and the staff are too focused on self-development and the development of the next generation product or service. As a result, the founder often draws more authority to him/herself and quickly realises that either leadership and management is boring or that s/he lacks the basic talents for doing the job well. At this point, the crisis of leadership occurs and the first revolutionary period begins. 'Who is going to lead the organisation out of confusion and solve the management problems confronting it?' The solution is to locate and install a strong manager who is acceptable to the founders and who can pull the organisation together. This leads to the next evolutionary period of growth through direction.

At this stage of development in an organisation, the first critical decision is to locate and install a strong business manager. This often leads to the hiring of someone who has all the founder/entrepreneur's trust. In family organisations, it's typically the brother or nephew who is called in, or the interim manager who will fix the leadership crisis. However, there's a tendency to oscillate between two extremes, leading to another type of crisis.

One of the most innovative companies is Google. Over a period of six years they went through all the crises described in this chapter. The big difference is that while it takes some companies 20 years to go through these steps, Google did it in record time. This is what one observes in a company that increased market value from close to zero in 1998 to $117 billion in 2006.

Their first major crisis that hit them was when the number of daily searches had grown to a level that could not be dealt with by just eight employees. So Larry and Sergey started to search for some investors, leaving them with a tremendous dilemma: they wanted as much money as possible while retaining as much power as possible 'Everyone in Silicon Valley knew that it was every entrepreneur's dream to land funding from one of the prestigious venture capital firms. The right money from the right people could make or break a technology business. At the same time, giving up control could destroy the vision of the founders and the long-term potential of the breakthrough technology.' And for Brin and Page there would be no compromise. Whatever happened they would keep the majority of shares and power. In his *Google Story*, Vise argues:

'It was a big dilemma for Brin and Page. On one hand, they needed money fast and had two offers. On the other, maybe they could raise cash without giving up control if they could persuade both firms to invest. It was a big "if", but that is the route they decided to pursue, even if it meant losing them'. And what they finally got, by having the controlling shares in their hands, was new money invested in Google that was needed to extend its growth at that time. It set the first steps in creating a family-like organisation where President Brin and CEO Page made their 85 employees work long hours and treated them like a family, including free meals, healthy fruit juice drinks, on-site laundry, dental and medical care, daycare and fitness facilities. But with further growth and temporary financial frustrations, even Google couldn't avoid the real leadership crisis. The investment firms were insistent that they hire someone more experienced and older than them. And with the hiring of Eric Schmidt in early 2001, the independent-minded entrepreneurs could focus on intriguing technical problems and leave the mundane tasks of running the business day-to-day to someone else. Vise comments: 'Schmidt arrived at Google to find a technology firm that nearly three years after its foundation was being run by technologists who put enormous time into people and products and users, but spent as little money and time as possible on the details of internal management … The underlying structure and strategy were good. The most apt description of what I (Schmidt) did in the first year or two was put a business and management structure around the vision and gem that Larry and Sergey had created'. In short, with the coming of Schmidt, the Incubator culture was transformed into a Family culture, without killing the eggs of the Golden Goose. And Google thrived on creativity and innovation. The way Schmidt played his role was a true case of transformational leadership.[10]

---

10 Vise, David A., *The Google Story*, Pan Books 2005, fully updated edition, pp.61–67, p.109

This issue was explored by Kevin Kelly, who did research on how one might best lead a connected network of professional people, each needing autonomy[11].

The crisis of leadership can be overcome by reconciling the typical leadership style tensions created between Incubator and the Family style leaders. We'll discuss the following dilemmas:

1 Leading participating employees versus respect for authority;
2 Team spirit versus individual creativity;
3 Effectiveness of teams versus creation of cultural knowledge about these teams.
4 Learning from team effectiveness

Dilemma 1: Leading participating employees versus respect for authority

We found that this tension came up frequently in our database of dilemmas. This concerns the relationship between the need for autonomy of the Incubator's staff and the need for direction provided by the Family culture. If you give too much decision-making power to the employees, it becomes a lost democratic leadership with too little left for management to direct. Conversely, once management get too much to say, employees are often constrained and feel overly dependent on the last mood of the managers, such as their need to go in their direction.

Obviously, reconciliation lies in a form of co-determination and empowerment. There are many aspects to the reconciliation of the paradoxes of leadership.

Authoritative, participative or transformational leadership?
James McGregor Burns differentiated transactional leadership from transformational leadership.

In the transactional style, there is a simple exchange of work for money, or votes for representation. Nothing new is created, and each party serves only self-interest.

11 See the experiment's details in: http://www.businessacrosscultures.com/Kelly experiment

In the transformational style, the leader transforms the consciousness of those led, and by their response, those led transform the consciousness of the leader. Each elicits a potential latent in others and brings to fruition a yearning or aspiration of which they were not previously aware.

Transformational leaders are present in business. Laurent Beaudoin transformed Bombardier from a ski-mobile company to a transport company and into an aeronautics company – a huge leap in complexity. Richard Branson leaves the mark of his personality on his entire portfolio of Virgin companies.

In Figure 4.4 we've expressed Burns' distinction as a dilemma. On the vertical axis is the authority of the leader, which becomes corrupted by the unilateral exercise of power from which the populace shrinks. On the horizontal axis is the degree of participation, which can lead to lost or abdicated leaders, whose authority is taken over by those who are sup-

Fig 4.4 Leadership styles

posed to lead. The incident pictured here actually occurred when Puritan pilgrims to the New World replaced their captain while at sea.

Between this arbitrary and failed leadership lies the transactional leader, as a kind of compromise, tolerated because they provide the necessities of life: routine work for routine pay. At the top right is the transformational leader, whose followers 'stand on the shoulders of giants' and are elevated through having experienced them.

Transformation is mutual, not unilateral. Leaders and followers resonate with one another. The experience of having thousands or millions of people pinning their hopes on you, identify with you, express themselves through you is profoundly significant for the leader, as well as for the led. S/he is collective determination writ large. The boundaries dissolve in a surge of human spirit, bound together by shared purpose. When you think of it, authoritative leadership grows out of widespread participation. How can you represent thousands of people if you are not deeply immersed in their aspirations and desires? How can they resonate with you unless you articulate their innermost feelings?

Jim Morgan, co-founder and former CEO of Applied Materials, created the phrase 'porpoise leadership'. From an Incubator culture he had created, he thought there was a way to overcome the leadership crisis. Just as a dolphin leaps and plunges, so must modern leaders move above the fray to see the corporation spread out beneath them, but also dive down deep to make a critical examination of the details. You can't always be at the top of the abstraction ladder, at a distance from concrete reality. You need to get your hands on the day-to-day minutiae of organisational life, to walk your talk, and be seen to actually do what you have been articulating.

An overview of leadership dilemmas can be seen at http://www.cultureforbusiness.com/leadership

The leader as authority, resource or conductor?
Does a leader teach the culture of the organisation how to behave or do they let the culture use the leader as an optional resource?

Theories of leadership have changed substantially as a result of the importance assigned to corporate culture. Increasingly, culture has been recognised as the secret of an organisation's success, a phenomenon almost impossible to imitate and very fragile in the hands of those who would acquire it, yet accumulating vital knowledge and learning from ongoing experience. More and more, an innovative leader is seen as managing the values of a culture, while the culture performs the actual work of the corporation, as a semi-autonomous living system with its own direction and purpose. How is such leadership exercised? Two metaphors spring to mind: the conductor of an orchestra, and the film director or narrator of an ongoing saga.

Certain modes of leadership are not permanent possessions. They have to be earned and re-earned. This is especially true of leading Incubator cultures in the process of innovation. You can only lead in such a culture by having your creative ideas applauded by others.

John Kao of San Francisco's Idea Factory calls it 'jamming', in his book of the same title. Roger Harrison, the Berkeley-based consultant, has likened the process to an improvising jazz band. Any member of the band can try out a new beat or number; the other players will follow the leader if they like it, and leave the leader hanging there if they do not. Improvised tunes are 'bids for leadership' which are accepted or rejected. The band wants to be led not by any identified person, but by novelty and improvisation as values. Leadership may change as new ideas and approaches come to the fore. You are 'as good as your last tune' (or, indeed, 'next tune').

In the dilemma shown in Figure 4.5 the jam session reconciles leading with following, as in the improvisational jazz band where would-be leaders vie for temporary leadership.

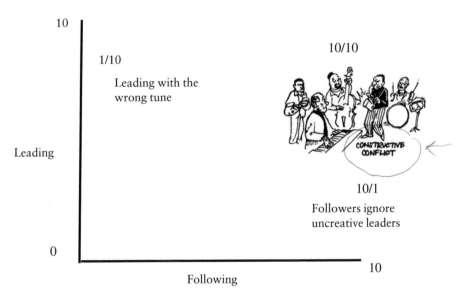

Fig 4.5 The improvising jazz band

Dilemma 2: Team spirit versus individual creativity

In the transition from Incubator to Family culture, we find that the leadership dilemmas can be reconciled, and that invention receives all the intention. But a simple change of leadership style is not enough. Working practice need to change drastically, and creative self-development needs to be reconciled with team spirit. This dilemma is perhaps one of the most common. Invention is likely to thrive on individual creativity, but it can develop from the idea to become an innovation when put to a team that can harness the idea. On the one hand, the organisation needs creative solutions where individuals take risks (as they often do in Incubator cultures). On the other hand, within Family cultures, one likes to develop loyal teams with a high long-term commitment. The second major dilemma is thus the tension between team orientation and individual creativity.

Businesses and people within businesses have long been exhorted to compete with one another. Out of this fray, it is conjectured, the better performers will emerge, and resources will be redistributed from those who perform poorly to those who perform better. Similarly more resources will be allocated to 'better' management. We can see further evidence of this phenomenon in countries like Japan, which, for communitarian reasons, do not let their weaker businesses fail, and therefore seem to suffer long recessions.

On the other hand, people within a corporation where Family culture dominates, and especially those in problem-solving teams, are expected to co-operate. Helping customers is largely a process of co-operation, as is harmonising different functions. This is all done in the common pursuit of company objectives. In due course, individuals may die, but the contributions they make to their families, their corporations and their communities outlive them.

So should you compete or co-operate? Recently the hybrid term 'co-opetition' has been used more and more to describe this reconciliation. Is it somehow possible to compete in order to co-operate? Is it somehow possible to co-operate more in order to compete? Many an innovation process does precisely this. In short, these teams co-operate with customers and with each other in order to compete with other teams and float

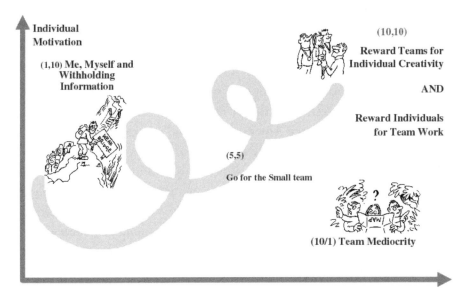

Fig 4.6 Co-opetition at Shell

the best solutions up to the top of the company, where senior managers can discover and disseminate them.

By inviting team members to exhibit their successes in public, a premium is placed on individual flair and self-exhibition. You get up on the stage and show off, but of course you are boasting of the success of the whole team. This process combines the imperatives of helping customers and helping fellow team members with the arts of self-display and self-assertion.

At Royal Dutch Shell, I was able to combine team (or communal) rewards with individual rewards. Half the rewards for good performance were distributed to all team members, while the other half were distributed to individual team members – in accordance with the team members' estimates of their relative contributions. So individuals received half the additional rewards, but only if their co-workers deemed this to be just. Where individuals contribute the winning edge to their teams, their popularity and self-esteem are greatly enhanced by the gratitude of team members. In this way, the social system applauds their individual contributions and does not grudge their subsequent promotion.

The reconciled dilemma is illustrated in Figure 4.6.

Dilemma 3: Effectiveness of teams versus creation of cultural knowledge about these teams

As we noted in Chapter 2, creative teams are a necessary but not sufficient condition of the creation of a sustainable culture of innovation. We've already demonstrated that a reconciling mindset between team roles is essential. In a large American financial services company (AFS), we found that there were plenty of *cross-cultural skills 'within teams'*. In fact the teams were much more skilled cross-culturally than was given credit by the company's own senior management. This was because, although great emphasis is placed on client needs *inside* their myriad teams, this knowledge tends to remain trapped at middle-management level and not disseminated. Great care had been taken to select team members who were culturally compatible with intimate knowledge of the clients' local situation and difficulties.

But while you may be more skilful than you realise, trapping cultural knowledge within teams may be hampering their capacity to learn from each other. Your company skill helps clients, but it does not accumulate internally as managed corporate knowledge.

As so often happens, your greatest competitive advantage can also be the source of your problems. AFS's informants believed they benefited hugely from their team structure. Small face-to-face groups would work for weeks or months on a client's problem, then break up and reconstitute themselves into other teams with other challenges.

Because these teams had a temporary life, you had all the advantages of novelty and intensity as they self-organised around the problem; you also avoided the staleness and repetition of long-standing committees, who soon bore each other.

Moreover, it was within teams were that cultural sophistication was most evident. A team visiting Madrid would typically have a Spanish-speaking relationship manager and would organise itself to match the client's problem profile as closely as possible. No challenge was ever like its predecessor. You rarely got bored. Every project brought you new team members with different expertise.

The company was as informal, pleasant, convivial and exhilarating as it was because the team atmosphere combined individuality with community. The team was small enough to respect and value each individual, and large enough to transcend self-concern and facilitate service to the community – both the AFS community and the client's community.

But we were surprised that team members who were relatively so-phisticated still faced cultural issues, and at how disappointed more senior managers were with AFS's transcultural progress. One interpretation, which would explain why both groups of informants were accurate in their description, is *that valuable cultural information was being trapped at the team level of the organisation, and was not being transmitted by senior managers into valued, captured and available knowledge, thus hindering the innovation process.*

While knowledge about the latest financial products was moving from team to team and from HQ to the field, knowledge of cultural issues (which was particular to each team) was not being generalised in ways useful to the wider corporation.

The dilemma looks like this.

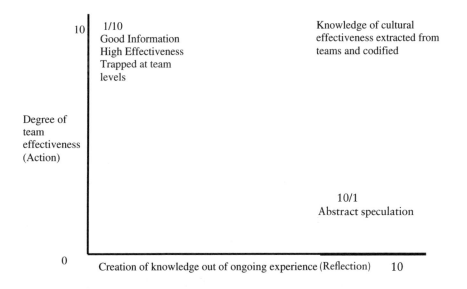

Fig 4.7 Learning from team effectiveness

Dilemma 4: Learning from team effectiveness

One of the roles of top management in an 'Innovative Learning Organisa-tion' is to create knowledge from information – to look at incoming data and ask: 'Is this relevant strategically to our future, and hence knowledge that should be managed?' Without this, AFS's teams were in danger of continually 're-inventing the wheel' and solving cultural problems only at the level of unique insights. In fact, many teams can learn from others as well as from their own experiences, and you need not repeat mistakes, provided you record such experiences and generalise. Cultural differences are systemic, not ad hoc interferences with successful deals. You can learn if you set yourself up to so do.

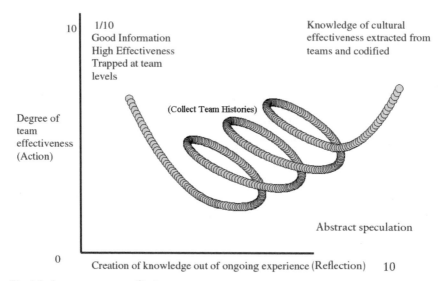

Fig 4.8 A route to reconciliation

Once again, you have to consider an anticlockwise helix, starting at 2/8 and spiralling three times to highlight the words 'histories', 'team' and 'collect'. The spiral that collects team histories and turns these into knowledge at 10/10 informs senior management and develops ongoing cases for in-company seminars and their successors. Why not have a 'historian' in every team, whose job it is to capture what is learned?

The anticlockwise helix spirals from Action (by a team for a client) to Reflection about that action, so that your transcultural knowledge steadily accumulates at 10/10 on the grid.

In this way, we can see how the first crisis of leadership, resulting from an over-growing Incubator, is resolved by reconciling through a new leadership style, where individual creativity is integrated into teamwork through 'conducting talents' in 'improvising jazz bands'. At that moment, the invention gets intention and it is captured into an enriched

Family culture, where vision reigns and teams work across boundaries. By the reconciliation on the vertical axis of the egalitarian and hierarchical, we soon see that, in the growing Incubating Family, the seeds of the next crisis are sown. This is the result of the increasing effect of the horizontal axis of person- and task-orientation. Both Incubator and Family cultures now inhibit sustainable innovation because of a lack of task-orientation.

From intention to invasion: growth through delegation

During this phase the new manager and key staff take most of the responsibility for instituting direction and intention; meanwhile, at lower levels, supervisors are treated more as functional specialists than autonomous decision-making managers. Again, a great deal of attention is given to the establishment of teams. This is in contrast with the loosely-coupled Incubator culture, where individual creativity reigned. With little respect for any authority except one's own, the main role of the leadership is to guide specialist teams with a 'tap on the shoulder' strategy and, if that doesn't work, a tougher hand. This 'management by subjectives' is a very personal leadership style, contrasting the 'free for all style' in the Incubator. The structure of authority is more centralised.

Finally, another sharp contrast between the Incubator and the Family cultures is the degree to which you appeal to the loyalty and personal commitment of the employees. In the entrepreneurial stage, loyalties are predominantly given to the founder/entrepreneur and one's own profession. In the Family culture, we see a clear shift toward loyalty and commitment to the larger organisation, and the leadership team in particular.

Through the more centralised and directive approach, invention gets intention and the chances of going to market increase significantly.

Although the new, directive processes direct employees' energy more effectively into growth, this eventually becomes inappropriate for controlling a more diverse and complex organisation. Lower-level employees find themselves restricted by the cumbersome and centralised hierarchy of the Family culture. According to Greiner, they have come to possess more direct knowledge about markets and machinery than the leaders at the top. Consequently, they feel torn between following orders and taking initiative on their own[12]. It takes too long for new ideas in the lower echelons to be discussed higher up, and the innovative teams feel a lack of sponsorship from the very top. As a defense mechanism, employees tend to start fulfilling their own personal and team goals and, before you know it, Family culture slips into becoming a comfortable Country Club.

As a result, the second revolution emerges from a '*crisis of autonomy*'. The solution adopted by most companies is to move towards more delegation. Yet it is difficult for top-level managers, who were previously successful at being directive, to relinquish responsibility to lower-level managers. Moreover, the lower-level managers are not accustomed to making decisions themselves. As a consequence, numerous companies flounder during this revolutionary period, because they adhere to ineffective, over-centralised methods, while lower-level employees become disengaged and disenchanted, and leave the organisation.

From intention to invasion: the need for a Guided Missile culture

The second crisis above jeopardises the innovative process significantly, and the leadership now faces many new dilemmas. The Family culture that was a platform for reconciling so much of the chaotic Incubator cul-

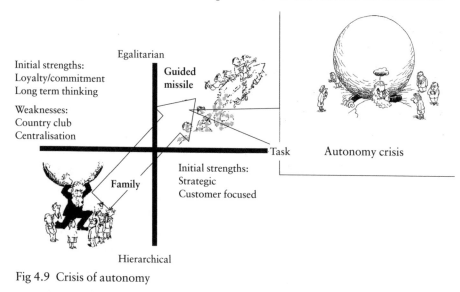

Fig 4.9 Crisis of autonomy

---

12 ibid, p.60

ture was effective, until growth made these more centralised approaches redundant.

Lower-level managers come to demand more autonomy, and this eventually leads to the next revolutionary period – the crisis of autonomy. This reveals itself through the development of a further functional organisational structure, where different departments are created. A formal communication system results, because of the hierarchy and the increased number of employees. Because of the centralising process, a lot of energy is expended on the inside world. So another area of challenge

> Google took the need for invasion literally. In many ways Google's financial success as a private company was the result of being the leader in figuring out a business model of how to make advertising on the Internet work, both for commerce and for computer users. Google and its venture capital investors were aware that the search engine generated $440 million in sales and $100 million in profits in 2002, although the world didn't know it, since Google was a private company with a family culture of many partners and affiliates. Once the information became public, competition would heat up.
>
> Google started to exceed the limits of federal rules requiring public disclosure of financial results by companies that have a substantial amount of assets and shareholders, including new hires and employees. The family had reached its limits. Going public was inevitable as Google would have more resources to grow to realise their vision. And that's what they did in their own egalitarian way, meaning anyone could participate in a 'Dutch auction'. It was a creative solution and irritated mainstream Wall Street as much as the unusual split between class A shares for regular investors and class B stock for Page and Brin protecting their absolute control. In that sense they reconciled the dilemma of being both lord and servant to their vision, well expressed in their accompanying letter to future shareholders:
>
> 'The main effect of this structure is likely to leave our team, especially Sergey and me, with increasingly significant control over the company's decisions and fate, as Google's shares change hands ... As an investor you are placing a potentially risky long-term bet on our team ... We believe a well functioning society should have abundant, free and unbiased access to high quality information. Google therefore has a responsibility to the world. The dual class structure helps ensure that this responsibility is met'. And in this way, the maximisation in profit orientation of the Guided Missile Culture was reconciled with the Intention of the family to realise their worldly mission. The stage of servant leadership was set for even further innovation.[13]

---

13 Vise, David A., *The Google Story*, fully updated edition, Pan Books 2005, pp.118–119, 177

is to open up the organisation again for the market. Thus we have the need for invasion.

The apparent solution to this crisis is usually greater delegation, so the next management response is decentralisation. So much so, that often the organisation goes public and there is a separation between ownership and management. However, once again, managers have difficulty relinquishing authority. The need to develop a more Guided Missile culture becomes evident.

The dilemmas created in the transition from Family to Guide Missile culture need to be reviewed in order for the innovation process to be sustainable. They include the following.

1   Lord, servant, or servant leader?
2   How do we centralise lessons reaching us from decentralised locations?
3   Social learning versus technological learning

Dilemma 1: Lord, servant, or servant leader?

Should leaders lord it over people, striking heroic poses as in Family culture, or serve the tasks as in Guided Missile? Or, thinking at a higher level, is there another way – leading by giving service to others?

In business, the concept of the 'servant leader' is appropriate wherever it is an inherent mission of the company to be innovative for customers. When any leader serves his or her subordinates, they are modelling how they should do likewise for customers. If the leader is not too proud or too high to serve others, why shouldn't employees imitate this by mirroring their behaviour? Servant leaders are forever trying to give away their status, only to get it back again through gratitude and admiration. The more you serve, the more you lead fellow servers.

Servant leadership is a powerful vehicle for the transition from the Family to Guided Missile culture. The leader 'gives' followers more than they could conceivably repay; thus they become obligated and even more compliant to the leader's wishes.

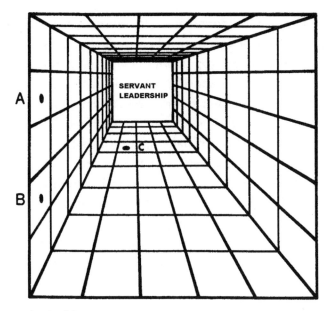

Fig 4.9 Servant leadership

Servant leadership is a highly ambiguous concept, since many typically confuse service with subordination and 'servitude'. We depict this in Figure 4.9.

Is the servant leader at the bottom of a deep shaft, or at the apex of a truncated pyramid? The answer is 'both'. The leader has reversed the organisational hierarchy and is serving subordinates as if they were superiors.

The apparent modesty of this style of leadership is especially important in reconciling the need for intention and the need for invasion. Those who have weight do not throw it around. Indeed, they behave as if they were eager to learn from you, as if they had nothing to boast about. High-status people exude modesty, which enhances their status. They have nothing to prove. We shouldn't underestimate the concept of servant leaders in making innovation sustainable to the next evolutionary phase.

Dilemma 2: How do we centralise lessons reaching us from decentralised locations?

A consistently vexed issue is where information originates and where and how it should be captured for greatest effectiveness. If a corporation is to communicate its knowledge, from where and to where should it travel? Should it move bottom up, top down, outside in or from inside to outside? Arguments about centralising versus decentralising never seem to end and are rarely settled. For several years on end, the watchword has been 'decentralise!' But those with memories can recall that 'centralise!' was once the cry. Will we ever make up our minds, or is the concertina with us for good? Obviously we've seen the need for centralisation in the second stage. Now there is a call for decentralisation that characterises the Guided Missile. And we must conclude that, at their extremes, both centralisation and decentralisation jeopardise the innovation process.

One way of avoiding this contradiction is to ensure that what is decentralised is subtly different from what is centralised. The slogan 'Think Global–Act Local' gives us a clue.

What we should decentralise are the activities across the organisation. What we should centralise is *knowledge* about these activities. The company has a central nervous system, through which impulses about its diverse, local activities travel. These become knowledge to be stored centrally. If we consider the dilemma step-by-step, it progresses as illustrated in Figure 4.10.

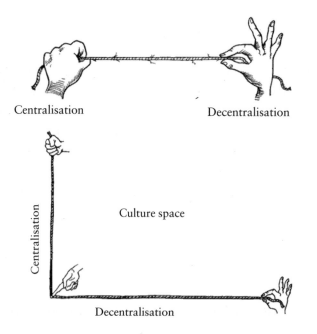

Centralisation

Decentralisation

Centralisation

Culture space

Decentralisation

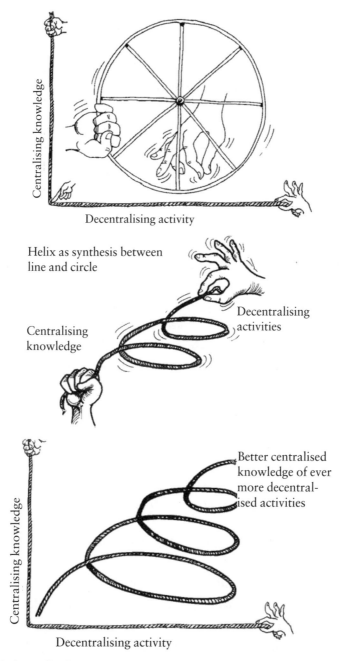

Fig 4.10 De/centralisation

We first polarise centralising and decentralising as in most debates, pulling first towards one pole and a few years later towards the other. But then we create a dual axis, using the same piece of rope. We now have a culture space in which to work. We then create a learning loop in which decentralising activity is followed by centralising knowledge about that activity. Then we turn our loop into a helix. A helix is part circle, part line, since it winds in either of two directions. As such it models centralising information from decentralised locations.

In the next step, we have a centralising axis and a decentralising axis, but the former controls the latter. Decentralised activities must be kept in check by the vigilance of central authorities. The system still lacks adequate local autonomy. The final stage gives full reign to decentralised initiatives, provided that the centre is always informed of these in good time. What we have is the most highly effective centralisation of the most highly decentralised and autonomous activities.

In fact, there is another, more mature phase, in which Centres of Excellence are themselves decentralised. Ideally, countries of the world should be allowed to specialise in what they do best. Hence Apple Computer's Centre of Excellence for skilled assembly and manufacturing is in Singapore, because this location is best for this function. Motorola's Centre of Excellence for software is in Bangalore. Sony chose to place its software centre in California; AMD's star Fab is in Dresden, East Germany. These 'centres' do not have to be in one place in a system. Different functions may look to their own Centres of Excellence. That's how innovation is extended.

Dilemma 3: Social learning versus technological learning

Is social learning different from technological learning? Can we achieve both?

In Incubator and Family cultures, we've seen a focus on the human side of innovation. Self-development was central in the learning Incubator, while the Family was very person-oriented. Innovation is stifled when there is no means for the de-personalisation of the process. The Family turns into a Country Club if no more formalisation is achieved.

Unfortunately, there has long been a split in our educational system between the Sciences and the Humanities or Liberal Arts. There are similar splits in business organisations between those qualified to understand machines (largely engineers), and those claiming to understand people (HR, Sales, etc.).

This venerable dichotomy was measured by Robert Blake and Jane S. Mouton. They tracked the development of managers on two 'opposed' axes: Concern with Task (or technology) and Concern with People. In short, technical and interpersonal competences were conceived and modelled as distinct. Our aim is to create a synergy of both types of learning.

The logic of their grid is re-applied below to the notorious cultures of many 'call centres'. These are often created as cost-saving, technical innovations located in places where land and labour are cheap, but are many miles distant from the things being discussed in the telephone calls. So flight bookings for Swiss Air may be routed through India. Call centres are often windowless, regimented and austere, with employees needing permission to visit the bathroom. The work can be isolating and stressful. Hence we see, in Figure 4.11, that high Concern with Task leads to a Sweatshop at top left, while high and exclusive Concern with People leads to a Country Club at bottom right. But there is no inherent reason why these two paradigms should not be combined at the top right, where Concern with Productive People combines technical with social logics.

Fig 4.11 The Guided Missile vs the Family – Concern with task versus Concern with people

This optimising of the socio-technical system is the long-standing mission of the Tavistock Institute of Human Relations in London.
The invention has gained intention through the directive infusion of vision and long-term commitment with the support of loyal people.

And now, with the reconciliation of Guided Missile culture, the intended inventions have obtained focus to the outside world and are ready for invasion.

From invasion to implementation: growth through co-ordination

When an organisation has arrived at the end of the delegation stage, it usually begins to institutionalise a decentralised organisational structure. This at least has the advantage of heightening motivation at the lower levels. In the dominant Guided Missile culture, greater empowerment of managers is achieved by a philosophy of 'Management by Objectives'. The establishment of profit centres is normal in the Guided Missile, and variable pay is an instrumental means to motivate and reward empowered employees. They are empowered to conquer the market with a diversification of products. Management has greater authority and has

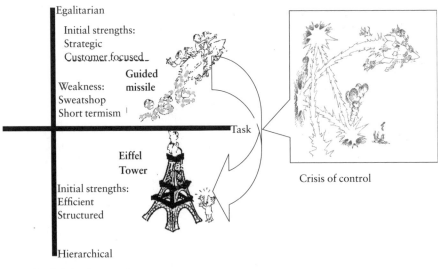

Fig 4.12 Crisis of control

incentives to penetrate larger markets, respond faster to customers and develop new and innovative products at any price. Top-level executives often limit themselves to 'management by exception' based on periodic management reporting. Communication becomes top-down and de-personalised.

It's no surprise then that the next crisis begins to evolve as the top management senses that it is losing control over a highly diversified field operation. Autonomous field managers prefer to run their own shows without co-ordinating plans, money, technology and personnel with the remainder of the organisation. Freedom breeds a parochial attitude[14]. Lower-level management begins running its own show without any co-ordination with the rest of the organisation. *Figure 4.12*

Soon, the organisation falls into a 'crisis of control'. This phase is characterised by the application of formal systems for achieving greater co-ordination and by top-level executives taking responsibility for the initiation and administration of these new systems. Management must again focus on control. The 'crisis of control' often results in a return to centralisation, which naturally is now inappropriate because it creates resentment and hostility among those who had been given their free-dom.

From invasion to implementation: the emerging Eiffel Tower culture

The task-oriented Guided Missile culture has been given a newborn ex-ternal focus to the market, and the 'right things' are again done since the 'politically correct' Family culture focused on the internal political processes of direction. The market invasion culture, however, was in its opportunistic drive, focusing on the 'right things'. However, because of the short-termism to satisfy clients, innovative new products came either too early for the market or with too high a price.

In the resulting control crisis, there's a call for 'doing the right things'. The invasion needs efficient implementation through the reconciliation with the role-oriented Eiffel Tower culture.

---

14 ibid, p.62

Going public with a Guided Missile mindset also posed a potential risk to Google's culture. Life at Google was informal and many people were known by their first names. With rapid growth and the public offering more traditional management and systems had to be implemented. No more off-the-shelf software to track revenue on the cheap. And it became time for auditing by major accounting firms. CEO Schmidt's biggest worry was to increase sales and headcount without destroying the culture that linked invention, with intention and invasion. And would the hundreds of Google millionaires (through the IPO) still have enough motivation left to be on the cutting edge of technology?

Vine observes: 'Things had started to change at Google after it went public and continued to grow at an extraordinary rate. For example, there were an increasing number of employees who had never met or talked one-on-one with Larry (Page) and Sergey (Brin) ... Some departments became more proactive to meet the numbers and insisting that their lead managers and directors were bringing numbers in ... It is really important, even if the company is making money hand-over-fist and reporting numbers beyond Wall Street projections, to run the business like every dime counts' (p.202).

And the major three dilemmas making up the crisis of control were reconciled brilliantly. The role of standards and benchmarks were continuously transcended both financially and technologically, by reinventing new standards. Despite the need for ever higher shareholder demands, the top three at Google kept on developing their people so much so that they hired a chef to look after their health rather than just shrinking the menus in the staff restaurants. And Brin and Page demonstrated that they were not only visionary leaders of a business and technologists for serving external customers but also hands-on managers and aggressive businessmen with a focus on internal processes. That's how they reconciled the Guided Missile with the Eiffel Tower prerequisites.[15]

The evolutionary co-ordination phase is characterised by the introduction of formal systems such as a job evaluation process, focus on product groups, formal planning procedures, initiation of company-wide programmes, investment centres, IT systems and extensive educational programmes to increase staff's professional knowledge. All these new co-ordination systems need to become useful for achieving growth through the more efficient allocation of scarce resources.

The invasion of the intended inventions is only implemented efficiently when the following dilemmas are reconciled.

---

15 Vise, David A., *The Google Story*, fully updated edition, Pan Books 2005, p.202

1   The role of standards and benchmarks: should we meet or transcend them?
2   Meeting financial criteria versus developing our people
3   Focus on external customers versus focus on internal processes

Dilemma 1: The role of standards and benchmark: should we meet or transcend them?

Most learning seeks to approximate the standards or benchmarks that authorities have preordained. 'Good' students get straight 'A's by answering questions posed by their instructors. But top marks are reserved for answers that mirror the conclusions their teachers have already reached. In industry there are benchmarks, professional standards, codifications of 'best practice', and tools like Six Sigma in which targets are pre-set. Could we not simply assess people against the company's strategic goals? Either employees 'come up to the mark' or they do not?

The difficulty we encounter in the innovation process is that strategic goals are, in themselves, constantly evolving and changing. If it takes three years to get an employee performing to the highest standards, during which time those standards must change anyway, then where are you? In the previous phase of placing the Guided Missile in the foreground, the standards of the 'Management by Objectives' system are frequently carved in stone for the period. As Peter Drucker once said: 'Efficiency focuses on doing things right and effectiveness on doing the right things.'

If you follow our logic, you will easily recognise that standards and benchmarks become obsolete because they are one-dimensional. You achieve them and then wish you hadn't! You've sacrificed one side of a dilemma to the other side. And the innovation process is stifled by it!

For the innovation to get through the next gate, you have to juxtapose two questions: 'Have our people lived up to our standards?' and, 'Have our standards lived up to the aspirations of our people?' Chris Argyris calls this Learning I and Learning II or, taken together, 'double-loop learning'.

We can also characterise 'living up to standards' as Doing Things Right. This is highly explicit, codified and objective. We can characterise 'our standards living up to our noblest aspirations' as Doing the Right Thing. That is tacit, uncodified and impressionistic. At top left on Figure 4.13 we achieve organisational goals but have little confidence in those goals. At bottom right, we make a bonfire of benchmarks deemed unworthy of customers or creative employees. In effect, this is Snowden's model of Knowledge Management, but he only conceived these as alternative strategies, with no attempt to reconcile these extremes.

Only at top right can we reconcile both values by creating Ever-Moving Goalposts as our people come up to current standards, which must themselves be subject to critique and updated as the environment shifts. This is a reconciliation between Guided Missile culture and Eiffel Tower culture.

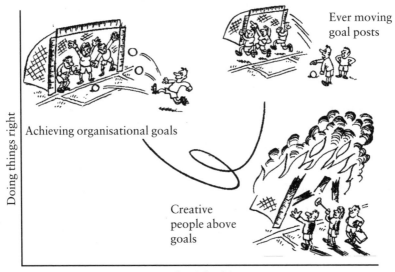

Fig 4.13 Dilemma 1 – Doing Things Right versus Doing the Right Thing

With the successful reconciliation of this dilemma, we have merged innovation as an outcome with innovation as a process. This a contrast to the way that innovation is often described in the literature, as comprising both of these components co-existing but in isolation.

In order to make the management system more effective and efficient in the new paradigm of the integral workplace, we offer the Integrated (rather than traditional 'balanced') Scorecard framework. We need to reconcile the two major cultural dilemmas that underlie the original Scorecard – The Past (Financial) and the Future Perspective (Learning and Growth), and the Internal (Business Process) and the External Perspective (Customer) dilemma.

Dilemma 2: Meeting financial criteria versus developing our people

Guided Missile culture has focused on shareholder return for the simple reason that, in the Incubator, inventions were often made for individual satisfaction and with a lack of business direction. With the introduction of Family culture, there was the quest to add intention into the invention. However, this person-oriented focus was rather internal, so with the development of the Guided Missile culture, the outside world came into focus and results for external shareholders came to the foreground. But then, because of the short-term focus shown in the next quarterly result, management development programmes were pushed to the background.

In our consulting practice, we have run Management Development programmes for many Anglo-Saxon organisations for more than a decade, only to have them cancel our interventions after just *one* bad financial quarter. What a contrast with some German Eiffel Towers, where we were asked to continue our educational programmes despite several bad quarters in succession. The point is not to 'balance' past financial performance with future learning goals, but to use those poorer financial results to learn – that is, to reconcile people growth with hard financial data.

In the Finnish organisation Partek, we found that financial surplus was reserved for the next year's learning budget, and the learning fed into the operations to improve future financial results.

In a European Insurance Company that we assisted, management became concerned because some very talented high-potential staff started to resign. From the exit interviews, it became clear that the severe budget cuts that followed 9/11 – of which training programmes were the first casualty – were the major factor in people leaving. High-potential people felt neglected, and felt that their expectations of being supported to develop further were not met. The dilemma underlying this incident is obvi-

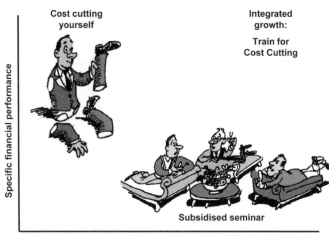

Fig 4.14 Financial Performance versus Learning

ously not reconciled, and the results are to be expected. But just ignoring shareholders' concern to save costs was not a good idea either.

The CEO reconciled the needs for short-term results and for the development of staff by increasing the training budget by 20% for the year to come. But with one condition: he required 20% of all training activities to focus on increasing the bottom line.

Dilemma 3: Focus on external customers versus focus on internal processes

To create sustainable innovation, we also need to improve the internal processes through the involvement of customers. Co-development programmes, where suppliers align strategically with their clients, are a great example. Applied Materials, as one of the main suppliers of microchips, has used this approach very effectively. Their survival is completely dependent on co-developing systems with AMD and Intel. This is quite different from 'balance' (as in the Balanced Scorecard). It supposes that value is not added by having high scores in each of the four perspectives and then adding them up; rather, it needs the added extra from a win-win solution that derives from the cross-integration of past and future, internal and external values.

A case in point is the Dutch electronics giant Philips. It faced the second, reoccurring strategic dilemma of innovation. This concerns the well recognised tension between technology push and market pull. Do we make something we want and know how to make, and then try to find a market to sell it; or do we let the demands and wants of customers feed back in to our R&D and product planning?

Fig 4.15 Internal processes versus External customers

Both extreme approaches on their own achieve do not achieve any sort of integrity once you strive for sustainable innovation. For many years, a pure push from technology worked successfully in internally controlled societies such as the UK, Netherlands and the USA. Conversely, a focus solely on the customer worked well in externally oriented cultures such as Japan and other Asian countries. However, technology push was doomed to failure when internationalisation accelerated in the 60s. American-produced and -conceived consumer electronics were wiped out by foreign competition, and Japanese products took their place.

A push strategy can work, especially in situations of low competition. In cases where competition is strong, this push approach leads to selling your fantastic products to the ultimate niche market to early adapter purchasers with a high disposable income. As it happens, this market has virtually no customers.

Dutch Philips is a splendid example of an organisation that still struggles with the marketing of awesome products such as the CD and DVD. Philips invents and Sony sells, say the cynics. It is typically Japanese to be fully empathetic with the customer. But this extreme 'market pull' approach also has its restrictions, because a customer often has no idea what s/he wants.

Bang & Olufsen also faced this challenge to develop an understanding of the evolving market and patterns of demand, before aligning its own products with this knowledge. 'We had to teach people how to think in business terms, without sacrificing their pride in their creativity and their products,' CEO Anders Knutsen recalled. 'Beauty, style and technical superiority were everything. No one had been paying attention to development costs or commercial success.' The product had actually taken the place of the people who were supposed to lead.

Knutsen regarded this imbalance as so serious that he made himself the Head of Marketing and Sales until an internationally experienced VP could be found. In this way, he was able to rediscover facts that the company had ignored for too long.

'Bang & Olufsen thought communication was a one-way process, and that its customers were dealers, not consumers. Of course, the dealers were passing on our arrogant treatment to the final customers.' Anders Knutsen had discovered that dealers used the Bang & Olufsen aura to upgrade the image of their dealerships, while putting most of their energies into selling rival products, better suited to the market, including Philips, Daewoo, Sony and Grundig. These appeared reasonably priced when compared to Bang & Olufsen's expensive, up-market offerings. 'There was a radical disconnection between the product and the market,' he recalls. 'It was as if we communicated with the product and not with the people.'

Through our WebCue tools, senior executives from Bang & Olufsen framed this dilemma in their own words as:

The Disconnection of Sales and Marketing from Research, Development and Production and the elevation of the latter functions to a dominant position, so that marketing commercial considerations were largely ignored[16].

Our Integrated Scorecard approach is intended to overcome the linear restrictions of the Balanced Scorecard[17] – although our intention is not so much to criticise it, as to improve it and offer the reader a vehicle for making dilemma reconciliation tangible and practical.

Corporate cultures often refuse, point blank, to value both ends of these polarities equally. You cannot order to them to do so. You can only show them that learning goals subsequently improve financials by a specific (X) amount.

A company can be paralysed by analysis or by 'lean and mean' cost-cutting. It can indulge itself in subsidised seminars and become the customer's creature, ignoring its own internal standards.

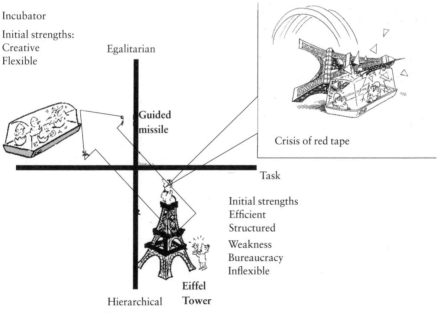

Incubator

Initial strengths:
Creative
Flexible

Egalitarian

Guided missile

Crisis of red tape

Task

Initial strengths
Efficient
Structured

Weakness
Bureaucracy
Inflexible

Eiffel Tower

Hierarchical

Fig 4.16 Crisis of red tape

16 Trompenaars, Fons and Woolliams, Peter, *Marketing across Cultures*, pp.286–287, Wiley, 2005

17 Trompenaars, Fons and Hampden-Turner, Charles, *People Management Across Cultures*, pp.105–106, Wiley, 2005

Or it can grow innovatively. Such growth requires more than balance. It requires a fusion and reconciliation of such contrasting values.

From implementation to inquiring: growth through collaboration

A more effective solution tends to initiate the next evolutionary period – the co-ordination stage. This period is characterised by the use of formal systems for achieving greater co-ordination with top management as the 'watch dog.'

Yet most co-ordination systems eventually get carried away and result in the next revolutionary period – the '*crisis of red tape*'. This crisis most often occurs when the organisation has become too large and complex to be managed through formal programmes and rigid systems. Procedures take precedence over problem solving since the organisation becomes too large and complex to manage formally. Answers take precedence over the quality of the questions, and that is bound to kill the innovative and learning spirit of the organisation. It all begins to accumulate into a nasty conflict between line management and staff.

If the crisis of red tape is to be overcome, the organisation must move to the next evolutionary period – the phase of 'collaboration', in which management must promote interpersonal collaboration. While the co-ordination phase was managed through formal systems and procedures, the collaboration phase emphasises greater spontaneity in management action through teams and the skilful confrontation of interpersonal differences. Social control and self-discipline take over from formal control.

And again, in this last stage-gate we've found that another series of crucial dilemmas needs to be overcome to sustain the innovation spirit of the organisation. We've now given 'intention to the invention', invaded the market and implemented the right processes whilst fighting crises of leadership, autonomy, control and red tape. With this last reconciliation, the infinity loop is finally closed and at the same time open to go outside of the organisation.

In Eiffel Tower culture, the formal systems depersonalise the authority system of management. Then spontaneity in management action is emphasised through teams and the skilful confrontation of interpersonal and intercultural differences.

The characteristics of the transition of the Eiffel Tower to the renewed Incubator is the integration of functional specialisations (e.g. task forces across functions). Teams are given the right sponsorship and span of discretion, and educational systems focus on behavioural skills for achieving better teamwork. Real-time information systems are integrated into daily decision-making processes, and experiments are allowed to become *serious plays* rather than *l'art-pour-l'art*.

And even egalitarian Google couldn't avoid their own version of the *red tape crisis*.

The Google advertising model started to show some of its weaknesses. That's OK, but more important is how you react on the challenges caused amongst others by being blamed for infringing on copyright and brand protection as well as for fraudulent clicks, where third parties deliberately inflate the number of clicks received by an ad.

The problems began in 2003 when Google was blamed for just flat-out ignoring advertisers completely relying on their superb technology. Yahoo tended to be more pro-active: This is why some advertisers tear their hair out and consultants get hired to help people create a case for what was looked at as a purely technological issue at Google. And the overriding Eiffel Tower mindset was well captured by Salar Kamangar, Google's product manager: 'We have a software system that filters out fraudulent clicks even before advertisers get billed for them. We are conservative with what we count, and throw out anything that looks suspicious. We also have a team of engineers and are continuously looking for ways to update the software ... So our main focus is catching it in the first place, detecting it, and giving advertisers the tools they need to track the effectiveness of their spending and the possibility of any click fraud' (p. 248).

But this automated response so characteristic for the sophisticated Eiffel Tower was less adept at detecting click fraud that uses sophisticated software to mask its identity. At the end of 2004 Google filed its first civil lawsuit against a Texas-based Internet company, Auctions Expert International, that it said defrauded Google and advertisers by systematically clicking on ads. But Stricchiola, who helps companies with paid search campaigns, said 'Google has been the most stubborn and the least willing to co-operate' with advertisers that complain about click fraud. She said the company is only now changing its tune because advertisers and recent media coverage have put pressure on the company to do more. Google had to reconcile it with the old Incubator culture of being close to the customer, whilst not giving up their great expertise employed by the Eiffel Tower. And that's what they did. They started to pose the right questions then just searching for traditional answers and they reconciled a crucial dilemma: should we strive to be right first time, or make errors and correct them quickly?

In 2006 they launched a new tool that let their advertisers track the number and percentage of clicks that are unintentional or the potential result of attempts to drive up advertising costs. Report author Alexander Tuzhilin says both he and Google were wary of revealing too much about Google's methodologies for fear scam artists would use the information to refine techniques and defraud more advertisers. 'This is really a tradeoff between advertisers' rights to know for what they have been charged and Google's right to protect their proprietary technologies from unethical users ... Google simply can't provide this information because they would open themselves up to massive click fraud.' (Business week, July 2006.)

Google's new system shows the company is reconciling between advertisers and Google. This is obviously a welcome step and it makes the whole thing more transparent. And with these steps reconciled one of the larger dilemmas it is facing with its business model. The client is back in the loop again integrating inplementation with innovation.[18]

Progression through this gate will be achieved through the reconciliation of the following dilemmas.

1   Authority of sponsor versus empowered teams
2   Questions versus answers
3   Should we strive to be right first time, or make errors and correct them quickly?
4   Do we learn explicitly or tacitly?

Dilemma 1: Authority of sponsor versus empowered teams

In the dominant Eiffel Tower culture, teams come about because an authority figure sponsors them. With continued growth, top managers have fewer and fewer answers. The world is simply too complex for the person furthest away from field operations to know what should be done next and then issue appropriate orders. So there is an increasing need for members to self-organise to solve a problem which is confronting and disturbing them.

---

18 Vise, David A., *The Google Story*, fully updated edition, Pan Books 2005, p.248

What senior managers are not likely to know are the issues or dilemmas facing the company. Of course, they may know the problem a company has to solve in order to move on, and they respond by sponsoring a team to find a solution. A typical sponsor must nominate team members, or approve those who volunteer, give the team access to information, provide the team's remit, pay the team's expenses, and receive the team's final recommendations before implementing them.

The sponsor of a team faces real dilemmas. This is because the success or failure of the team reflects on its sponsor and is therefore a very public exhibition of good or bad judgement. Teams can go spectacularly wrong and, if they do, the mistake is costly, advertising the sponsor's error to all and sundry. A team that has worked hard on an impractical proposal is not easily silenced, and is likely to blame its sponsor for the poisoned chalice and non-implementation of any proposals. Because so much is at stake, sponsors will sometimes cripple their teams by over-control, or make the opposite mistake of letting the team take over completely. This is illustrated in Figure 4.17.

The sponsor may try to create a Captive Team (top left) by seeding it with informers, but such a team, full of people anxious to please the boss, is very likely to prove stagnant and unoriginal. What the sponsor fears is shown at bottom right – a team that runs away with the mandate it is given and ties its sponsor in knots! Only with care and skill will the sponsor be provided with a creative solution of genuine novelty.

Here an empowered team presents an innovative solution to its sponsor.

Perhaps the most famous team sponsor was Jack Welch of General Electric. At the height of team processes at GE, Welch was debriefing four to five teams a week and taking their conclusions on board. He would implement up to 75% of their suggestions. Sponsorship is no easy task. The sponsor knows the question, the issue or the dilemma but not the answer, and must be prepared to let the team be a source of enlightenment. Those who do know the answers are wasting huge amounts of money by asking expensive teams of experts to post-rationalise their prior decisions.

Although the sponsor does not know the answer, they often know what an answer would look like and what it would have to accomplish in order to solve the problem at hand. While the sponsor should never

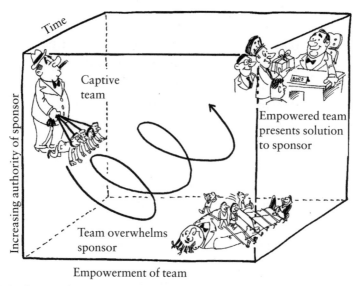

Fig 4.17 Authority of Sponsor versus Empowered Teams

spy on the team's deliberations, they should encourage team members to confer if they fear they are going beyond their remit into new territory. Sometimes an otherwise 'good' solution will not work because of barriers of which the team is not aware. Sponsors must help their teams surprise them.

Some teams self-organise around a problem they all find irksome and wish to solve because of the challenge! This spontaneous process is often a very intelligent reflection of their own concerns. A sponsor may decide to back a self-organising team if they approve its composition.

A big advantage of the self-organising team is that it evolves out of the culture where the problem lies. Many consultant-based solutions fail because the 'tissue graft' refuses to 'take'. Consultants are seen as foreign: their solutions are 'not invented here'. But, in this example, the team taken from Accounts Payable remained part of that culture and its solutions were generally welcomed.

Dilemma 2: Questions versus answers

Is sustainable innovation a matter of having answers, or is it about asking the right questions?

The dominant Eiffel Tower culture is very much focused on answers. The best answers will reduce the high risks the organisation is taking. And procedures do the rest. The Incubator culture, on the contrary, is very much about asking questions.

Values of innovation are, as we have seen, processes in the mediation of differences. A corporation risks its money so that it can secure additional monies. Risking-securing are on two ends of a continuum and with enough skill, money is risked and more is then secured, then more risked, in a spiralling process of innovation.

In the corporation, there are also many people faced with challenges who need help. They have questions, but have little idea whether the answers they seek are buried in the mass of data collected. Lots of data without questions and lots of questions with answering data do not constitute knowledge, but rather a mess. Instead of leaving employees to beg for help from other employees, senior managers should be posing questions to which employees as individuals or as teams should be supplying the answers. Questions form the context to which answers and data are the text. Knowledge consists of questions, hypotheses, propositions and conjectures to which customers, or those dealing with customers, provide the answers.

Does this new way of serving customers provide more or less satisfaction? Is it really possible to cut late deliveries by half? Can three successes by three different business units be generalised to other units? If so, why don't they act on it? Has our formal strategy learned from these successes, and is it being modified?

An innovative organisation worthy of the name is, above all else, an *inquiring system*. This means that top managers, far from knowing all the answers and issuing orders on the basis of those answers, are rather *chief inquirers*. They know what questions are crucial, what dilemmas need answering, what customers need to be won back; but they do not know, in most cases, how this should be done. After all, they are some distance from the action and from personal engagement with markets. What they can and must do is preside over the ongoing processes of inquiry, and derive vital knowledge from them.

An inquiring system belongs at the reconciliation end of our culture quadrants, because it integrates egalitarian and personalised Incubator with hierarchical and depersonalised Eiffel Tower cultures. If you are asking questions, you need to show respect and appreciation for the answers. Theory cannot be 'better' than data, nor are conjectures superior to refutations/confirmations. Those asking questions and those answering them need each other to make sense, and engage in dialogue to do so.

In the previous dilemma, we considered the sponsorship of teams, whose task it was to get to grips with complex issues, devise solutions and report back to their sponsors. This is one form that inquiring systems can take.

Some seemingly humdrum activities can be given added meaning by being turned into questions. Suppose you have to deliver many gallons of heating fuel to contractors each day. This is pretty routine work, not enough to keep the mind alive! Yet you can turn it into a question: 'By deliberately varying my delivery route, can I find the quickest and most economic way of delivering fuel? Can I save time by calling ahead so the depot is ready to receive me?'

The process of questions and answers can be framed in Figure 4.18. At top left, we have employees (vainly) asking for help, with the requisite answers irretrievable from the mass of 'objective' information. Perhaps the answer is somewhere, but where exactly? And does it fulfill our pur-

Fig 4.18 Questions versus Answers

poses? At bottom right, we have Pandora's Data Bank, a massive box of answers for which no one has a question and for which the original questions are lost.

Genuine knowledge is portrayed at top right. It consists of strategic questions answered by employees and customers, or texts within contexts. The whole process of continuing inquiry unwinds in a helical pattern of ever-more probing questions answered by the most up-to-date operations of the company, which culminates in vital knowledge about the corporation and its environment.

As the American mathematician Paul Sally (University of Chicago) extols: 'The question is the answer and the answer is the question.'

Dilemma 3: Should we strive to be right first time, or make errors and correct these quickly?

Our dominant Eiffel Tower thrives on being objective. The knowledge that's easiest to objectify is the self-sealing technique or experiment, which can be tested and replicated by others before being sold in the market place. This is what most people mean by the Knowledge Revolution: that is, a mass of discrete tools, which are thoroughly tested and are right the first time when they are installed. It is this type of knowledge that is idealised by the university and academics in the utopia of Knowledge Management.

But there is a quite different kind of learning, very widely used in business and everyday living. Here we learn by successive approximations. It's on this logic that the Incubator bases its reason for being. We make errors in our early attempts but we quickly correct them. Getting to know customers, learning languages, trying to love or to help someone, crossing cultures to engage foreigners, and virtually all entrepreneurship and innovation consist of trial and error.

But trial and error doesn't simply occur with inexact ways of inquiry in softer subjects; it becomes very important when issues grow complex and never making mistakes is an impossible demand. This is where model-making and simulations come in. You correct errors in simulations so that you do not have to make them in reality. Knowing that mistakes are inevitable and needing to learn from mistakes, you set up simulations and dry runs. Once you've eliminated errors one by one, you can employ this technique with confidence in real situations.

This process has been called 'serious play'. Remember the old saying about all work and no play making Jack a dull boy? World-class companies today need play – serious play – if they want to make truly innovative products, argues Michael Schrage: 'When talented innovators innovate, you don't listen to the specs they quote. You look at the models they've created.'[19] Whether it's a spreadsheet that tests a new financial product or a foam prototype of a calculator, what interests Schrage is not the model itself, but the behaviour that play – be it modelling, prototyping, or simulation – inspires. Schrage examines the approaches to successful prototyping at companies such as AT&T, Boeing, Microsoft and DaimlerChrysler, and describes the kind of culture that's needed for encouraging innovation. The essential message of 'serious play' is that tomorrow's innovations will increasingly be the by-products of how companies and their customers behave and misbehave around this new generation of models, prototypes, and simulations. The distinction between serious play and serious work dissolves as technology gives innovators ever-increasing opportunities to simulate and prototype their ideas. As the media for modelling radically change, so will the organisations that use them. He lays out rules of serious play, including:

- be willing to fail early and often,
- know when the costs outweigh the benefits,
- know who wins and who loses from an innovation,
- build a prototype that engages customers, vendors, and colleagues,
- create markets around prototypes, and
- simulate the customer experience.

The play occurs when inexpensive errors are made in simulated environments. The seriousness occurs when the perfected techniques are put to use in real situations. As an added precaution, the techniques themselves can be cybernetic and self-correcting, so that 'Houston, we have a problem' can be put right after it occurs. You build into a system the

---

19 Schrage, Michael, *Serious Play: How the World's Best Companies Simulate to Innovate*, Harvard Business School Press, 1999

capacity for retrieval. Sergey Brin of Google stresses the importance of serious play very clearly: "We run Google a little bit like a university. We have lots of projects – about 100 of them. We like to have small groups of people, three or so people, working on projects ... So we do lots of varied stuff. The only way you are going to have success is to have lots of failures first."[20]

In order to stay competitive, business often has to act before all the data can be gathered; hence, decisions must be made on imperfect information and the situation rapidly retrieved. The famous method of 'Case Learning' introduced at the Harvard Business School, and long used in British and North American law schools, recognises that every case is unique, and that the precedents may not be clear until after a decision has been made by a judge or by a business executive. We can then consider whether or not that decision was erroneous or correct. This dilemma is shown in Figure 4.19.

Note that those who insist on their own Immaculate Perception may be denying the possibility of serious error. Like one-eyed giants, they tend to blunder on in absolute certainty (top left), punishing mistakes and so driving these underground, as is common with the Eiffel Tower. Yet someone forever tripping up and never grasping the truths over which they stumble is of little use to us either (bottom right). Business succeeds by getting it right in the shortest possible time, using the logic of the integral organisation.

Dilemma 4: Do we learn explicitly or tacitly?

In the process of finishing the infinity loop and overcoming the red tape crisis, Greiner observes the need for stronger interpersonal collaboration, where subjective social control and self-discipline take over from the objective measures of formal control through procedures.

Another way of distinguishing 'objective' information from personal knowing is via a distinction made famous by two Japanese researchers, Ikujiro Nonaka and Hirotaku Takeuchi. They contrast explicit, codified knowledge with tacit knowledge, shared intuitively between people. The

---

20 The Google Story, p.16

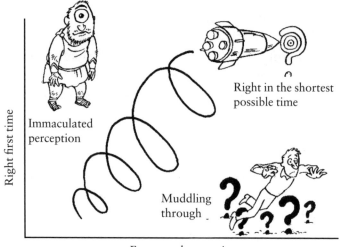

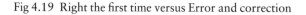

Fig 4.19 Right the first time versus Error and correction

latter is inseparable from the personalities of its creators, although it may later be turned into a codified technique and separated from them.

Tacit knowledge may be metaphorical, as in the case of an aluminium beer can which gave a team the idea of building a cheap, disposable drum for a home copying machine; or it may be a form of manual dexterity, as when the hands of master bakers twisting dough were filmed and then copied by engineers designing a dough-mixing machine for home baking. The tacit knowledge was in the bakers' hands, which the machine made explicit, just as the analogy was in the empty beer cans, which the disposable drum codified and objectified. This work is important because it reveals that the origins of new knowledge and creativity lie in cultural relationships between people; see the dilemma illustrated in Figure 4.20

The Buried Treasure lies in a shared meeting of minds (bottom right). This may in time become explicit Intellectual Property (top left) to which the owner has the key, in the manner of Microsoft. Knowledge moves from being tacit to being (in part) codified and explicit, although the process of actual creation – along with its tacit understandings – may not be shared; what is made explicit has been torn from its roots like a flower put in water and then sold as an object, soon to wither since its roots are lost.

Fig 4.20 Explicit knowledge versus tacit knowledge

Corporations make innovation flourish by interweaving the tacit with the explicit. This is sometimes done by use of a narrative or 'learning journey', in which knowledge is generated and made explicit. Here we use the example of Moses leading the Children of Israel across the Red Sea. On the far side is the Land Flowing with Milk and Honey. A stirring narrative with explicit and tacit meaning holds the experience of an entire ethnic group together. The story has the effect of eliciting new meanings until the end of time. You never know quite what the story 'means', because it is there to help you create new meanings. Knowledge leaders embark on journeys of endless discovery, sharing and codifying as they create knowledge. John Sculley of Apple wrote Odyssey[21] about his time with the company. His slogan was: 'The journey is the reward.' Like Odysseus, he saw himself on a wandering adventure without end. Computers were 'the wings of the mind', navigating through seas of knowledge. You never finally arrive, but you keep inquiring. He called himself the Chief Listener.

21 John Sculley, *Odyssey,* Stoddart, 1989

G-Star

What could be a better example than a fashion organisation to show the importance of innovation for success and global brand awareness. The success story of the Dutch company G-Star is amazing.

From its conception in 1989, G-Star has been known for its innovative and cutting edge style in the world of denim. Its strong following worldwide is based on pure product innovation combining continuous experimentation and product development. G-Star is extremely product focused, and people are struck by the close attention to detail. First, they use Japanese denim produced exclusively for the label. Each pair of jeans is positioned as a work of art; each style is an 'authentic original'. Among the vast range of styles and finishes, there is an overall theme of high-quality, durable comfort with a strong, characteristic allure. Currently the label focuses on complete men and women's collections: tops, bottoms and accessories. Acolytes of the brand are typically well-educated, well-travelled architects, designers or photographers, who appreciate the extraordinary craftsmanship.

Founder and major shareholder Jos van Tilburg is quite clear when describing the two main logics that turned G-Star from a one million Euro company in 1989 to a 500 million Euro company today.

'Just the product' has always been G-Star's philosophy and market approach. Through the development of innovative products like Raw Denim, which has had major influence on the jeans market, and the newer styles, G-Star has continuously worked on a strict sense of identity. In order to achieve that G-Star has always tried to combine emotions and the rational side of the buying moment focus on a particular segment (jeans) of the market with complete creative freedom within that segment.

And the product itself reconciles orientations that seem contradicting, like futuristic and cautious, far-reaching and experimental, alternative and traditional.

G-Star is about making eccentric combinations, whilst maintaining authenticity.

In an interview with Jos van Tilburg, it became clear that, despite the gradual and almost harmonious growth of the company since 1989, there were some crucial gates the owner had to pass. When starting in 1989 with a greatly successful portfolio of products, G-Star grew dramatically fast. In the first years, Jos surrounded himself with a small group of people he could trust, so that he could go on innovating. And he still works with designer Pierre Morisset, who was there from the very beginning.

The first crucial gate was that too many responsibilities were accumulating for this small group of people to face – a crucial dilemma between the qualitative and quantitative aspects of the business model. This *leadership challenge* was solved by increasing and professionalising the management, and Jos' role was to focus this team on listening skills through internal training and a focus on people. By keeping the focus on the product and avoiding politics, based on people you trust, the corporate culture could be enriched and the gate closed.

The next phase of growth as a Family culture created another main challenge that could be described as how to be innovative on the one hand and commercial on the other. It was the introduction of a Guided Missile culture, supported particularly by the very serious analysis of data coming from the markets, through a variety of panels giving up-to-date market information.

There was a re-emphasis of the marketer in the driving seat. The *autonomy crisis* was resolved by giving staff more managerial responsibilities on top of their professional expertise. This led to some problems like demotivation, burn-out and people leaving. With a continuous effort to educate professionals for a managerial job, the gate could be closed and the positives of the Guided Missile culture came to fruition. The importance of strategic focus was re-emphasised and G-Star kept growing.

This lead to a *control challenge,* which came to the surface because a genuine need developed for deepening the knowledge and expertise of the support functions such as HR, Finance and IT. The importance of keeping and attracting the best people was symbolised by appointing a full-time recruiter. Systems were also put in place to support the golden triangle of Production, Sales/Marketing and Design, resulting in a military-style set of processes, allowing for lots of creativity to come to fruition. It is the creative clashes between these three main functional disciplines within the very clear and focused mission and vision reinforced by Jos that G-Star is seeking to exploit for the next growth phase. 'And these clashes will soon be in a war-room-like setting with the help of the most advanced technology to shorten the cycles and increase the creative clashes,' Jos said enigmatically.

From inquiring to innovation: growth through external connections

What is the next stage the leaders of organisations need to enter, now that the predominantly internal dilemmas have been reconciled?

The stages of invention, intention, invasion, implementation and inquiring have been entered in a continuous enrichment process, leading to an organisational culture that supports sustainable innovation. Greiner anticipated that the next revolution might centre around the 'psychological saturation' of employees – when employees grow emotionally and physically exhausted by the intensity of teamwork and the heavy pressure for innovative solutions. But Greiner was doubtful himself, and admitted that he might be wrong.

His original article was written as far back as 1972 and, though some organisations have indeed tried to focus on sabbaticals and the like, we observe with him that: 'Instead, we think the crisis is one of realising that there is no internal solution, such as new products, for stimulating further growth. Rather, the organisation begins to look outside for partners or for opportunities to sell itself to a bigger company.'

A possible sixth phase may be evolving in which growth depends on the design of extra-organisational solutions, such as creating a holding company or a network organisation composed of alliances and cross-ownership[22].

This new phase would be supported by the networked organization, with an emphasis on the market rather than hierarchy. It will look for alliances for learning, and access to complementary resources, where the organisation may choose between keeping activities in house and outsourcing through a clear identification of a set of core competencies.

---

22 ibid, p.65

As such, the dilemma between disaggregation and vertical integration is reconciled and new innovations will sustain it.

We admire his predictions because, in the 2006 IBM study, the main conclusion was that in their conversations with 760 CEOs, a persistent, worldwide, sector- and size-spanning push toward a more expansive view of innovation was found – with a greater mix of innovation types, more external involvement and extensive demands on CEOs to bring it all to fruition[23]. Yet all too many companies approach innovation without a gameplan that positions them for success. Instead, they take the strategies that worked in the past and try to execute them better[24].

When asked which sources their companies relied on most for their innovative ideas, CEOs held some surprises. Business partners were right near the top of the list – just behind the general employee population. And customers were third, which means two of the top three significant sources of innovative ideas lie outside the organisation!

Business model innovation matters
Leaders frequently define their businesses in terms of the products and services they take to market and naturally focus their innovative energy there. But with technological advances and globalisation presenting so many new opportunities – and threats – CEOs are now giving business model innovation as prominent a place on their agendas as products/services/markets innovation and operational/process innovation.

Christiansen et al. describe the need for 'thinking catalytically', as existing players have resources, processes, partners and business models designed to support the status quo. This makes it unappealing for them to challenge the prevailing way of doing things. Therefore, the catalytic innovations that will bring new benefits to the most people are likely to come from outside the ranks of the established players[25].

---

23 The Global CEO Study 2006, *Expanding the Innovation Horizon*, IBM Global Business Services, p.2

24 Anthony, Scott D., Eyring, Matt, and Gibson, Lib, 'Mapping your Innovation Strategy', *Harvard Business Review*, May 2006

25 Christensen, Clayton M., Baumann, Heiner, Ruggles, Rudy and Sadtle, Thomas M., 'Disruptive Innovation for Social Change', *Harvard Business Review*, December 2006

Organisations who strive for sustainable innovative culture are candid about the need to search out new competitive differentiators – even if that means confronting a sacrosanct business model. Major strategic partnerships and organisation structure changes top the list of the most significant business model innovations. Innovating with respect to business models and operations will not only create opportunities for cost savings, but will also lead to additional revenue generation opportunities.

It is vital to combine the different types of innovation – products/services/markets, operational and business model – to meet objectives of innovation and help establish sustainable differentiation. And if business model change is not already part of your innovation agenda, it should be. Internal R&D, on the other hand, was conspicuously buried much further down the list. Only 17% of CEOs referred to it in the IBM study.

Encouraging collaboration inside and out

Regardless of the type of innovation undertaken, collaboration and partnering are very important to innovation. But leaders striving for innovation have a problem – and it is not a small one. As many CEOs in the IBM study explained, collaboration and partnering are 'theoretically easy', but 'hard to do in practice'. Whether it involves crossing internal or corporate boundaries, collaboration requires serious intent. In that sense, collaboration is a discipline. When reflecting on the collaboration gap, CEOs spoke about lacking the skills and expertise needed to collaborate and partner externally.

Despite all the potential challenges encountered when collaborating externally, *internal* collaboration sometimes proves even more difficult. In fact, the inability to collaborate internally can foil companies' attempts to deliver innovative value propositions for their clients.

CEOs described a broad spectrum of benefits from collaboration and partnering – both predictable and unexpected – and cost reduction was clearly top of their mind. But this was just a start. Moving down the list, the majority of benefits were actually drivers of top-line growth.

The higher customer satisfaction generated through collaboration ultimately results in more revenue, because in a commoditised market, you can command greater customer loyalty because of collaborative innovations. This implies both higher revenues and lower risks.

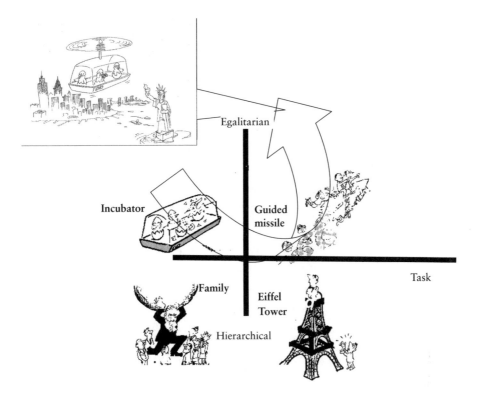

Figure 4.21 Crisis of internal focus

The upside of collaboration is underscored by the financial perform-ance of companies with extensive collaboration capabilities. Extensive collaborators outperform the competition in terms of both revenue growth and average operating margin. When we analysed operating margin results, for example, over half of the extensive collaborators out-performed their closest competitors.

To outgrow the internal and systemic phase of innovation, when eve-rything is centrally co-ordinated, to a more modularised and networked phase of innovation, the leader faces the following dilemmas.

1   Internal versus external innovations
2   Investing in Research and Development efforts versus co-operating with rival companies
3   Hi-tech versus 'hi-touch' in virtual teams
4   Systemic versus modular innovation

And to complete the Google success story of making the company into a sustainable innovation culture: Google has been a master in creating a network composed of alliances, where learning and access to complementary resources is the central part of the game. In their reconciliation process Google is still working with teams consiting of three to five people cutting out all layers of middle management. Google created 'Founders' Awards', multi-million stock awards to be presented regularly to small teams of people that developed the best new ideas. And being an information publisher delivering a mission of 'don't be evil' makes it a spider in the Web.

Quite some examples make clear that Brin and Page have ambitious long-term plans for Google's expansion far beyond their own boundaries. Detailed health knowledge is no longer the sole possession of the medical elite. Google are angling the consumer line, proposing that patients should have full power over how their own personal health and wellness data is used and managed. The medical professionals have been scrapped and the consumer is king in Google's online healthcare vision. Their goal is to empower millions of individuals and scientists with information that will lead to healthier and smarter living. They are even considering sponsoring the maverick biologist Dr. Craig Venter, to help him to make a library of all human genes.

Among other innovations Google wants to support is the production of clean-burning fuel by sponsoring a US company that is developing solar cells for commercial, residential and utility use. Given that one of Google's potential limitations on growing is the availability and cost of electricity this investment is a logical part of Google's future plans. In that context Google announced the Climate Savers Computing Initiative, a joint effort with more than 30 organisations to save energy and reduce greenhouse gas emissions by using more energy-efficient computers and computer equipment.

And the Google Print program announced agreements with the libraries of Harvard, Stanford, the University of Michigan, the University of Oxford and The New York Public Library to digitally scan books from their collections so that users worldwide can search them in Google. Later Princeton and the University of Austin joined this prestigious project.

Offering Google Apps in Africa means more to Google than connecting students and teachers to conduct that special exchange of ideas, innovation and creativity so unique to universities. In Africa and in the developing world, it also means doing our part to make sure that everyone has access to the same services wherever they live, whatever their language, and regardless of income.

What's next from Google? It's hard to say. Google doesn't talk much about what lies ahead, because as their site says: 'We believe one of our chief competitive advantages is surprise. And then there's innovation and an almost fanatical devotion to our users. These are the things that fuel us and, we hope, fuel your own dreams.' And we are sure that cross-cultural mapping and increasing the awareness of and competence to deal with cultural differences is high on the list.

Dilemma 1: Internal versus external innovations

When working with this type of base, the organisation changes from a well-defined entity consisting of fixed structures of managing systems into an entanglement of network systems with fuzzy boundaries[26]. Here the focus shifts from products and companies as units of analysis to people, organisations and the social process that binds them together in ongoing relationships. Most firms now realise that a key factor in obtaining lasting innovations is not the ability to administer existing knowledge, but the capability to constantly generate new knowledge.

The network perspective is essential in understanding the process of idea generation. The locus of innovation has shifted from individual firms to networks of inter-organisational relationships, where participation in and invitation of knowledge exchange are essential[27]. As a result, organisations are slowly evolving from 'well-structured and manageable systems into interwoven network systems with blurred boundaries'[28]. This trend will presumably continue, making the process of idea creation and the transfer of new knowledge into network structures, rather than the work of one individual, thus blurring the borders of internal and external innovations[29].

---

26 Seufert, Andreas, von Krogh, Georg and Bach, Andrea, 'Towards knowledge networking', *Journal of Knowledge Management*, September 1999

27 Powell, Walter W., Koput, Kenneth W., Smith-Doerr, Laurel, 'Interorganizational Collaboration and the Locus of Innovation: Networks of Learning in Biotechnology', *Administrative Science Quarterly*, Vol. 41, No. 1, pp.116–145, March 1996

28 Seufert, A., Von Krogh, G and Bach, A., 'Towards knowledge networking', *Journal of Knowledge Management*, 3, pp.180–190, 1999

29 Vintergaard, Christian and Husted, Kenneth, 'Enhancing selective capacity through Venture bases', CKG Working Paper No. 13, 2003

At Cisco, for example, we observe that subscribers are increasingly demanding 'many services to many screens'. They want the convenience of having services available anytime, anywhere, and on any device. To offer such services, cable operators must transform themselves from 'service providers' into 'experience providers'. An experience provider is a company that integrates internal and external innovations to deliver a 'connected life' to consumers and businesses. The experience provider manages constant and rapid innovation to provide differentiated products and services[30]. This is very similar to the way Google, Yahoo and Microsoft trial their internet-based services in 'beta' mode, before the service rolls out to widescale production: that is, measuring the readiness and viability of a service based on the experience that a customer would receive.

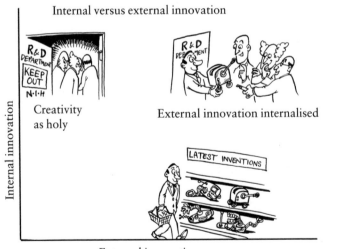

Figure 4.22 Modern corporations increasingly mixing internal with external innovations

---

30 'Living the Connected Life', *Cisco White Paper*, http://www.cisco.com/application/pdf/en/us/guest/netsol/ns705/c654/cdccont_0900aecd8057eead.pdf

Dilemma 2: Investing in Research and Development efforts versus co-operating with rival firms

This dilemma can best be reconciled by a concept called *open innovation*. We define open innovation as systematically encouraging and exploring a wide range of internal and external sources for innovation opportunities, consciously integrating that exploration with firm capabilities and resources, and broadly exploiting those opportunities through multiple channels.

The open innovation paradigm is often contrasted with the traditional vertical integration or 'proprietary' model, where internal research and development activities lead to products that are developed and distributed by the firm[31]. This challenge involves quite a number of dilemmas. Why would firms spend money on research and development efforts if the results of these efforts were available to rival firms?

Earlier models and 'fully integrated innovators' or 'systemic innovators' like AT&T (now Lucent), Bell Labs and IBM conduct basic research through commercial products. By contrast, open innovation celebrates success stories like Cisco, Intel and Microsoft, which succeed by leveraging the basic research of others. Under this paradigm, internal innovation is supplemented by systematic scanning for external knowledge, with firms maximising the returns that accrue from both sources. We observe four strategies that firms employ:

1   pooled R&D or product development,
2   spinouts.
3   product-centric approaches, and
4   attracting donated complements. [32]

Pooled R&D or product development
Organisations leveraging internal and external innovation often need to change corporate culture to realise the benefits of shared research and development. An open culture is essential for accepting external innova-

---

31 Chandler, A.D., *Scale and Scope*, Cambridge, MA: Belknap, 1990
32 Cohen, W. M. and Levinthal, D.A., 'Absorptive capacity: a new perspective on learning and innovation', *Administrative Science Quarterly*, 35, 1, pp 128–152, 1990

tions, overcoming 'not invented here' biases and building trust between firms. For example, Novell acquired Ximian, an open-source startup, to transform its internal culture in order to become more outwardly focused and to work better with external open-source projects.

Spinouts

Since spinouts are valuable for technologies locked in the laboratory, they are most relevant to larger firms, which have both the largest innovation budgets and the largest bureaucracies to defeat commercialisation. While Xerox PARC has exemplified such obstacles, in some cases Xerox spun out the technology and participated financially in its commercialisation[33].

In this context, we can consider the whole concept of *co-opetition* as the way organisations and individuals can compete for better co-operation. We have seen at Sematech how the co-operation between competitors such as AMD, Intel, Philips and National Semiconductor has lifted the American semiconductor industry to unprecedented levels and wiped out its Asian competitors.

Product-centric approaches

Many innovations require a combination of goods and service to provide buyers with a 'whole product solution'. In computers and electronics, the base innovation ('hardware') requires an investment in producing complementary goods ('software') specialised for that innovation, in order to make the entire system useful. In some cases, a system architecture will consist of various components – with mature components highly commoditised, while other pieces change more rapidly or are otherwise difficult to imitate, thus offering opportunities for capturing economic value. In other cases, the complementary products are more valuable than the core innovation – as when videogame console producers deliberately lose money on the hardware so that they can make money from software royalties.

---

33 Chesbrough, H. and Rosenbloom, R.S., 'The role of the business model in capturing value form innovation: evidence from Xerox corporation's technology spin-off companies', *Industrial and Corporate Change*, 11, 3, pp 529–555, 2002

Attracting donated complements

In this approach, essential complements to a product include not only other products, but services to buyers and (often invisible) activities within the producer's value chain. In other cases, firms make their money from the core innovation but seek donated labor for valuable complements.

Today, the PC game industry has a proven model, in which the game developer provides the core technology and some 'customer-facing' complements, while encouraging users to develop their own complements, known as game modifications (or 'mods'). To allow users to update and modify their games, publishers release editing tools for their games to encourage user mods; the users then freely distribute the mods on the internet. Frequently, this is followed up with the release of the core game itself under an open source license, as with Id Software's *Quake*. While mods do not directly generate publisher revenues, the novelty of the mods extends the relatively short demand-period for most computer games. Meanwhile, the mods keep the name of the game in front of consumers for additional months, while publishers prepare follow-on products, keeping the product current without tying up internal innovation resources.

Of course, in other cultures, the whole notion of intellectual property may be completely different. In countries like China, the motive to disseminate rather than control (some) knowledge may derive from the belief system that it should be shared to benefit society as a whole, not just the individual or organisation that invested in its creation and development.

Dilemma 3: Hi-tech versus hi-touch in virtual teams

In the development of an open culture to support the combination of business models and partners, the use of virtual teams has become increasingly important. The use of geographically dispersed virtual organisations, however, comes loaded with dilemmas. In particular, the role of a culture of trust and commitment in the virtual organisation is paramount.

Multiple relationships arising from alliance-based structures require clear commitment to enable the development of trust as a basis for longer-term partnership. Paradoxically, the perceived low level of commitment from the organisation does not engender the high level of trust and commitment required from virtual teams to maximize their performance[34]. Charles Handy argues that it is easy to be seduced by the technological possibilities of the virtual organisation, but the managerial and personal implications may cause us to rethink what we mean by an organisation. At its simplest, the managerial dilemma comes down to the question: How do you manage people whom you do not see?

The simple answer is, by trusting them, but the apparent simplicity of this idea disguises a turnaround in organisational thinking. The rules of trust are both obvious and well established, but they do not sit easily with a managerial tradition that believes efficiency and control are closely linked and that you can't have one without a lot of the other[35].

This is perhaps the area in which balance is most crucial, from both a personal and a corporate point of view. The distant hi-tech extreme can lead to disruption, and the diffuse hi-touch extreme to a lack of perspective; a collision between them results in paralysis. It is the interplay of the two approaches that is the most fruitful for the virtual team: recognising that privacy is necessary, but that complete separation of private life leads to alienation and superficiality; that business is business, but stable and deep relationships mean strong affiliations.

Let's take the development of internet trading. We can reflect on how financial consultants were getting very nervous by what was initiated by Charles Schwab and much cheaper internet trading.

So what about all the years it had taken to set up these deep, diffuse relationships with clients? We know him and his wife. We know that they like risks and we know what kind of risks they like. That can never been replaced by more impersonal internet and e-commerce technology. What are the possibilities? First of all, the role of specific, anonymous inter-

---

34 Lee-Kelley, Liz, Crossman, Alf, Cannings, Anne, 'A social interaction approach to managing the "invisibles" of virtual teams', *Industrial Management & Data Systems*, Volume 104, Number 8, pp.650–657(8), 2004

35 Handy, Charles, 'Trust and the Virtual Organization', *Harvard Business Review*, May/June 1995

net trading will be appreciated differently across cultures. Specific low-context cultures might like it regardless; more diffuse and high-context cultures might prefer diffuse contact with the broker. But what will happen with the internationalisation of these services? Can you imagine an internet site where the clients can get all the necessary data? And when a question needs to be asked, you click on the little portrait of your broker who then gets in touch with you? Wasn't it great that your bank installed a video conference facility on your computer? And you, as a client, know just how to scroll down the data screens. It is your financial consultant who is in personal contact with you through the internet. Every two weeks you could even select a training session given by your broker.

This is what happens in the USA. For example, Merrill Lynch regained its lost market share within six months by integrating the specific internet advantages with the deep relationships their brokers had built up – a reconciliation between hi-tech and hi-touch, and it was reached by combining business models through virtual teams.

Trust
Virtual teams might not meet organisational expectations and achieve the same levels of performance and success as those that are able to meet at critical times. The organisation's core players need to create a chance to build trust in each other's presence by discussing cross-company objectives and the processes and style they want to apply to achieve these objectives.

Paradoxically, the more virtual an organisation becomes, the more its people need to meet in person. The meetings, however, are different. They are more about process than task, more concerned that people get to know each other than that they deliver. Such meetings have been termed 'presenteeism' (in contrast to absenteeism). Attendance of the entire team at such meetings is a prerequisite. Obviously, such meetings need to be organised in such a way that many business issues can be discussed effectively and sufficient time is available for informal contact.

Video conferences are more task-focused, but they are easier and more productive if the individuals know each other as people, not just as images on the screen. Work and play, therefore, alternate in many of the corporate get-togethers that now fill the conference resorts out of season. These are not perks for the privileged; they are the necessary lubricants of virtuality, occasions not only for getting to know each other and for meeting the leaders but also for reinforcing corporate goals and rethinking corporate strategies.

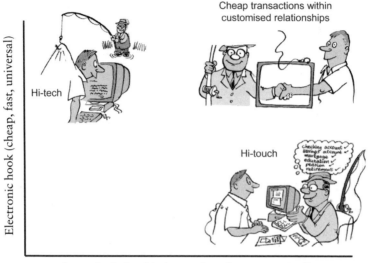

Fig 4.22 Cheap transactions within customised relationships

Communication

The manager could facilitate the discussion of the various communication styles and the concurrent dilemmas may emerge, but there are some basic conditions for reconciling core dilemmas when managing remotely.

How can people from a high-context culture – where intonation, non-verbal communication and the holistic perspective determine the meaning of a particular message – communicate with people from a low-context culture who explicitly say what something is about?

The little quality literature there is on remote management pays much attention to the benefits of using the right communication channels, like internet, email, voicemail and video-conferencing. Combining two processes can make the communication process more effective, by increasing the context. When using low-context means like e-mail, it is recommended to call afterwards, to expand the available resources, the scale or the context. The low-context information channel gets context by adding high-context communication channels, like tone of voice, etc. This is not about the separate, individual means that are at your disposal, but about combining them. A brief phone call after the e-mail you sent to your Japanese colleague may work wonders.

If virtual members further agree to meet once a week on a special internet instant messaging site or by telephone conference (taking time differences into consideration), in order to discuss mutual challenges, this often works very well.

Clarity of roles and objectives
In a virtual team, the articulation of objectives and roles of different team players is crucial for success. Unexpected misinterpretations of roles can be fatal. For example, during remote surgery a surgeon, located in Brussels, asks the nurse, located in Düsseldorf, to turn the scalpel 20 degrees. To the dismay of the Belgian surgeon, she refuses, using the words: 'A nurse in Germany does not have permission to do that.' The surgery was a failure.

It is important for the manager of 'virtuality' to make clear which criteria will be used to judge the performance of the team and the individual, including how this will be monitored and how cross-company team members will be given feedback. According to Handy, without some real sense of belonging, virtuality looks like a very precarious state and a perilous base for the next phase of innovative capitalism, whatever the economic and technological advantages.

Learning
Finally, the process of learning and (continuous) improvement should be installed in the virtual team.

An organisational architecture made up of relatively independent and constant groupings pushes the organisation toward the sort of loosely coupled structure that is becoming more common everywhere in the cross-organisational development of innovation. A necessary condition of constancy, however, is an ability to change and learn. The constant groups must always be flexible enough to change when times and customers demand it. They must also keep themselves abreast of change, forever exploring new options and new technologies. They must create a real learning culture. The choice of people for these groups is therefore crucial. Every individual has to be capable of self-renewal. Recruitment and placement become key, along with the choice of group leaders. Such topics will require the serious attention of senior management – they should not be delegated to a lower echelon of human resources.

Dilemma 4: Systemic versus modular innovation

In its years of expansion, Lego, the Danish toy company, wanted to improve their instruction booklets for the American market to help increase sales. They wanted to be as successful as they were in Germany, which they took as their role model. When the research group videotaped German kids playing with Lego, the children would carefully cut out the sticker from the new box, then start sorting out the different elements and organising them according to the colours in which the parts came. With the same extreme care, they then took the instruction booklet and read it from cover to cover. Then they built exact replicas of the models shown in the booklet. When the observers undertook similar observations with the American kids, the results were completely different. The majority of the American children took the box of building blocks and immediately started to tear it apart in great excitement. The pieces dropped on the floor and created a mess from the very beginning. Then they started to experiment without looking at the instructions; they didn't seem to care about them at all. Action was what they wanted, making their own things and following their own ideas – and their mothers praised them for their creativity and unique constructions (German kids, on the other hand, were praised for following instructions). American children had a more practical focus and could learn by doing and by making errors.

American children seem to love a box of Lego because they see it as having infinite possibilities. In Germany, Lego is a means of learning how to follow instructions and perform tasks in a prescribed manner. The difference here is creativity by making unique combinations versus following universal instructions to re-create the pictures in the booklet.

Clotaire Rapaille eloquently showed that Lego found reconciliation in combining boxes for the international markets:

'Lego repositioned itself as a source of developing creativity and imagination. If they explained, however, that with one box of Lego there exist infinite possibilities, consumers would only buy one box, creating a loop. Lego needed to create a spiral, with possibilities for children to create more with two boxes than one, and still more with three than two. Instead of an instruction booklet, they needed a growth map, showing how a child's creativity grows from one box to the next.'[36]

The dilemma is shown in Figure 4.23.

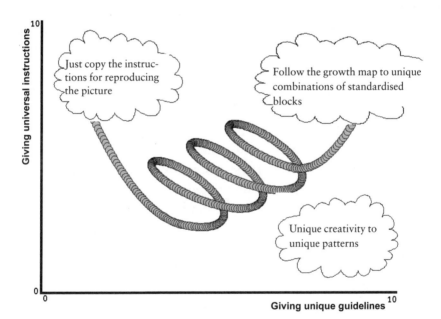

Fig 4.23 Unique continuations of standardised blocks

This is a wonderful example, where the unique guidelines and infinite possibilities are combined with a universal and standardised brick. The international success of this creative tool is unprecedented, and has been described by top management as the Tool of the Century. It was cynical to see that at the end of that same century Lego ran into trouble. Their

36 Clotaire Rapaille, G., *7 Secrets of Marketing in a multi-cultural world*, p.204, USA: Executive Excellence Publishing, 2001

standardised bricks and tools/instruments were combined with templates of standardized solutions: sales went down, and the rest is history. With the introduction of the internet-driven 'Mind-games', Lego has put itself ahead of the game again, by combining universal parts with infinite combinations.

The success story of IKEA is very similar. As the following analysis clearly shows, making the parts relatively modularised and standardised to make them cheap, while putting them together to the customers technical skills and taste, made these unbeatable products.

Very much in line with the previous set of dilemmas, we can distinguish between innovation activities that are clearly separable/modular or strongly interdependent/systemic in nature[37]. It is common knowledge that organisations involved in autonomous modularised innovations benefit from decentralised approaches in virtual companies. Largely through the marketplace, they co-ordinate the information needed to integrate an autonomous innovation with existing technologies, which in most cases will be well understood and possibly codified in industry standards. Such codified information is difficult to protect.

Conversely, in the case of systemic innovations, where the reaping of economic benefits depends on related complementary innovations, benefits are said to take place best within a centralised organisation, i.e. in integrated companies that have control of the activities that need to be co-ordinated by means of a hierarchy. Achieving control of innovation activities is necessary in order to control co-ordination and facilitate rapid mutual adjustment[38].

Distinguishing between different types of innovation according to their systemic nature dates back to Henderson and Clark, who distinguish between innovations that change only the core design-concepts of a technology, but leave the interfaces between concepts and components unchanged, and innovations that change the interfaces between

---

37 Chesbrough, H.W. and Kusunoki, K., 'The Modularity Trap: Innovation, Technology Phase Shifts and the Resulting Limits of Virtual Organizations', pp.202–230 in Nonaka, I. and Teece, D.J. (eds), *Managing Industrial Knowledge*. London: Sage Publications, 2001

38 Chesbrough, H.W. and Teece, D.J., 'Organizing for Innovation: When is Virtual Virtuous?', (HBR Classic), *Harvard Business Review*, August, pp.127–134, 2002

components[39]. With regard to the former, standards codify interactions among components. Modularity may be influenced by companies that apply specific standards later adopted by other key players in the industry. However, as such interfaces become the accepted standard in the industry, they also become an inherent part of the industry characteristics, setting the boundaries for the scope of these modularity decisions.

For instance, in the case of bicycle manufacturers, interfaces between components are clear-cut and global standards prevail. Thus, a company like Batavus or Raleigh can develop new types of gears irrespective of wheel manufacturers or other complementary components manufacturers. One component can be changed without having to adjust the rest of the system which the component is part of – hence the label modular or autonomous innovation. With an innovation of the second type, a change in one component also implies changes in the linkages between components, due to the complex nature of interrelations among the components constituting the whole. For instance, the construction and development of fighter jets represents a technology which is clearly systemic, since changes in the functionality of almost any component – from weaponry systems to the landing gear – are intricately related to a range of other components in the jet. The label systemic (or integrated) thus refers to innovation that requires subsequent alterations in the system of which it is a part.

In an article by Houman Andersen and Drejer[40], a very eloquent reconciliation can be seen in the description of the case of the very successful Danish wind turbine industry.

The case clearly illustrates that systemic innovations can also occur successfully in distributed innovation networks.

Part of the answer of this paradox is found in the organisation of innovation activities, where there is an emphasis on co-ordination as a result of more or less formalised co-operation among the various parties.

---

39 Henderson, R.M. and Clark, K.B., 'Architectural Innovation: The Reconfiguration of Existing Product Technologies and the Failure of Established Firms', *Administrative Science Quarterly*, 35, pp.9–30, 1990

40 Houman Andersen, Poul and Drejer, Ina, 'Systemic Innovation in a Distributed Network: Paradox or Pinnacle?', DRUID Working Paper No. 06–13, 2005

The presence of local customs, as well as the importance of reputation for further collaboration, explains why collaboration appears to have been preferred over integration as a co-ordination mechanism among subcontractors in the Danish wind turbine industry.

Because the industry is characterised by a high degree of interdependence between elements, there is little room for modularity in most parts of the system. This means that industry-wide component standards defining the interface between the various components are lacking.

How to approach this dilemma?
In the case of suppliers of parts (e.g. blades, glass fibre and turbines), the ability to draw on, as well as contribute to, knowledge and technology development in other industries was a core aspect of their reconciliation strategy. Thus, these companies saw the possibilities for maximising continuous learning and functioning as a knowledge broker across industries as a core feature in their strategic positioning. The ability to re-use and renew knowledge across industrial sectors plays a decisive role in understanding the underlying dynamics of distributed innovation activities in the wind turbine industry.

Especially in a learning economy, where the focus is on the ability to exchange and develop knowledge, co-ordination through collaboration may come to play an increasingly important role.

The dilemma between society's interest in sharing and diffusing knowledge, and the individual firm's interest in protecting knowledge in order to reap the economic benefits from investments in knowledge creation, is classic. But the insights from the Danish wind industry presented suggest that individual firms may also see advantages in sharing knowledge. As long as technological resources can be applied to solve similar problems in a variety of contexts, the single firm will be able to appropriate benefits from technological contributions through a redeployment of competencies in a range of industries.

As value creation becomes increasingly dependent on learning and the development of new knowledge, it is crucial to improve our understanding of the complexity of the reconciliation mindset in relation to the possibilities for engaging in knowledge-producing interactions. This poses new challenges for management, since corporate strategy must take account of how to support the ability to enter into the right kinds

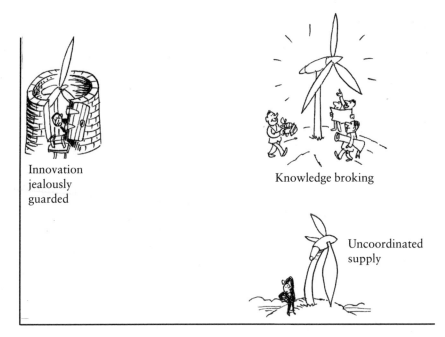

Fig 4.24 Knowledge management

of knowledge-creating interactions, and how to maximise the scope for appropriating the benefits in different contexts. This thus calls for openness in two dimensions: openness towards collaboration partners; and openness towards alternative uses of newly developed knowledge, i.e. developing new knowledge with a heterogeneous rather than homogenous demand structure in mind.

The carousel

After the dominant mindsets of *homo apprendis* in the Incubator, *homo socialis* in the Family, *homo economicus* in the Guided Missile and *homo efficientis* in the Eiffel Tower, the time has come for an organisational mindset where actors integrate opposites: the *homo reconciliens*. It is the actor who works in organisations where opposites, dilemmas and trilemmas are being reconciled on higher levels. Only then is innovation sustainable.

It is not surprising that recently the value of shares is completely dominated by financial and therefore historic numbers. These determine the rate of the share in combination with the expectations of that same share. Now expected and actual numbers alone can hardly be trusted; we need to find more reliable indices. We have always wondered how the value of an organisation where employees, suppliers, clients and shareholders meet, can be determined by a relatively small group of short term movers of money.

But what is a better means of determining value?

Much in line with the criteria of good individual leadership and innovation, we need to fundamentally redefine and rebalance the criteria for the quality of the collective organisation. Many traditional methods for determining leadership qualities and their creative powers base their score on a number of criteria, where the extremes of the scales are mutually exclusive. The ISTJ (introvert, sensitive, thinking and judging) score, for example, is the most popular typology amongst successful managers based on the Myers Briggs model. With Shell it was the more analytic and realistic 'manager with helicopter' quality that prevailed.

But all of these qualities exclude their mirror images. It is not that we proclaim that the extrovert, emotional and perceiving manager or an integrating and imaginary leader with a landing gear should get more chances. In order to ascertain the essential qualities of a leader we need to judge how well this person integrates opposites in tension. The innovative leader will use emotions to increase his or her power of thinking, use analysis in order to test the larger whole and use imagination in order to make realistic decisions. The same applies to organisations in which these leaders operate.

In our consulting practice, we've recently analysed and codified over 7,000 such tensions and dilemmas with which organisations wrestle. We've applied clustering and factor analysis type methods to reduce these thousands of outputs to a core set of ten golden dilemmas of innovation (see our website: innoscan). In parallel, we've undertaken many experiments in this area with ten blue chip organisations. We researched how we could map the value of an organisation in an alternative way, by the degree to which these organisations integrated the tensions over and above conventional linear measurement KPI-style indicators. We sought to discover if such new measurements could give us a much better insight than through the standard pure financial and technical analyses.

In this way the reconciliation of the dilemma between efficiency of the internal organisation and the development of the employees is of prime importance for the innovation power of an organisation. Here *homo efficientis* meets *homo socialis*. On the playing field of tension between financial short-term results and investments of people for the long term, *homo economicus* meets *homo apprendis*. The development of technology needs to reconcile itself with the demand of the market in such a way that the market helps decide what technologies to push. On the other hand, the push of technology will need to help determine by what markets one wants to be pulled. The need for consistency in the creative organisation needs to be fine-tuned with the need for local flexibility and sensitivity. In other words, *homo apprendis* needs to be integrated with *homo efficientis*.

The last example relates to a simultaneous high score on both specialisation in supply and the value added of the organisation by a broad assortment of products.

In due course we will ask the representatives of the four dominant organisational perspectives – management, clients/suppliers, society and financial analysts – to provide their opinions and score the organisation on the ten golden dilemmas according to the methodology and format described below. This is a type of 360° evaluation at the organization level, akin to 360° competence profiling of individual employees by their peer group. On each of the ten scorecards, we will ask the relevant group to indicate the relative importance of the dilemma for the future sustainability of the organisation's innovation on a Likert scale, so that we can weight the relevance differently for different organisation sectors or categories.

Our quest is to arrive at a new, alternative 'ROR' index that will eventually push away financial-technical analyses and reconcile the various perspectives. Historical indices will be enriched by future potential. Return on Investment (ROI) will finally be replaced by the much more penetrating Return on Reconciliation (ROR).

Let's be just a little creative in the approach and assessment of the creativity and innovative powers of our organisations.

It is time.

CREATING A CULTURE OF INNOVATION IN PRACTICE

Through the course of the journey in this book, we have travelled from the creative individual, through how these individuals can work together and be lead in diverse teams to be creative, to how the leadership of the organisation must reconcile the dilemmas any team faces as the organisation grows and develops. The development of skills and knowledge in all these areas will help an organisation develop a hyper-culture.

But overall, this book is about a mindset change that requires thinking in terms of resolving dilemmas. The organisational innovation process that we provide through our consultation work for clients builds on our own philosophy: that, ultimately, success derives from enabling leadership to define and implement organisational values in such a way as to increase performance for innovation. The value of a 'value' rests in how much it helps your organisation to reconcile the basic innovation dilemmas its leaders and staff are facing.

Our multi-step methodological framework, which includes 'dilemma thinking', is central to bringing people together to discover which values and behaviours they share and where they differ. We have tested many variations in our search for a means that both is reliable and has high validity. Our research and consulting practice reveal that a genuine and successful organisational innovation process requires four components:

1   Recognition of organisational cultural differences
2   Respect for those differences

3   Reconciliation of both innovation and cultural dilemmas resulting from the first two phases, and finally
4   Realisation and rooting, in which the business benefits of sharing core values and behaviours and connecting different viewpoints are embedded throughout the organisation.

Together our extended MBTI-type indicator, the extended Kirton Innovator-Adapter, and our own Intercultural Competence Profiler, based on the above four components, provide an overall evaluation that enables an individual to reflect on their overall competence to innovate and how they approach dilemmas.

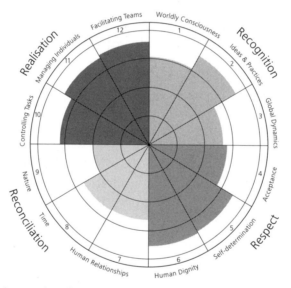

Fig 5.1 Typical Intercultural Competence Profiler

It is, of course, important that the human aspect is fully integrated with the business aspects of the process. Maximum innovative power from an organisational culture is only achieved when strategic, structural, systemic, human resource and supplier-and-client processes are aligned. In this wider context, our approach is defined as a process of reconciling divergent goals and values, and structural, functional and cultural differences for maximum innovation.

In order to achieve this, we have designed a process that consists of the four main phases above, comprising a total of 10 steps (access to further information and examples of these steps and tools is available from www.ridingthewhirlwind.com). Each step comprises an analytical phase supported by the appropriate diagnostics, codification and outputs that inform and link to the next step.

Phase 1: Recognition of organisational cultural differences

During the diagnostic stage, the current and desired cultures are measured with the Organisational Value Profiler (OVP). The four-quadrant model of corporate cultures described in Chapter 4 is at the meta-level. In practice, we drill down by subdividing each quadrant into three, making a total of twelve segments. This provides a more comprehensive analysis of corporate cultures and helps us to use our dilemma databases not merely for benchmarking, but more as predictive tools, which draw upon known examples of successful reconciliations from our client portfolio. This is particularly valuable in cases of creating sustainable innovation in mergers and acquisitions, through the values-driven organisation, and of course fundamental innovation management when growing from stage-gate X to stage-gate Y.

Let's take an example of a hi-tech company that is facing a crisis of autonomy. This is clearly diagnosed through the OVP and validated by face-to-face interviews and the Personal Values Profiler (PVP), which looks into the values of the staff themselves.

Phase 2: Respect for those differences

In order to create a basis for change, it is crucial that the existing culture is appreciated as much as the desired culture. We are at the phase of defining the dilemmas between the stages. The intention is to collect some examples of the challenges staff are confronted with, so that we can address the issues being faced by the organisation and how the staff relate to these issues.

We apply both a deductive and an inductive approach to reveal the dilemmas of innovation staff are facing. While the latter set of dilemmas represents an inductive set through an open question, the deductive

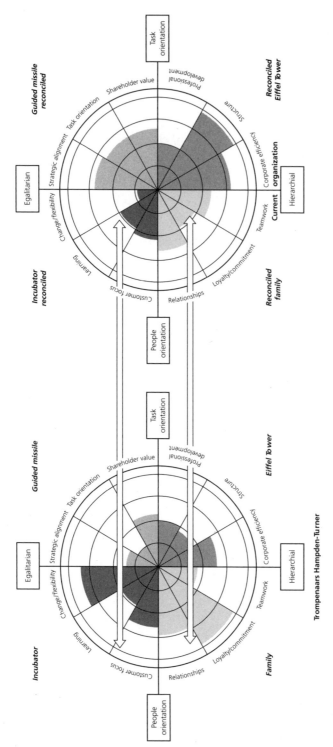

Fig 5.2 Current culture: what hinders and supports

Most frequently selected values:

1.Entrepreneurial ◄——————— Top scoring value

2.Professional

3.Winning

4.Creative

5.Performance-oriented

6.Initiating

7.Reliable

8.(Self) Critical

9.Open-minded

10.Results-oriented

Fig 5.3 Personal Values Profiler

set looks at the following organisational stakeholders and the tensions between them.

These conflicting interests are potential sources of tension between each possible pair of components, giving rise to ten catogories of dilemma.

On the one hand	On the other hand
What made us great was our unique way of thinking	We have to grow up and implement structure, processes and rules
We need to keep our entrepreneurial atmosphere within the company	We need to grow this organisation
We need to maintain the entrepreneurial 'spirit'	We need more (formal) control and accountability as the company expands in size
We need to allow for creative chaos to generate ideas	We need to be rigorous in our processes and execution
We want to be an entrepreneurial can do fast organisation from the days of 'small'	We are growing big – more people = more structure = slower whilst the stakes get bigger: monetary and other

Fig 5.4 The challenge of the guided incubator (as expressed by participants)

Component	Sectional interest
Business Processes	Corporate Effectiveness
Employees	Employee Development and Learning
Shareholder	Shareholder Return, Financial Performance and Growth
Client, customers and suppliers	Satisfatcion
Society at large	Contributions to society

Fig 5.5 Component: Sectional interest

The deductive gathering of dilemmas

Throughout our research and consulting, we invite respondents to identify the dilemmas which, if resolved, would have the biggest (innovation) benefits to their organisations. Having captured some 7,000 dilemmas online, we have clustered these into a number of 'Golden Dilemmas' in several domains. We invite participants to consider these Golden Dilemmas and their significance to the innovative capabilities of their organisation. We use an analysis to the responses to these types of questions to offer insights that can help identify decision-making priorities for action steps to a new future.

Phase 3: Reconciliation of both innovation and cultural dilemmas

In our workshops, participants work on both dilemmas of innovation and corporate dilemmas as described under phase 2. To do this, we use a Dilemma Reconciliation Process, which stimulates a series of constructive dialogues, resulting in some suggestions for action.

Phase 4: Realisation and rooting

At this stage, the organisation is ready for the actual change process. Actions to reconcile major dilemmas are defined, and measures are taken to be able to monitor progress. It is crucial at this stage that systemic actions are taken, ranging from implementation of integrated scorecards and reward systems to redefining the job-evaluation systems and advertising campaigns.

Finally, in this implementation stage, it becomes crucial to involve the client, along with other possible stakeholders from outside the organisation.

And the change all boils down to creating constructive dialogues to jointly reconcile the dilemmas – individual, team and organisational – that unleash the unlimited creative powers of us all.

Good luck in applying it – if, in your culture, you believe in luck!

INDEX

BASEMENT